Economics and corporate strategy

T0318155

Economics and corporate strategy

C. J. SUTTON

Sheffield City Polytechnic

CAMBRIDGE UNIVERSITY PRESS

Cambridge
London   New York   New Rochelle
Melbourne   Sydney

CAMBRIDGE UNIVERSITY PRESS
Cambridge, New York, Melbourne, Madrid, Cape Town, Singapore, São Paulo

Cambridge University Press
The Edinburgh Building, Cambridge CB2 8RU, UK

Published in the United States of America by Cambridge University Press, New York

www.cambridge.org
Information on this title: www.cambridge.org/9780521226691

© Cambridge University Press 1980

This publication is in copyright. Subject to statutory exception
and to the provisions of relevant collective licensing agreements,
no reproduction of any part may take place without the written
permission of Cambridge University Press.

First published 1980
Re-issued in this digitally printed version 2008

A catalogue record for this publication is available from the British Library

Library of Congress Cataloguing in Publication data
Sutton, Clive Julian.

Economics and corporate strategy.

Includes bibliographical references.

1. Corporate planning – Economic aspects. I. Title.
HD30.28.S92 1979   658.4'01   79-4198

ISBN 978-0-521-22669-1 hardback
ISBN 978-0-521-29610-6 paperback

Contents

v

Illustrations

Preface

This is a book about corporate strategy written for industrial economists. It is intended for students who have already completed an introductory course in economics, and who, therefore, have some familiarity with the conventional theory of the firm. They may also be acquainted with some of the modern revisions to the conventional theory, although such knowledge can probably be treated as an optional extra.

Corporate strategy is concerned with long-term decision taking. It reflects the firm's need to prepare for an uncertain future in an uncertain environment, which may be subject to almost continual change. By contrast, formal economic analysis often concentrates on equilibrium conditions in a world with little or no uncertainty, and, although equilibrium analysis is a powerful tool, it sometimes seems to be far removed from the world of the corporate strategist. Indeed, in casual conversation I have often heard businessmen explaining why they had to reject an "economic" solution for "strategic" reasons. In reality this conflict is more apparent than real, but the appearance is both misleading and unfortunate: misleading, because it ignores the deep insights into strategic behavior which can be developed from the analytical and empirical work of many economists, and unfortunate, because it simultaneously denies the potential usefulness of those insights. I hope that this book may help to dispel some of this misunderstanding by synthesizing a fairly broad range of economic and management literature and relating the economic analysis directly to its strategic context. As a bonus, I would also hope that the synthesis may help economics graduates to contribute more effectively to long-term decisions in the firms for which they work or, at least, to understand why their bosses take such decisions.

The book is concerned with the way in which firms may choose the direction and the method to be followed in their future growth, and it concentrates on the analytical reasons behind these strategic decisions rather than on the management problems of implementing the decisions. It also concentrates on the aspects of strategy that are most amenable to general economic analysis, and leaves aside those areas that require more specialized knowledge. It, therefore, avoids the intricate details of (say) financial strategy. The topics are touched upon, for example, in the discussions of mergers and diversification, but the treatment is unashamedly designed for the generalist rather than the specialist. This implies a fairly narrow definition of strategy, which may seem to be unnecessarily restrictive to some readers. But there is no universal agreement on the limits of any definition of strategy, and the definition adopted here is consistent with the views of at least one eminent management specialist and at least one eminent economist. For example, P. F. Drucker suggested that top management's strategic challenge relates to "size and complexity, diversity and diversification, growth change and innovation" (1974, p. 603), while O. E. Williamson defined strategic planning as being concerned with "diversification, acquisition, and related activities" (1975, p. 149).

The first part is an introduction. It assumes no knowledge of corporate behavior, and is therefore presented as a fairly elementary guide to strategic planning. Subsequent chapters draw more heavily on economic analysis and are a little more advanced. The second part (Chapters 3, 4, 5, and 6) deals with integration and diversification: that is, it deals with the direction of growth. Initially in Chapters 3 and 4 the analysis ignores national boundaries; Some specific problems of multinational strategy are, however, discussed in Chapter 6. The main emphasis is on the range of factors that may influence such strategic decisions rather than with detailed decision-taking processes, but Chapter 5 does attempt to show how different aspects of the analysis are appropriate at different stages of the process. The third part (Chapters 7 and 8) deals with mergers and innovation and is therefore concerned with the method by which growth can be achieved. As with the second part, it concentrates on the background factors that help to shape decisions, but it includes brief discussions of the decision-taking procedures for mergers and of the problems of handling nonquantifiable criteria in assessing innovation projects.

Many colleagues and students have influenced this work, and I should like to thank them all; they are too numerous to mention individually. More formally, my thanks are due to the Cambridge University Press for permission to reproduce the data in Table 1. Various parts of the book were read in draft by Frank Bradbury, Richard Davies, Neil Kay, Brian Loasby, and Richard Shaw, and I am most grateful to them for their comments and suggestions. I should also like to thank June Watson, Catherine McIntosh, and Eileen Cerrone for their help at various stages in the preparation of the typescript, and above all, my wife for her unfailing patience, encouragement, and coffee. My thanks are due to all these people for their contribution to the work. It goes without saying, however, that all the errors are entirely my own.

June 1979   C. J. SUTTON

Part I
The nature of corporate strategy

Introduction: What is strategy?

Corporate strategy is concerned with the long-term survival and growth of business organizations. It involves the choice of objectives, the search for developments which may help to meet those objectives, and the identification of those developments which are most likely to be feasible with the organization's existing resources. But the process is unlikely to end with a set of detailed plans or blueprints for the future. It should be more concerned to establish the general form of long-term developments, and to set the guidelines against which future plans can be judged. Formal model building may help in this process, but it will have to be complemented by less formal analysis of a wide range of factors, many of which have to remain unquantified because they cannot be measured in any meaningful way.

The tasks of the strategist are discussed more carefully in Chapter 2, but there are two points which must be emphasized right at the beginning. The first is that strategy is concerned with long-term developments rather than with the cut and thrust of day-to-day operations: that is, it is not concerned with the current production and sale of particular products, but with the possibility of new products, new methods of production, or new markets to be developed for the future. The second point is that strategy is relevant precisely because the future cannot be foreseen. If firms had perfect foresight they could produce a single plan to meet all future developments. Without such foresight they must be prepared to face the unknown, but they can still build on what knowledge they have and act so that they can take advantage of whatever unforeseen developments do arise.

It is probably true that all successful organizations have always followed some implicit strategy of this sort, but as a separate field of study, the analysis of strategy for business firms is still fairly young. It is perhaps for this reason that there is no single definition of corporate strategy which is universally acceptable, and the terms "strategy," "policy," and "long-range planning" are sometimes used interchangeably by different authors: The literature is rich if not profligate in its use of jargon but is not always unanimous as to its interpretation. One definition which will satisfy most interpretations has been given by Andrews. He defined corporate strategy as

"the pattern of major objectives, purposes or goals and essential policies and plans for achieving those goals, stated in such a way as to define what business the company is in or is to be in and the kind of company it is or is to be. In a changing world it is a way of expressing a persistent concept of the business so as to exclude some possible new activities and suggest entry into others. (Andrews 1971, p. 28)

This definition will be accepted throughout our analysis.

Our major purpose in this book is to discuss some of the more significant ways in which analytical and empirical economics can contribute to an understanding of strategy, and it is immediately obvious that if strategy is concerned with business objectives and the methods used to realize those objectives, it may have something in common with the debate about objectives and the theory of the firm which has captured the attention of microeconomists for some time. We therefore start in Chapter 1 with a brief review of this debate, in order to identify the points which may help subsequent analysis. Our purpose is not to summarize the alternative theories of the firm in detail, but to provide a link between the textbook theory and the less rigorous but more wide-ranging work of the corporate strategist. Subsequently in Chapter 2 we shall build on this introduction to explain the nature and purpose of corporate strategy in more detail.

1

Strategy and the theory of the firm

We begin this chapter with a brief critique of the traditional theory of the firm which assumes that firms are motivated to maximize profits in the short run. We then turn to consider the alternative optimizing and behavioral theories so as to pick out the major features to which we shall want to refer in later chapters.

1.1 The traditional theory

The traditional focus of economic analysis was the small owner-managed firm which operated in only one industry. The firm was assumed to be a price taker that was forced to pursue its objectives by adjusting output and internal efficiency in the light of a set of prices that it could not hope to influence significantly by its own actions. It was also assumed that the personal motives of the owners and the pressures of an inhospitable environment would combine to enforce a search for maximum profit, and although the emphasis was on long-run equilibrium, the analysis implied that the managers would adopt a short time horizon, because they would know that their current actions could not affect the market prices they would have to face in the future. The traditional analysis was therefore based on models of firms which sought to maximize short-run profits in highly competitive markets, and although it was recognized that a few firms might possess monopoly power, the convenient assumption of profit maximization was generally retained for the analysis of such firms, even though it was then more difficult to rationalize.

This way of characterizing firms as one man bands playing other people's music may have been a reasonable approximation to reality at one time, and may still be justified if it allows us to make useful predictions of the aggregate behavior of groups of firms, but it has grown more and more suspect as the typical firm has grown in size and complexity. This growth has led to changes in the character of firms, and any attempt to analyze their behavior must be prepared to allow for the consequences of these changes. Two points are of particular importance.

First, it is misleading to think of all firms as price takers. Firms often acquire market power as they grow larger, and so gain some control over the prices charged for their products. But firms which can influence current prices can also influence future market trends, and so can no longer ignore the long-term consequences of their current decisions. Unfortunately, these long-term consequences are more difficult to predict, and because they are more distant in time, must be partially discounted before they can be compared with the more immediate effects. In consequence the behavior of firms is more strongly conditioned by the quality of information which can be made available to the decision takers, and will reflect their attitudes to risk and their time preferences.

Secondly, it is no longer correct to equate the firm with the owner-manager. Large firms, in particular, are collections of people who may each have some degree of control over the decisions that are taken. These people may all have different objectives, and as a result the behavior of the firm will depend upon the relative influence of different groups or individuals, including shareholders, managers, employees, or others with a direct interest in its affairs.

The people who can influence decisions may be interested in a number of objectives. Financial motives will be important for many people, and some shareholders and employees may feel that the income they derive from a firm is primarily dependent on its profitability. Others, while similarly stressing the financial aspects, may believe that their incomes are more closely related to the size of the firm, whereas shareholders who are looking for capital gains may be more interested in the immediate prospect of a takeover bid than in longer-term profitability. But financial gain is rarely the only objective. Most people are also motivated by other factors, including their security, their status, their professional pride, and the respect of others who may have no active involvement in the firm. Sometimes these objectives may still be served by an increase in the firm's profits, as when profitability is taken as a sign of technical excellence. But profits are rarely a sufficient condition for satisfaction. For one thing, managers whose objectives require the accumulation of resources by the firm may be more interested in cash flow than in profitability. Further, at times, the pursuit of financial gain will conflict with other objectives. It may be, for example, that the objectives can be met by increasing current sales or investment at the expense of profits, by emphasizing the stability rather than the profitability of activities, or by giving up activities that may have undesirable external effects, such as pollution.

Clearly there is a range of objectives which may be relevant, and there is no evidence to suggest that any one of them is likely to dominate the others in all circumstances. As a result, economists have developed a range of alternative models of behavior, but have been unable to develop a single dominant model. The models may be classified conveniently into two groups: optimizing and satisficing.

1.2 Alternative optimizing models

Optimizing models are based upon two fundamental assumptions: (i) that decision takers will behave *as if* they had sufficient information to identify the decisions which are appropriate for optimization, and (ii) that the effect of the varied objectives of decision takers can be analyzed by positing a single objective function for the firm as a whole. The functions used for economic analysis are often fairly gross simplifications, with very few variables. These are usually financial variables and are chosen partly because they seem to provide clear analytical links with the firm's commercial operations. But they may also be selected to represent some nonfinancial variables. For example, decision takers may seek to enhance their status and security. Neither of these is amenable to economic analysis because they cannot be measured in economic units, but they may both be correlated with (say) the size of firm, and the latter may therefore be taken as a proxy for both objectives. It is then assumed that the firm will behave as if it sought this proxy objective.

Some of the optimizing models retain the central interest in price and output behavior that was the original focus of the theory of the firm but seek to investigate the effects of using substitutes or complements for profits in the objective function. Examples include the sales-revenue-maximizing model (Baumol 1959), or the managerial-preference model (O. E. Williamson 1964), which explicitly allows for management's attempts at empire building through (say) excessive staff recruitment. The main interest in such models is that they provide alternative predictions of the response made by firms to external stimuli such as tax changes (see, for example, Crew 1975), but in many cases the differences are slight or indeterminate, and so the assumption of profit maximization is commonly retained as a more convenient working hypothesis for initial analysis. It is used in this way in later chapters: for example, in analyzing the effects of rivalry on the incentive to innovate.

A second subgroup of optimizing models concentrates on the relationship between managers and shareholders of firms, and typically assumes that managers will identify their interests more closely with the growth of the firm, whereas shareholders retain a stronger preference for dividends (Marris 1964, 1971; J. Williamson 1966). Models of this type can assist our understanding of mergers (see Chapter 7) and of the way in which the stock market may constrain managerial behavior. They are generally less concerned with the allocative effects of price and output decisions in particular product markets.

The continuing life of the optimizing models may be taken as circumstantial evidence of their usefulness, and noneconomists are often surprised by the mileage which can be obtained from models which make little or no claim to descriptive accuracy. The models can be particularly useful if we wish to analyze the general behavior of industrial systems, because in this case the precise characteristics of individual firms may not be very important. In this way, the models may help us to identify the likely effects of (say) changes in the degree of competition in an industry. In turn, such information would be valuable to a corporate strategist who had to consider the consequences of alternative new-product developments by his organization, and so the optimizing models can provide valuable inputs to the strategic-planning process. As was suggested in the last two paragraphs, subsequent chapters will identify further examples of this sort of use.

On the other hand, the ability of the optimizing models to produce conclusions that are generally applicable has to be bought at the price of descriptive accuracy, and this can be a real limitation when we need to understand the behavior of individual firms. The increased sophistication of quantitative techniques for planning and control may make it easier for firms to optimize their short-run behavior if they wish to do so, but generally it does not help them to reconcile conflicting objectives nor does it contribute much to long-run optimization: The quality of information about far distant events is usually so poor that calculations which purport to be optimizing are really no more than crude guesses at possible results. In these circumstances, managers may favor procedures that do not maximize anything explicitly, but that seek to ensure decisions that are reasonable and acceptable to those most directly affected. This is the main rationale of the behavioral or satisficing theories of the firm, which we now consider.

1.3 Behavioral models

The main alternatives to the optimizing models are those based on the satisficing or behavioral approach (see, for example Simon 1952, or Cyert and March 1963). The basis of this approach may be summarized as follows. It is assumed that the existence of uncertainty and the problems of agreeing and imposing a single set of objectives on all the members of a large organization will make optimizing behavior impossible. Instead it is suggested that organizations will define a target or an aspiration level for each objective, with the level set by extrapolation of past experience or by observation of comparable organizations. Its achievements will then be compared with its aspirations. Existing policies will be maintained if the achievements are satisfactory, but a shortfall below the target will prompt a search for an improved policy. The search may be successful, in which case the improved policy will be adopted and the search will be stopped. However, the organization may have to revise its aspiration levels downward if prolonged search fails to discover any. method of improvement.

This type of behavior was developed into a formal model of firms' price and output decisions by Cyert and March (1963). The model is not concerned directly with strategic behavior, but it incorporates a number of basic principles or relational concepts which are of more general relevance. These are (i) quasiresolution of conflict, (ii) uncertainty avoidance, (iii) problemistic search, and (iv) organizational learning. Since we shall wish to refer to these concepts in later chapters it is appropriate to describe them briefly at this stage.

Quasiresolution of conflict

We have seen that firms may wish to pursue several objectives. We have also seen that if we are interested in making general predictions for broad groups of firms, it may be convenient to replace this range by a small number of proxies which are more amenable to formal analysis. However, this analytical device cannot be used so readily to guide the decisions that have to be taken in individual firms, because the detailed effects of small variations in objectives are then more significant.

In principle, the multiple objectives can all be included in an optimizing model, provided that we can specify the appropriate trade-off between the different objectives. For example, if a firm seeks both profits and growth of sales as separate objectives, it can solve any decision problem, provided that it knows the marginal benefit derived from each: that is, provided that it can decide whether a particular increase in (say) the growth rate can justify any consequential drop in profitability. Individual business managers are frequently faced with decision problems of this sort, and they can usually resolve them even though they may not make their marginal values explicit.

On the other hand, the problem is less tractable if the different objectives are sought by different people who are trying to pursue different policies. In this case, the trade-off must be established by explicit bargaining if the decisions are to be consistent with a single set of objectives. This is not necessarily impossible, but it may be very time consuming, and may leave managers with little time to manage anything. The costs of reaching agreement will be particularly high if the bargain has to involve a large number of people, or if it has to be negotiated frequently as new members join the group, and as existing members change their priorities. Further, any agreement will be difficult to sustain if the trade-off involves qualitative objectives that are given different subjective measurements by different people.

Firms must find some way of living with these problems, but they may well find that it is unnecessary or impossible to eliminate all sources of conflict. For example, they may ignore the potential conflict and give individual managers a fairly free hand to pursue their own objectives in their areas of responsibility. Unavoidable disputes will then be dealt with as they arise, but no attempt will be made to ensure that all the decisions are consistent. Alternatively, the firms may allow each major objective to appear as a constraint on decision taking. Instead of seeking a single optimum solution, the decision takers may set a target level for each objective, so that any possible solution can be classified in only one of two ways: satisfactory or unsatisfactory. They therefore establish their aspiration levels as a set of constraints, so that any outcome will be acceptable to all members of the organization if it meets the minimum target for each objective, and any problem can be solved satisfactorily if there is at least one solution which satisfies all the constraints.

Uncertainty avoidance

It is suggested that firms will generally react to uncertainty by trying to avoid it. Where possible, they will emphasize flexible procedures that enable them to react quickly to any change in the environment. "They avoid the requirement that they correctly anticipate events in the distant future by using decision rules emphasising short-run reaction to short-run feedback rather than anticipation of long-run uncertain events" (Cyert and March 1963, p. 119). Alternatively they may try to control their environment so as to minimize the unpredictable changes. Perfect control will be impossible but many features of the environment may be influenced by negotiation. For example, long-term contracts with suppliers or customers may provide some guarantee of stability, whereas the standardization of costing methods or the use of a conventional price/cost markup may help to reduce the risks of unpredictable actions by competitors. In this way firms may rely upon a "negotiated environment" to reduce some of their uncertainty.

Problemistic search

In a satisficing model, an organization is assumed to take decisions by choosing the first alternative that it can find to meet its aspirations, and the model must therefore include details of the search process that determines the sequence in which alternatives will be discovered. These details are not required for an optimizing model, in which the organization is assumed to know all relevant alternatives before it makes its choice, but they are necessary for a satisficing model, because the choice of policy may then depend upon the sequence in which the firm considers a number of potential alternatives.

Cyert and March used a concept of problemistic search, which involves three related assumptions: first, that firms will only search intensively for new information when they have a specific problem which demands a solution; second, that the search will favor simple solutions that involve minor changes in existing practices, and will only admit radical alternatives as a last resort; and third, that the search will be biased by existing experience and by objectives, so that, for example, we might expect salesmen to seek to increase profits by increasing sales, whereas engineers would be more inclined to look at the efficiency of manufacturing processes.

Organizational learning

Organizations may learn to adapt their behavior as a result of earlier experience. In the simplest possible terms, such learning might encourage organizations to believe that successful behavior should be repeated because it will lead to further success, whereas unsuccessful behavior should be changed. Obviously this learning may influence the search procedures already mentioned. It may also affect the organization's aspiration level, because the results achieved in the past are likely to influence strongly the targets set for the future.

It must be emphasized that these four relational concepts do not comprise a behavioral model, because a model would need to specify the rules and procedures which were used to reach operational decisions in the organization concerned. Nevertheless, the concepts do help to explain the general nature of behavioral models, and the way in which these differ from optimizing models.

The behavioral approach is usually treated as an alternative to the optimizing theories, but the generality of any conclusions it yields is necessarily reduced by the failure to specify a general objective function and the need to allow for individual reactions that depend upon specific experience. For example, Crew (1975, p. 117) suggests that "the Cyert and March behavioral theory might be criticised most severely on the grounds that it is questionable whether it is a theory at all. Normally a theory is expected to do more than deal with an individual case . . . It is still not clear that Cyert and March have not done much more than modelled particular cases rather successfully." Nevertheless, the behavioral approach does provide many valuable insights into the process of organizational decision taking. Further, we shall see that although most behavioral models have been concerned with short-run decisions, the basic concepts can also help our understanding of strategic behavior. We shall use the first two relational concepts (quasiresolution of conflict and uncertainty avoidance) to explain the function and role of strategic planning in Chapter 2; the concept of organizational learning will be used extensively to explain some of the constraints on strategic planning, which are considered in later chapters. In general (although at the risk of some oversimplification) we might say that we shall be using optimizing theories to provide inputs to the strategic-planning process, but will lean towards a behavioral approach to explain how these inputs may be exploited in practice.

2
The purpose of strategic planning

The previous chapter reviewed some developments in the theory of the firm in order to provide some early pointers to the way in which economic analysis may assist our understanding of corporate strategy. In this chapter, we first consider the role of the corporate strategist in a little more detail, and then seek to justify that role in principle (section 2.2) and by reference to the experience of corporate planners (section 2.3). At this stage we are still concerned with a very general view of strategic planning. Specific planning problems will be dealt with in later chapters.

2.1 The role of the strategist

Our initial definition suggested that the strategist is concerned to identify policies which contribute to the long-term goals of the organization. Implicit in this definition are several intellectual tasks that must face all managers involved in the formulation of corporate strategy. First, they must identify the value systems and the long-term objectives that are to be sought by the members of the organization, including the obligations that are acknowledged to outsiders. Secondly, they must define the current and expected future state of the environment in which the organization operates, so as to pick out the opportunities which may arise and the threats which may have to be faced. Thirdly, they must consider the organization's relative strengths and weaknesses in responding to those opportunities and threats. Fourthly, they must seek to identify the direction in which the organization should try to move in order to achieve its objectives, given its competence and resources, and the state of the environment. Generally, the formulation of strategy would not tie the firm to any immediate action nor would it imply that future decisions had already been taken, but it would attempt to fix the more desirable future alternatives that are open to the firm, so that current decisions can be better informed. A full statement of strategy might include the set of short-term plans and

11

targets which had been selected, but the selection itself is not normally thought of as being part of the process of strategy formulation.

In selecting alternative avenues for development, the firm must consider the resources which will be needed, and must ensure that the critical resources can be marshaled in the right place at the right time. In this context, the critical resources "are both what the company has most of and what it has least of" (Tilles 1963, p. 115). If critical shortages can be identified, it may be possible to take some action to improve the future supply position, but this takes time and may require special skills that are not readily available. As a result, the current choices are generally constrained by the current resource base. This constraint is clearly emphasized by Drucker's reference to a firm which appraises new products by asking which of its competitors could exploit a particular product most effectively (Drucker 1974, p. 702). The intention is not to encourage collaboration but to emphasize the need for a clear match between the product and the firm's competitive strengths. These strengths may also include the size of firm: Small firms generally have advantages of agility and good internal communications, whereas larger firms are not so fast but have more staying power. The different attributes are likely to be of value in different contexts and, for example, Rolls-Royce was clearly successful at filling a small but prestigious niche in the car market though at the same time it may have been too small for the range of operations that it believed to be necessary for its objective of world leadership in aero-engines.

These components of strategy seem to be universally accepted, but there are two further points on which agreement is less common. First, we have so far implied that strategy formulation is a recognizable exercise leading to a formal statement of objectives, threats, and opportunities. This may be misleading. Often it is found that although a consistent strategy can be identified in a firm, it has come about as a result of a fairly informal process and is not made explicit. Further, it is sometimes argued that strategy is like pricing policy and must be kept as a trade secret from competitors. This argument has some merit, but it may conflict with the need to find a stategy that is recognized and contributed to by many different individuals in the organization. Second, different analysts prescribe different degrees of rigor for the process of strategy formulation. Some see it rather loosely as a method of approach to a problem rather than a formal process (e.g. Guth 1976). By contrast, others have sought to prescribe a complete set of decision rules for strategic planning (e.g. Ansoff 1965). We shall not attempt to mediate between these alternatives, although it will become clear that the treatment in this book is not intended to define decision rules for strategists. We must note, however, that any formal system must ensure that its plans are not so rigid that they cannot be adapted to meet changing circumstances.

2.2 The general case for strategic planning

The formulation of strategy is designed to identify feasible avenues for development, but at the same time it introduces a number of constraints and may exclude some alternatives from any further consideration. These constraints may be stated positively rather than negatively. For example, in simple terms, they may say, "Concentrate on the chemical industry," rather than "Ignore anything outside the chemical industry." But they remain as constraints. It is therefore appropriate to ask why the members of a firm should be prepared to act in a way which appears to restrict their freedom of choice. The argument will be pursued under three headings: (*a*) uncertainty, (*b*) multiple objectives, and (*c*) internal cohesion.

Uncertainty

We saw previously that some early behavioral studies suggested that firms would react to uncertainty by ignoring it, and would concentrate on short-run problems rather than long-term strategies. However, while this behavior may be feasible for firms which expect to go on doing in the future what they have always done in the past, it becomes increasingly dangerous if competition encourages them to consider a wider range of alternatives. The long lead time required for many of these alternatives may eventually force them to look further and further into the future.

Formal model building may then help the decision takers to identify some of the future states of the world in which they may have to operate, and to predict some of the long-term consequences of their current decisions, but the models are inevitably imperfect. "There is only one fully accurate, comprehensive and implemented 'model' of firms and their environment – and we live in it" (Cantley 1972). The best that a model can do is to produce a list of possible future events. If the list is thought to be comprehensive, it may be possible to use formal calculations to indicate the preferred decision. For example, the firm will know that each strategy will lead to a range of possible payoffs, with the range depending upon future events which are beyond its control. If it has a complete list of all possible events, and can attach a probability to each event, it may be possible to treat the apparent uncertainty as a problem in risk analysis. Such analysis can help to supply a single value (a "certainty equivalent") in place of the range of possible payoffs for each strategy. One possible way of doing this is to use the numerical probabilities as weights and calculate the weighted average or "expected value" of the possible payoffs. Alternative methods may allow more explicitly for the decision takers' attitudes to risk, and the way in which they balance out (say) the near certainty of a small gain against the slight risk of a large loss. (For further details see, for example, Schlaifer 1969). However, in many cases it will be inappropriate to treat uncertainty as a formal problem in risk analysis. Even if all the relevant decision takers could agree on a single decision criterion and a single attitude to risk (which is hardly plausible) they are unlikely to be able to identify all the alternative future states of the world. There will be gaps in their knowledge of the future, and the extent of their ignorance will increase with the time horizon that is necessary for planning. Nevertheless they must reach some decisions, and the decisions must reflect their uncertainty about the future. There are several ways in which a statement of corporate strategy may help.

A. Even if the decision takers cannot foresee all the results of their decisions, they may be able to emphasize their shorter-term targets or competitive strengths that are believed to contribute to their long-term objectives. To some degree, such actions are comparable to those of a military strategist. A field commander cannot guarantee success, but he may well recognize that control of some geographical feature may be decisive, whereas other areas are likely to be indefensible except at very high cost.

In business, the appropriate choices are rarely obvious, but some clues may be gained from experience or by observing and analyzing the actions of other firms. In practice, the observations may be fairly casual, but we should note that the analysis can also be the basic subject matter of industrial economics. The observations may suggest, for example, that although profits are unpredictable, the prospects for long-term profitability can be improved by more immediate efforts to increase market share. The latter then becomes a major strategic objective, and in pursuit of this objective, the firm may decide that it should move out of some markets and concentrate on others. Alternatively the observations may suggest that the firm can respond more readily to unforeseen changes if it concentrates on the business areas that it knows well, and in which it has some competitive advantage. In each case, the argument indicates that the firm should concentrate on certain types of development to the exclusion of others. This specialization cannot guarantee success, but it may significantly reduce the chances of failure.

B. At the same time, the firm may be able to reduce the consequences of potential mistakes by reducing its dependence on the outcome of a single decision, and this desire to spread risks must clearly be balanced against the advantages of specialization (see Chapter 4). Adverse consequences may also be reduced if the firm can increase its flexibility and develop more versatile resources. In terms of the old analogy of eggs in baskets, we might note that the dangers are not caused simply by the thin shells on the eggs: They also depend on the number of eggs in any one basket, on how long they are going to stay there, and on whether one can still make an omelet with the broken eggs.

C. The decisions that are taken will depend not only upon the objectives but also on the quality of information available. Unfortunately, it is impossible to measure this quality if we do not already know what a perfect answer would look like, but we might guess that, in some sense, information would be better if it was obtained from someone with long experience or by a thorough search of all known sources. If this is accepted, then it follows that firms will be better informed, and so will be able to take better decisions, if they stick to the business areas they already know or if they concentrate on a relatively few new areas, so that they can economize on search expenditure.

D. If a firm can find some way to influence the future actions of consumers, governments, or other firms, it may be able to control some features of its environment and so may be able to shape the future instead of waiting passively for it to arrive. In the language of behavioral theory, it may seek a "negotiated environment" in order to reduce uncertainty. In the longer term, for example, a firm may consider mergers to limit competition, or vertical integration to control input supplies and markets. But in each case, its ability to control the immediate environment will be limited by the less tractable characteristics of the "superenvironment" in which it operates. Given its size and its financial strength, it is likely to be more successful if it concentrates on the business areas in which it understands the requirements needed for success, whereas it is less likely to succeed if it dissipates its resources by taking on too many different areas.

Multiple objectives

As we saw in our earlier discussion of behavioral theories, it may be impossible for the members of a large complex organization to agree on a single set of objectives with a clearly defined statement of priorities. Instead it may be more feasible to allow an aspiration level for each relevant objective to appear as a constraint on decision taking. In the same way, the constraints embodied in a statement of corporate strategy may help to ensure that the organization is directed to serve the objectives of its members.

As an example, consider the need for goals to reflect social obligations. There is clearly a growing view that firms must concern themselves with the wider needs of society, and that this must be done as an integral part of the firm's activities, not simply as a charitable donation from profits. Relevant objectives might include the advancement of social minorities, the control of pollution, the provision of secure jobs, or the conservation of energy. The pressures on firms are illustrated by the activities of Nader's Raiders in the United States, or by the long campaign in the United Kingdom against low wages paid by international firms to labor employed in the less-developed countries. The arguments have been accepted in principle by the Confederation of British Industries, which sought to establish a set of precepts to guide business conduct (see, for example, C.B.I. 1973).

The motives for firms to respond to these pressures may be a genuine concern for the interests of society or a narrower self-interest. "Business is only tolerated by society as long as it is a net contributor to community welfare . . . To pre-empt excessively harsh controls it is in the interests of large companies to go at least part of the way to meeting the legitimate objections of their critics" (Lowes 1977, p. 23). However though firms may wish to serve the interests of society, the objectives and methods of achievement are never clearly specified: Even the society whose interests are to be served cannot reach unanimous agreement on the objectives. As a result, firms cannot hope to optimize their contribution. The best that they can do is to make some attempt at progress in specific areas while avoiding the more obvious pitfalls. These areas and pitfalls should therefore be identified as part of their corporate strategy.

Internal cohesion

It has long been accepted that firms may benefit from the use of fairly loose employment contracts, which leave some future tasks to be ordered as the need arises. The contracts are more efficient for the firms than are the alternatives of specifying every future contingency in advance or of renegotiating the contract to cope with every minor change in the environment (see, for example, Coase 1937, O. E. Williamson 1975). At the same time, however, the contracts will be more acceptable to an employee if he can see in advance that his future tasks will be ordered so as to contribute to objectives which he believes to be important. A clear concept of corporate strategy should, therefore, "help to weld an organisation together by developing among the members of the management team both a shared belief in the efficacy of major action programmes and a shared commitment to execute those programmes successfully" (Vancil 1976, p. 1).

Similarly Christiansen, Andrews, and Bower (1973, p. 112) refer to strategy "as the focus of organisational effort, as the object of commitment, and as the source of constructive motivation and self-control in the organisation itself." The commitment will be easier to achieve if the strategy is clearly discernible and accepted by all concerned, but in complex organizations it may depend on a continuing iterative process in which a number of influential people or groups develop semipermanent agreements with each other. In these conditions, the individual commitment is not to a single statement of strategy but rather to a belief in the way in which strategy is likely to evolve in the future.

If strategy is to have a lasting effect on the cohesion of the organization, then it is clear that the reward system used by the firm must be consistent with the same long-term objectives. For example, if the objective is to encourage risk taking, then managers who take risks must be rewarded more highly then those who play safe. Unfortunately it seems that this consistency between stated goals and actual rewards is not always achieved in practice. "Everyone talks about the importance of management development, staff training and investment in plant and equipment that will pay off in the long run. But when salaries are decided and promotions are arranged, there is a tendency to look at performance against the profit target *this year*" (Taylor 1977, p. 7. Italics added).

2.3 The payoff from corporate strategy

The use of corporate strategy is spreading, and although not all firms benefit from its introduction, there is a growing body of evidence to confirm the potential benefits of formal strategic planning. For example, Thune and House (1972) reported the results of a survey of six U.S. industrial groups. They studied formal and informal planners for varying periods around 1955–65, and measured their performance in terms of increase in sales, increase in earnings per share, increase in stock price, increase in earnings on common equity, and increase in earnings on total capital employed. Their results suggest that formal planners performed significantly better than informal planners and also improved on their own pre-planning performance. Subjective estimates of success were also obtained in a survey of planners in Australia, Canada, Italy, Japan, the United Kingdom, and the United States, made by Steiner and Schollhammer (1975). In all countries except Japan (where a majority of corporate planners were dissatisfied with their planning systems) at least seventy-five percent of the planners were not dissatisfied with the results they had obtained. Their satisfaction was generally greater in firms which used more formal planning procedures and which had more experience of corporate planning. Further evidence in favor of strategic planning in specific contexts is reported in later chapters dealing with mergers and innovation. See also Steiner and Miner (1977, p. 114).

However, although there would seem to be clear evidence to support a general case for corporate strategic planning, some doubts and dissatisfaction remain. Steiner and Schollhammer (1975) attempted to identify some of the causes of poor performance, and reported widespread agreement that the major problems arise because relevant staff are not involved in the formulation of strategy, and so lack any real commitment to the outcome. A common complaint was that top executives concentrated too much effort on short-term problems, while delegating corporate strategy to planners who were isolated from other decision-making channels. Similarly a survey by Taylor and Irving (1971) stressed that corporate planning was not taken seriously unless the chief executives were personally involved and line managers could see a specific personal payoff from higher job satisfaction or help in overcoming operating problems.

It seems that the case for an explicit strategy is weaker if firms can survive and grow by adapting slowly to meet gradual changes in the environment, whereas more formal procedures are needed for rapid changes if different departments or divisions are not to pursue contradictory policies (see, for example, Ansoff 1972). Taylor and Irving (1971) confirmed that in the United Kingdom, strategic planning was frequently adopted because firms found it difficult to handle rapid external or internal changes by more familiar methods. Similarly Thune and House (1972) found that formal planning had the least effect on the performance of firms in industries characterized by a low rate of innovation: Formal planners consistently outperformed informal planners in the drug, chemical, and machinery industries; but no clear association between planning and performance could be found in the food, oil, and steel industries.

Clearly, formal strategic planning can pay off in the right circumstances, and to this extent, it is tempting to think of it as a nonquantitative optimizing technique, in the same way that continued learning may allow short-run satisficing rules to yield optimizing price and output decisions in the long run (Day 1967). This interpretation is very appealing to an economist. However it may be misleading. In conditions of true uncertainty, it is very difficult to define what we mean by the optimization of nonrepeatable strategic decisions.

Part II
Strategy, specialization, and diversity

Introduction: Defining the problem

This part discusses the many factors influencing the range of activities which may be undertaken by a firm, and especially the range of final and/or intermediate products. Our main purpose is to see how changes in the range of activities may contribute to the firm's strategic objectives, either by encouraging a more effective use of existing resources, or by developing a more secure and fruitful resource base for subsequent development.

The different activities are usually linked in some way, and it is often convenient to classify these linkages as being either vertical or lateral. Vertical linkages are involved when one activity provides some of the inputs required for another. By contrast, activities are said to be laterally related when they occur at a similar stage in the process of production, and often the activities will share a common vertical linkage with some third activity. For example, lateral linkages exist when two products share a common input or are both sold through the same distribution channels.

Common examples of vertical linkages include the production and refining of crude oil, or the common ownership of breweries and public houses for the production and distribution of beer. Conversely, examples of lateral linkages are common in the chemical industry, in which firms typically produce a wide range of products from a limited number of basic chemical building blocks. Firms which exploit lateral linkages of this sort are said to be diversified, while the term "conglomerate diversification" is used to imply that a firm undertakes a wide range of activities with very little linkage between them. On the other hand, firms which internalize vertical linkages are often said to be vertically integrated, although the term "integration" is sometimes used for all vertical linkages whether these occur within individual firms or involve market transactions between independent firms. In an attempt to avoid confusion, we shall refer to these market transactions as vertical or market *coordi-*

nation and reserve the term "vertical *integration*" for linkages occurring within firms.

We turn in Chapter 3 to the strategic problems of vertical integration, and then consider diversification in Chapter 4. In each case, the emphasis is on the general range of factors that may influence success or failure – what we have previously called the inputs to the strategic-planning process – but Chapter 5 attempts to explain how an understanding of these factors may be exploited in practice. These three chapters are concerned primarily with behavior within national boundaries, and the behavior of international firms is then introduced as an additional feature in Chapter 6.

For the most part, Chapters 3 and 4 treat integration and diversification as separate strategies. This is convenient for exposition, but there is one sense in which it may be misleading. As a firm grows, or as its environment changes, so the importance of specific activities will vary, and the firm will wish to change the mix of its activities, expanding some and contracting others. At any one time, the mix may include a range of vertical and lateral linkages, but when it seeks to change this mix by further integration or diversification, it will find that these represent competing uses for its financial or managerial resources. We must, therefore, accept that the opportunity cost of choosing any one direction for expansion must include the benefits of the excluded alternative. It would be tedious to repeat this point at every stage of our discussion, but we must remember that it is implicit in the argument. If firms have limited resources, we cannot make a complete case for any one strategy without considering the alternatives.

3
Vertical integration

When a firm chooses to become more vertically integrated, it is choosing to take on activities that might otherwise have been covered by a market transaction in which it acted as either customer or supplier. This is in direct contrast to the process of diversification, which involves the addition of activities which were previously outside the firm's areas of direct interest and influence, although the activities may have been related as substitutes or complements in the eyes of consumers.

There are many possible motives for integration, and any attempt to classify these motives may involve some ambiguity. Nevertheless it is often fruitful to recognize at least two broad alternatives. First, integration may be undertaken consciously to reduce the costs of manufacturing or distributing existing items. Second, integration may be undertaken for longer-term strategic reasons, to improve the general competitive position and to reduce the risks faced by the firm. However, almost as a third category, we should note that, in some cases, it may be difficult or impossible for a firm to develop at all unless it does so as an integrated unit, because the existing sources of supply are inadequate and cannot develop quickly enough to offer a realistic alternative.

For example, in the early stages of development of the motorcar industry in the United Kingdom, the domestic light-engineering industry was unable to provide satisfactory component supplies, and car manufacturers had to provide capital and know-how to manufacture their own components. It was not until the 1920s and 1930s that independent component suppliers grew to offer a genuine market alternative to vertical integration in the United Kingdom, whereas in the United States, a more highly developed light-engineering industry was able to offer this alternative from the outset. (For further details see Rhys 1972).

More recently, similar problems forced an integrated structure on the firms which helped to set up the U.K. watch industry after

23

the 1939–45 war. In 1945, the U.K. Government decided for strategic reasons to try to establish a domestic industry that would have the capacity and expertise to produce very small precision mechanisms in large quantities. It therefore encouraged the development of a watchmaking industry. The opportunity was taken up by a small number of firms, most of whom had had some prior experience of related activities. For example S. Smith and Sons had a broad manufacturing base, which included clocks and motor accessories, while Ingersoll had previously been concerned with the import and distribution of watches. However, there were virtually no U.K. suppliers of the components and tools required for watch manufacturing, and prolonged imports were ruled out by the Government's strategy. The entrants were therefore forced to provide most of their own requirements This was in marked contrast to the structure of the long-established Swiss watch industry, in which many manufacturers were primarily assembly firms obtaining standardized or precisely specified components from a large number of competing suppliers. In the United Kingdom in the 1940s and early 1950s, such alternatives did not exist, and it was simply not possible to create them overnight. "An industry cannot be started by the integration of a large number of small firms across the market if few people have the necessary technical knowledge, organising knowledge and enterprise" (Edwards and Townsend 1962, p. 242).

It is clear that, in cases like this, the firms may see no realistic alternative to integration. However it is probably misleading to emphasize the purely technical problems of manufacture. Commercial problems and risks may be even more important (see section 3.1 cost savings). Further, it will generally be true that the viability or nonviability of a market alternative to vertical integration is not so clear-cut as has been implied so far. Typically, a market alternative may exist, but may seem to be inadequate, especially in times of rapid growth, when existing suppliers are unwilling or unable to expand capacity rapidly enough to avoid periodic shortages. Firms may then seek to integrate in order to protect their existing sources of supply. This point has been emphasized by Adelman, who argues that "a firm does not normally integrate into a market when it can buy unlimited quantities at the going price and when the producers are receiving a normal (or subnormal) return. A firm does integrate into a broadening market whose service is scarce and expensive" (Adelman 1955, p. 319). For the rest of this chapter we shall therefore assume that the firm has a genuine choice between integration and market coordination. Section 3.1 concentrates on the major incentives for integration, starting with the objective of cost reduction and then turning to the broader stretegic objectives. Subsequently, in section 3.2 we shall look at some of the problems which lie in wait for the overoptimistic integrator.

3.1 The incentives for vertical integration

Cost savings

Potential cost savings are often cited as a possible reason for vertical integration (see, for example, Pickering 1974, pp 57–8, or Reekie 1975, Chap. 11). These savings may arise in many different ways, but fundamentally there are two alternatives: Either there can be an improvement in technical efficiency, reducing the quantity of resources required at constant market prices, or the prices of the resources may change in the firm's favor as a result of the change in market structure. In practice, these may occur simultaneously, but we shall consider them separately.

Technical efficiency: sources of cost savings. Resources may be saved in several different ways. It may be that production techniques are such that linked processes are best operated in a single plant, or that marketing and distribution costs can be saved by the elimination of intermediate transfers, or that production can be planned and coordinated more efficiently within a single administrative unit. However, as we shall see, all such cases have one thing in common. Regardless of the operating characteristics that dictate close physical links or careful coordination, and so appear to be the proximate causes of the cost savings, the essential point is that market coordination involves higher costs than does administrative integration. Ultimately, we must therefore ask why some production systems cannot be coordinated by market transactions between independent parties, without excessive transactions costs for at least some of the people concerned. This point will be developed more fully in due course, but first we shall look at the proximate sources of cost savings in a little more detail.

The standard example of technically induced vertical integration is the manufacture of steel. Many of the processes for this product have to be carried out at high temperatures, and so if the processes were geographically dispersed, manufacturing costs would be increased significantly by the expense of reheating cold metal or transporting hot metal over long distances. As a result, a typical large steel mill is not restricted to the manufacture of steel but includes some preparatory processes, such as the production of pig iron, and some later-stage processes, such as initial rolling of the hot metal. On the other hand, once the metal has had to be cooled as part of the production process (for example, in annealing) or loses heat in processing (for example, after initial rolling) then the purely technical argument for vertical integration becomes less imperative.

The steel industry may appear to be an extreme example, but similar conditions involving very high temperatures exist in other basic-material industries, and, in general, it is quite common to find that transport costs discourage the dispersion of vertically related activities. As a further example, consider the various stages involved in the manufacture of metal castings. To the layman, these stages may be simplified as (1) preparing molds in boxes with impacted sand; (2) pouring hot metal into the mold and allowing it to cool; and (3) removing the castings from the molds and undertaking initial surface treatment. From a purely technical point of view, there is no reason why these stages should be integrated, but they are usually performed in a single foundry, because of the significant transport problems which would arise if they were separated. For one thing, additional handling would increase the risk of damage to the molds. Further, there is a clear incentive to minimize the handling of the boxes and the sand (including recycling from the third to the first stage) because none of this material is required by subsequent users – ultimately it is only the space contained in the material that is wanted. In general, we should expect that processes will be linked so as to reduce the need to transport intermediate products whenever further processing involves a significant reduction in weight or volume before the product is shipped to the final consumer.

Further savings in distribution costs may arise when firms integrate forward, that is toward the market or "downstream." In recent years, many large manufacturers of consumer goods have chosen to become increasingly involved in distribution, especially for food products. They have taken on their own wholesaling activities, distributing direct to large retailers although possibly continuing to rely upon independent wholesalers for distribution to smaller retailers. In some cases, these links may yield strategic advantages, but they can also produce cost savings if redundant activities can be eliminated. Traditionally, the independent wholesalers have provided services of particular benefit to smaller retailers. These include merchanting advice, stockholding, and breaking bulk to meet the delivery sizes most appropriate for the retailers. However, many branches of retailing have become dominated by larger shops or larger organizations owning chains of shops, and these larger units may be large enough to accept bulk deliveries direct from the manufacturers, thus eliminating the need to break bulk, and they may also find it more efficient to develop merchanting strategies to meet their own needs, independently of any wholesaler's advice. However, although it is possible to eliminate some of the wholesalers' services, others such as transportation and (possibly) stockholding are still essential and may be provided by vertical integration, either by the manufacturer or by the retailer.

Problems of market coordination. Each of the examples (steel, castings, or wholesaling) therefore illustrates a possible motive for integration, but as yet the explanations remain incomplete. Manufacturers do not have to provide their own wholesaling services just because they want a package that is a little different from that offered by conventional wholesalers: They may be able to persuade unconventional wholesalers to do the job for them. Similarly in the metal casting and steel examples, the fact that the separate stages have to be in close physical proximity does not automatically mean that they must all be under common ownership. There are certainly other cases when divided ownership is commonplace. As an example, consider the domestic use of electricity. In most houses, the electricity meter and (say) a washing machine are vertically linked (in that they represent distinct stages in the distribution and use of electricity) and are in close physical proximity, but they remain under separate ownership. In spite of occasional widely publicized cases in which domestic consumers claim that they are being charged for the local street lighting, the separate ownership does not cause any problems, because the rights and responsibilities of the electricity authority and the domestic consumer can be specified clearly and unambiguously in advance.

However while this ability to specify things in advance appears to be critical in such cases, it is not always possible. If closely linked activities are to be coordinated, then it must be possible to specify the appropriate actions to be taken by all those involved in the activities. Within a firm, this coordination may be achieved by the central management, which has the power to monitor all activities and to make adjustments as the need arises. Provided that all members of the firm trust the managers' decisions, they do not need to know all those decisions nor do they need to keep a running check on all the other activities. On the other hand, the system may react differently if the same activities are to be coordinated by means of market contracts. Each participant will then act only if he has a specific incentive to do so. Before he commits himself to a particular type of activity, he will want to know what he is expected to do in different circumstances, and what incentive he has to act in that way. At the same time, he will want a reasonable assurance that other participants will provide appropriate complementary activities.

As an example of the problems involved, consider again the case of metal castings. In principle, the molds and subsequent castings could be made by different firms. But because the two stages must be physically linked, neither firm would have any choice but to supply to or buy from the other. Before either would accept such a situation, they would want a firm contract that would not only give reasonable guarantees of quantities and prices but would also specify how prices were to be fixed if patterns or other technical characteristics were to change, and would provide for arbitration in the case of dispute over (say) the quality of the molds or the causes of any imperfections in the castings. This type of contractual relationship may be feasible if the range of alternatives to be covered is fairly narrow, and if the actions of each party can be monitored fairly easily, but there is no reason to suppose that either of these conditions is inevitable. It is therefore appropriate to look at some of the unsatisfactory features of market coordination in a little more detail, and then to ask whether administrative integration may provide a basis for improved operating conditions.

The problems of achieving coordination will be considerable if it involves a large number of activities which can work in many different ways. Market coordination then requires a large number of interdependent contracts, with considerable expenditure of time and effort to ensure that the contracts cover all the alternatives that are thought to be relevant. But even so, the contracts will never be completely comprehensive, and there will be occasional events which throw up problems that they do not cover. These omissions will arise either because the costs of providing complete coverage are unacceptable, or because of what is called "bounded rationality": that is, because even the best planners cannot foresee everything. This would not really matter if all the excluded alternatives were covered by established case law, so that disputes could be resolved quickly and easily in line with established principles. Indeed, if the case law is unambiguous there may be no need for formal contracts except as a way of confirming that the parties recognize the law and accept its implications. This appears to be true of many transactions at the retail level.

However, case law depends upon precedent and is therefore most appropriate for repetitive events. The more significant problems arise with unpredicted events that are not covered by case law. If such events are covered by the contracts, then the agreed solutions must have been accepted by all parties when the contracts were signed. However, if the events were not foreseen even as possibilities, and were not covered by the contracts, then an appropriate level of prices or an acceptable distribution of profit may have to be negotiated *after* the event when some of the parties involved will have a vested interest in preserving the existing distribution, while others will wish to change it. Agreement is then more difficult. Exceptional goodwill, or exceptional trust in the judgment of an independent arbitrator will be required if all parties are to be satisfied. If some remain dissatisfied, or even if they just fear that they might be, then they have two alternatives. They may be prepared to pay the higher costs involved in getting more comprehensive contracts. Alternatively they may opt for vertical integration in place of market coordination if this seems to offer a cheaper alternative.

Even when the contracts are fully specified, in the sense that they cover all possible outcomes, the trading parties may still end up in dispute if they cannot agree on the facts of the case. For example, if the contract says that one party shall act in a specified way to change output whenever there is some change in the quality of inputs, then it must be possible for *both* parties to judge when the quality of inputs has changed and whether the appropriate change in output has been made. But, in many cases, such observation could not be made without some more or less permanent check involving detailed measurements. This may be especially true if observations relate to changes in quality or involve several different components of a complex system.

The case for integration. Market coordination may therefore prove to be unsatisfactory in some cases, either because the transactions costs are too high or because the results cannot be monitored satisfactorily. The problems may sometimes be reduced if the linked activities are integrated within a single firm. By assuming powers of arbitration in cases of dispute, the central management may avoid some of the problems of incomplete contracts. Foward planning may still pose problems, but because the firm can more easily adapt to situations as they arise, it is not necessary for the firm to anticipate all possibilities in advance: It may be able to postpone the less immediate decisions and so use a sequential decision process that economizes on the need for advance information. Further, the central management of a firm can perform an audit or otherwise monitor the performance of each activity more effectively than independent trading partners could do for themselves in a system of market coordination, and as a result the firm may be able to raise the performance of each separate activity.

Vertical integration may therefore offer some advantages over market coordination. But the benefits are not universal. For example, the gains will be less marked if organized commodity markets provide a firm base for market coordination by setting acceptable criteria for measurement and arbitration. Conversely, in large firms it may be necessary to find some way to measure the performance of subunit managers, and this may limit the scope for detailed intervention to coordinate the subunit's activities. Further, it may be that vertically linked activities require different skills, which are not easily controlled by a single management. In such cases, integration may reduce the efficiency with which some of the activities are operated.

However, these administrative problems are unlikely to be troublesome in the sort of cases which we were discussing at the start of this section, because processes which have to be in close physical proximity are unlikely to have widely different operating characteristics. Further, although the problems of market coordination are not confined to any particular product, they are likely to be greatest when there is strong technical interdependence between closely linked activities. That is, activities with strong technical linkages are likely to be vertically integrated because of the high transactions costs that would be involved in market coordination.

Similar arguments apply to the general management problem involved in planning the sequence of operations required to produce a particular product. Arm's length coordination may be quite adequate when standard components are purchased in polypolistic markets, and yet may be suspect when a single supplier provides a special purpose component to a single user. In the latter case, the unique product may make it more difficult to agree on a price, and hence on a fair division of profit between the two parties, or to establish agreed criteria for testing performance. Coordination of the two activities is essential, and will require close cooperation. However, it is less certain that this necessarily requires integration. (This latter point will be taken up again in section 3.2.)

Changes in input prices. It is clear that integrated firms may be able to reduce costs by increasing their technical efficiency. They may also be able to achieve lower input prices. Integration may contribute to this end if it allows them to avoid or exploit any distortions caused by quasimonopolistic markets for intermediate goods. We must therefore look at the relationship between integration and the prices that are paid for inputs.

Economic analysis recognizes that a firm that wishes to maximize profits will achieve its objective if marginal cost is equal to marginal revenue. This is not a particularly good description of the managers' decision-taking processes, but it remains as a useful analytical device. It implies that a firm which is committed to making its own components will achieve the most profitable output of components if the marginal cost of manufacture is equal to the net marginal revenue (marginal revenue net of all other marginal costs) received from sales. The possibility of internal transfer between subdivisions of the same firm does not affect this argument, although if accounting procedures require that notional prices should be attached to these internal transfers, and if these transfer prices are likely to influence the profit-motivated decisions of the subdivisions, then the transfer prices must also reflect marginal costs if the local decisions are to be optimal for the firm. Strictly, the argument relates to marginal opportunity costs rather than marginal cash costs. If the firm could sell the components on the open market, then it is the price or marginal revenue obtained from these sales which determines the marginal opportunity cost of using the components internally. However, for convenience, we shall assume that the manufacturing costs are true opportunity costs.

This line of reasoning suggests that a firm should compare the marginal outlay on inputs against the marginal cost of their manufacture. A firm might consider increased vertical integration to provide inputs which were previously bought out, whenever the marginal outlay on the bought-out items exceeds the marginal cost of producing them. But clearly the relevant marginal cost is that achievable by the purchaser, not the current supplier. Integration would be an immediate nonstarter if the suppliers have specific patents, technical know-how, or other advantages which are not available to the purchaser: that is, if there are some absolute cost barriers to entry to the industry supplying the inputs. Similarly, integration may be discouraged if there are economies of scale in the manufacture of the inputs. A firm whose internal requirements are too small to absorb the capacity output of an optimal plant may be unable to match the suppliers' prices unless it has unrestricted access to the market to offload its surplus production.

It is possible to identify various circumstances in which integration would be prevented by cost barriers of this nature, even though imperfect markets for intermediate goods may result in a large margin between marginal cost and price. Some of the more obvious cases of price distortion may therefore have trivial effects on integration. For example, if many small firms buy from a single monopolistic supplier, no one buyer could integrate backwards to produce the intermediate product unless the monopolist has no protection from entry barriers, and therefore has only temporary monopoly power, or the buyer in question has unique advantages which offset the general entry barriers. Conversely, perfectly competitive suppliers are unlikely to be able to integrate to avoid restrictions imposed by a well-entrenched monopsonistic buyer.

The choices facing the monopolist in such cases may be more complex, and will depend upon the buyers' ability to find substitutes for the monopolized inputs, and so vary the mix of inputs used in production. A monopolist selling to perfectly competitive buyers will have no incentive to integrate if there are no effective substitutes for its product. The buyers will process the input and set their selling prices equal to their marginal costs, and if they have to use their inputs in fixed proportions, the monopolistic supplier of one input will receive the same marginal revenue (net of all other marginal costs) whether he processes the intermediate product himself or sells it to the perfectly competitive firms for processing. The monopolist's profit: maximizing output will be the same in each case. However, this would not be true if the buyers can find an effective substitute for the monopolized input, and the monopolist may then wish to integrate forward in order to secure the use of its own product rather than the substitute. Although this choice had proved unprofitable for the original buyers, it could be profitable for the integrated monopolist, because the latter's decisions should reflect the marginal cost of producing the input rather than the higher price at which it had been sold to the nonintegrated buyers.

The practical importance of this point, however, is uncertain. Perfect markets are rarely observable, but in general those industries which remain polypolistic in structure will have some feature which restricts the growth of individual firms. The restriction may arise because of (say) market fragmentation, or uncertainty, and is likely to limit the intermediate monopolist's ability to integrate with all end users of the input, just as it limits the growth of the end users themselves. The monopolist's initial incentive to integrate is therefore likely to be offset by increases in costs, especially if different managerial skills are required for the intermediate and final products.

In general, the more significant cases would seem to be those involving bilateral monopoly or bilateral oligopoly, with a degree of monopoly on both sides of the intermediate market. Unfortunately "the theory of bilateral monopoly is indeterminate with a vengeance" (Scherer 1970, p. 242). No general predictions can be made. However, it is possible to identify the more significant points by concentrating on two alternative cases: (A) joint profit maximization, and (B) myopic monopoly.

A. Joint profit maximization. If a monopolist sells to a monopsonist, and they wish to maximize their joint profits, they should select the same output as an integrated monopolist. To ensure that this output is in fact produced, and that the monopsonist does not change his purchases unilaterally after a fixed price has been agreed upon, the contract between the two firms must specify both the price and the quantity of the intermediate good. The price would determine the allocation of profits between the two firms and this would reflect their relative bargaining strengths and negotiating skills.

In these circumstances, there is likely to be relatively little incentive for vertical integration, except insofar as either firm may try to improve its bargaining position, and so may undertake some limited integration in order to increase its knowledge of the other stages and/or to show that it can operate at all stages if it has to. Once the bargaining positions have been established, neither firm should be able to gain significantly from further integration, no matter how much it may wish to do so. Its ability to displace the other in open competition will already have been reflected in its bargaining strength, and the alternative of acquisition is unlikely to be profitable because the price paid would simply capitalize the expected profits. The only major exception might arise if shareholders lacked the information needed to estimate the true profit potential of either firm. With the better information that it gets from its direct contacts, a firm may be able to exploit the market's undervaluation of its suppliers or customers, and may use a takeover bid as a basis for profitable integration. However, we should note that, in such cases, the firm's gain would simply reflect its superior information: Integration would be coincidental.

B. Myopic monopoly. The other major alternative arises in the case of what Scherer (1970) calls two-stage myopic monopoly. In this case, a monopolistic supplier of an intermediate product faces a monopsonistic buyer, who also has a monopoly in the final product market. It is assumed that the intermediate monopolist sets a price for its product, and that the monopsonist then determines its purchases on the myopic assumption that those purchases will have no effect on the price of the intermediate. The output of the intermediate may then be less than that required to maximize joint profits. A formal proof of this result is given in Appendix A, for the limited case of linear cost and demand functions. Verbal explanations are inevitably tortuous, but the result may be understood intuitively, once it is accepted that the demand curve for the final product is necessarily more elastic than the derived demand for the intermediate product. The result must hold for any monopolistic producer who seeks to maximize profits, on the assumption that input prices are fixed. Such a firm would respond to any change in input prices by adjusting output until the new input price is again equal to the marginal revenue product of the input. The buyer's marginal revenue product is therefore the same as the supplier's average revenue at every level of output for the intermediate product, but the buyer's marginal revenue function is less elastic than his demand function because of his monopoly position in the final product market. The supplier therefore faces a less elastic demand than he would if he controlled both stages of production, and he will restrict his output accordingly.

In principle, the opportunity to avoid this restriction may seem to provide an incentive for integration. In a pure bilateral monopoly, it may be more reasonable to expect that the firms would learn to overcome their myopia and negotiate a joint maximizing alternative, but the so-called myopic solution may be plausible in bilateral oligopoly, because it will then be more difficult to identify and preserve the prices and quantities required to maximize joint profits. Even in these conditions, however, the buyer who recognizes the consequences of myopia may be able to obtain price concessions by using the threat of integration without actually integrating. The threat would seem to be more plausible in oligopoly than in monopoly because the ability of more than one firm to survive has already been demonstrated. It will also be most effective when made by oligopsonists who would have a guaranteed market for their own intermediates. Examples are common in the United States, and have been summarized by Scherer. For example:

Tin-plated steel prices have been restrained by the ability of the tin can manufacturers to begin plating their own steel, while tin can prices have been held in check by the threat (and in some cases the actuality) of upstream integration by large food canners. The auto manufacturers have kept downward pressure on glass window, electrical component, fabricated parts, and even cold-rolled steel sheet prices by their demonstrated willingness to produce for their own use whenever the prospect of cost savings becomes attractive. (Scherer 1970, pp. 246–7)

In general, therefore, it seems that noncompetitive markets for intermediate goods may not provide a very common incentive for vertical integration. Examples of such integration are rare, or at least are not well documented. One pertinent exception, however, has been analyzed by Oi and Hurter (1965) who argue that noncompetitive transport prices in the United States may have encouraged firms to provide some of their own transport needs rather than relying on common carriers. As possible examples of noncompetitive prices they quote (i) prices which purport to reflect the value of the service to the customer without considering the cost of alternatives, and (ii) prices which are based upon suppliers' average costs for a range of distances or time periods. In the first example, any customers who were charged discriminatorily high prices would have a clear incentive to provide their own transport fleets, whereas, in the second example, customers may choose to provide their own fleets for normal business while using common carriers for exceptional loads or peak periods when the carriers' prices may be below their true marginal costs. However, Oi and Hurter also point out that while integrated users often claim that their transport costs are below the common-carriers' prices, they are generally unwilling or unable to give details of those costs. Their decisions may reflect formal analysis, but it may be that general cost differences are used to provide simple post hoc rationalizations for decisions taken for other reasons. These other reasons may include the strategic factors to be considered in the next section.

Strategic motivation

We turn now to the strategic consequences of vertical integration. These are generally less quantifiable than the cost savings, and are sometimes less amenable to formal analysis. As with the discussion of costs, however, it is convenient to divide the discussion into two parts for exposition. We shall first consider the effects on a firm's market power, and then some aspects of risk and uncertainty.

Market power. It is possible that vertical integration may raise entry barriers against potential future competitors, or more generally, that it may enable the integrated firm to discourage aggressive moves by rivals by using predatory pricing practices or cross-subsidization. However, we shall see that in practice the strategic gains are not unambiguous.

Entry barriers. Consider first the situation in a bilateral oligopoly. Provided that the established firms do not integrate across the market, any potential entrant to either of the bilateral stages need only consider the entry conditions for that stage. The bilateral structure will affect his estimate of potential profitability, but it does not represent an additional barrier protecting high profits for the established firms. The entrant does not need to enter both stages simultaneously. By contrast, entry may be difficult if the two stages are dominated by a small number of vertically integrated firms. The potential entrant must then attack both stages simultaneously so as to obtain the necessary inputs or outlets for his products, or must at least ensure that entry occurs simultaneously at each stage so that other entrants can provide the complementary services, unless by chance one of the existing firms is seeking additional capacity for intermediates or outlets for surplus intermediate production, and is prepared to trade with the entrant.

In general, the capital or the knowledge needed for effective entry will be greater if it is necessary to enter in an integrated form. For example, in the United Kingdom, the tied-house system, under which many public houses are owned by the major breweries, reduces the outlets available to any potential entrant. Any entrant who is unable to trade through the existing breweries must either provide increased capital to create outlets or accept a restriction to the carrry-out trade through independent off-licences. However, the capital requirement would not constitute an entry barrier if the supply of capital were perfectly elastic to every potential entrant. The problems for the entrants arise because of imperfections in the capital market, which make it more difficult to raise the finance needed for integrated entry. They are likely to be especially significant for relatively small firms which have limited internal sources of finance. But although integration may enable established firms to exploit such imperfections, it cannot create them if they do not already exist.

Similar general results may follow if integrated firms enjoy operating advantages which make it more difficult for nonintegrated firms to compete, and restrict them to less-profitable market segments. As an example, consider pharmaceuticals. New products offering significant therapeutic advances can be highly profitable but may only enjoy a short life before they are displaced by competitive products. Their marketing requires direct contact between company salesmen and doctors, supported by heavy advertising, to ensure rapid acceptance of potentially successful products. The problems facing smaller firms are undoubtedly increased by the need to integrate marketing with production, given that a marketing organization that is large enough to gain rapid market penetration involves a high fixed cost. Many small firms are therefore confined to the less-profitable market segments which deal with long-established drugs (Shaw and Sutton 1976).

Further advantages may follow if integration appears as a prerequisite for price discrimination. Discrimination may enable a monopolist to exploit differing demand elasticities by charging different prices in different market segments, but it is not feasible if the buyers can resell from the low- to the high-priced segment. Forward integration to gain control of one market segment may enable the monopolist to prevent resale and thus preserve a discriminatory price structure.

It is, therefore, clear that integration can yield strategic advantages. However, unless the integrated firms can obtain clear operating advantages or exploit entry barriers at both stages, the vertical integration *by itself* may have little direct impact on market power. For example, Adelman (1972) has argued that this was true of the world petroleum market during the 1950s. World supplies of crude oil were then controlled by a handful of international companies, who had integrated forward into refining. These major companies chose to maintain overall profitability by charging high prices for open-market sales of crude, while taking a relatively low paper profit on their refining operations. This squeezed the profit margin available to independent refiners and gave the impression that the entry barriers faced by independent refiners had been increased by the majors' integration. It was certainly true that the entry of independent refiners was restrained during this period. However, the entry barriers declined as increased supplies of crude in the 1960s weakened the majors' ability to maintain high prices for crude on the open market. It became clear that the entry barriers had depended upon control of crude oil supplies. Vertical integration appears to have had no separate effect either way.

Predatory pricing. Predatory practices designed to squeeze nonintegrated companies have not been confined to the oil industry. It has occurred in other primary industries, such as aluminum. For example, in the United States in the 1930s, Alcoa, as a major market supplier of both virgin aluminum ingots and aluminum sheets, was reputed to have set the price differential between ingots and sheets so as to ensure that independent rollers were unable to manufacture sheet at a reasonable profit (Blair 1972, p. 29). In such cases, the primary producer's profit depends upon monopolization of the input, not upon vertical integration, and the motive for predatory pricing is sometimes obscure. Explanations remain speculative. Two alternatives are feasible. The primary producer may wish to squeeze the fabricators' margins so as to encourage long-run penetration of the market for fabrications, and hence increased sales of the primary product, without sacrificing current profits. Alternatively, the primary producer may be seeking deliberately to weaken the independent fabricators, so as to reduce any risk that they may develop significant buying power. In either case, it may be forced eventually into further integration if the predatory pricing deters further investment by the independent fabricators.

Cross-subsidization. A related but more general problem concerns the possibility of cross-subsidization, by which an integrated producer uses monopoly profits from one stage to subsidize operations in more competitive stages. Such cross-subsidization is not confined to vertical integration. It may be feasible for any firm which operates in a number of markets with different degrees of market control. But the gains are not automatic. The integrated firm may well be able to use profits from one stage to subsidize competitive losses elsewhere, but to do so it may have to give up preferred alternative uses for those profits. Further, while some managers may be prepared to use cross-subsidization to satisfy their own egos by winning an immediate competition battle, they cannot hope to recover the costs out of increased profits, growth, or market penetration in the subsidized areas if the competition reappears as soon as the subsidy stops. If a firm expects to make any long-term gains, it must believe that ultimately competition can be deterred by the *threat* of cross-subsidization. This is possible, although the threat may lose its force if competitors can respond in the same way. It is therefore unlikely to be effective against other integrated firms. On the other hand, the ability to sustain losses is one of the factors which determines a firm's bargaining strength in oligopolistic markets. The ability may remain latent without being any less effective if erstwhile competitors appreciate the potential threat, and this might allow a firm to act as a price leader even when this would not be justified by its relative position in any one market. Occasional demonstrations of power might then be appropriate, as Voltaire suggested, *"pour encourager les autres."*

Risk and uncertainty. The final strategic motive reflects a desire to avoid the uncertainties involved in market transactions. It is true that partial integration may sometimes aggravate the situation, because it may take the firm into competition with its own customers, but in many cases integration is seen as a way of avoiding some of the worst effects of uncertainty. The uncertainty may arise because information channels are imperfect, so that existing information is not readily available to all users, or it may reflect our general inability to foresee future events with perfect clairty. In turn, integration may reduce perceived uncertainty by improving information flows; it may enable a firm to eliminate some uncertainty because interdependent decisions can be internalized and controlled by a single organization, and it may redistribute the consequences of uncertainty in a way which at least benefits the integrated firm.

Market information. Integration may help to promote stability. It will not normally affect the stability of the aggregate market, although integration between a large supplier and several smaller customers selling in turn to consumer markets may do so by encouraging increased expenditure to stabilize demand. This may occur if the change in structure of the final-product market facilitates advertising. Larger firms may advertise more intensively either because of economies of scale in marketing or because a significant part of the gain from stabilization would appear as an externality to a smaller firm. The externality would imply that any one small firm would by paying for advertising which yielded benefits for its competitors. The benefits could be captured or internalized by a firm with a larger market share, but would not encourage a smaller firm to advertise unless it was guaranteed reciprocal benefits in a cooperative agreement.

However, even if aggregate market stability is not increased, vertical integration may provide suppliers with improved knowledge of the market and thus enable them to plan ahead to avoid the costs of sudden changes in output. Similar benefits may arise from the integration of research with production and marketing. Innovations are less likely to succeed if they are developed without adequate knowledge of user needs. Integration may help to provide that knowledge and may also ensure that the users recognize the need for innovation. Innovation by suppliers may be further encouraged if forward integration helps to provide guaranteed outlets for the products of the new equipment. For example, in the textile industry, Courtaulds argued that its integrated structure encouraged modernization in this way (see, for example, Knight 1974). Further, in some circumstances, integration may help firms to reduce oligopolistic uncertainty by making it easier for them to maintain the tacit collusion required to suppress unprofitable competition. For example, Adelman has suggested that so long as control of crude oil supplies remained highly concentrated, vertical integration into refining encouraged stability by making it more difficult for any one of the oligopolists to plan for an increase in market share without publizing the fact. Given that there were few significant independent refiners, no company could increase its output of crude oil without first building refineries and distribution systems, which telegraphed their plans to their competitors (Adelman 1972).

It is therefore clear that a search for market information may encourage integration, but uncertainty may also encourage integration in other ways. In particular it may do so if interdependence between customers and suppliers leaves one in a weak bargaining position, of if arm's-length trading seems to increase the variability of demand or supply for individual firms.

Interdependence and security. Section 3.1, in the material on cost savings, suggested that market coordination of closely linked activities may be hampered by incomplete knowledge of what is actually happening or poor predictions of what is likely to happen. This incentive to integrate may be increased if there is no acceptable way to allocate the costs between the trading partners, because, in that case, one of the partners may have an incentive either to take over the other or to withdraw from the transaction, thus forcing the other to integrate. The incentive will be greatest when a market transaction would leave one of the partners with a very limited range of future options. This might happen, for example, because the transaction requires specific and nontransferable assets or because one party acquires a monopoly of relevant market or technical know-how. Market coordination may still be feasible in such cases, but sometimes the risks become too great to be acceptable. Oi and Hurter have suggested that integration of production and transportation is likely whenever transport facilities are specific to one firm. In principle, the facilities could be provided by a common carrier for sale to the firm, but the carrier would then face considerable risk unless he can first negotiate a long-term contract to guarantee an acceptable return on his investment, or unless the buyer has no other source of supply, which might be true, for example, of dock facilities or a rail siding. In general, the seller is in a weak bargaining position as soon as he has acquired the specific facilities. The buyer may insist on revised prices which only cover the suppliers short-run variable costs and make no contribution to the intial equipment costs.

A similar risk may have discouraged initial market coordination in the U.K. motorcar and watch industries. In the case of car components, independent suppliers were almost certainly deterred by the rapid changes and diversity of design. These would have forced close contact between buyers and sellers without guaranteeing any long-term market for the latter, and clearly it would have been difficult to allocate the costs of this uncertainty between the firms. Similarly in the watch industry, any potential component suppliers faced a very narrow domestic market, with buyers who were obviously capable of manufacturing their own components. In this case there were no significant scale economies to deter vertical integration. However, in the motor industry, the increasing standardization of components from the 1920s onwards allowed independent suppliers to realize economies of scale and so provided an incentive for increased reliance on market coordination.

Guaranteed markets. Finally, we may note that vertical integration may reflect a search for security of supply of inputs or security of market outlets. Following the supply shortages caused by the oil crisis in 1973–4, many U.S. chemical companies have chosen to integrate backward in an attempt to secure future supplies of the basic chemicals which they need for further processing. In part, this security may be provided by long-term contracts, and these are now spread among several suppliers and include price-escalation clauses in an attempt to avoid a repetition of the breakdown of contractual supplies that occurred frequently in 1973–4. However the companies are also trying to provide enough of their own capacity for key materials to meet the input requirements of their major profit earners (Carruth 1976). This cannot give complete security against shortages of crude oil, any more than firms which manufacture (say) their own metal components are secure against a breakdown in the supply of metal, but the integration does provide greater security against one possible cause of supply restriction.

Conversely, forward integration may help to guarantee market outlets. "Vertical integration, by tying users to particular suppliers, eliminates demand variability felt by suppliers due to users shifting supply sources. The size of this effect is great when user concentration is great since then individual transactions will be great relative to market" (Bernhardt 1977, p. 215). A particularly clear example occurred in the U.K. steel industry in the early 1960s. With the exception of Richard Thomas and Baldwins (R.T.B.) which was still owned by the state, the major steel producers had then been denationalized following the initial moves towards nationalization in the 1950s. One of the major producers, Stewarts and Lloyds (S & L), had excess capacity for the manufacture of steel billets, and were seeking tied outlets among the independent rerolling firms who purchased billets for further processing. S & L therefore proposed to take over Whiteheads Iron and Steel Company, and they made an offer to buy in December 1962. However Whiteheads were a major customer of R.T.B. which was in grave financial difficulties. The Government feared that R.T.B. would collapse if it lost access to Whiteheads, and therefore empowered R.T.B. to acquire the company as a defensive measure to protect its market (Vaizey 1974). Subsequently in 1963, and with much less publicity, S & L took over the Wolverhampton and Birchley Rolling Mills, and thus obtained at least some compensation for their failure to acquire Whiteheads (Keeling and Wright 1964).

3.2 Problems of integration

We must now add a word of warning. Our discussion of the possible motives for integration has included occasional reservations, but it has concentrated on the potential benefits, and may have given the impression that vertical integration is the "normal" business structure. This could be very misleading. It is true that every firm internalizes some vertical linkages, in that it performs for itself some activities which in principle could be bought out, but it is also true that even the largest companies depend upon outside suppliers for many key inputs or services. Further, in spite of many individual examples of increased integration, there is no clear evidence that vertical integration has been increasing in industry as a whole. An American investigation for the period 1929–65 could find no trend in the degree of vertical integration in manufacturing industry. Indeed when some allowance was made for changes in the relative prices of inputs and outputs, the results were consistent with a general decline in the degree of vertical integration (Laffer 1969). Clearly, there must be some factors which reduce or offset the potential gains in many cases.

Integration may sometimes prove to be inefficient because it increases the demands placed upon management's expertise and reduces an organization's flexibility. Alternatively, it may be restricted by the high costs of operating some processes at small scales. These problems are discussed below. But first we should remember that even if it is not clearly inefficient, integration may not be adopted if firms can identify more attractive uses for their scarce resources. Integration might then seem to be beneficial when viewed in isolation, but involve a net opportunity loss when compared with alternative strategies.

This possibility becomes increasingly probable if some of the advantages of integration can be obtained by close cooperation between independent firms, involving very much closer contacts than are implied in the "arm's-length transactions" assumed by much conventional economic theory. Among examples of such cooperation, Richardson has cited the links between large retailers and independent suppliers of goods that are sold under the retailers brand. For example:

Not only do Marks and Spencer tell their suppliers how much they wish to buy from them, and thus promote a quantitative adjustment of supply to demand, they concern themselves equally with the specification and development of both processes and products. They decide, for example, the design of a garment, specify the cloth to be used, and control the processes even to laying down the types of needles to be used in knitting and sewing. In the same way they co-operate with Ranks and Spillers in order to work out the best kind of flour for their cakes and do not neglect to specify the number of cherries and walnuts to go into them . . . Yet all this orchestration of development manufacture and marketing takes place without any shareholding by Marks and Spencer in its suppliers and without even long-term contracts. (Richardson 1972, pp. 885–6)

Such cooperation does not depend upon the dominant power of one firm, although this may appear in some cases. More generally, it requires that both firms recognize their mutual interests and have sufficient mutual respect to trust each other. This seems to be common, and the incentives to cooperate are increased if there are barriers in the way of full integration. Further, in some cases, the apparent risk of dependent status may be offset by more tangible incentives as, for example, is sometimes true of suppliers who find that their business with Marks and Spencer may help them to get other contracts. On the other hand, as we have already seen, the cooperation will be unstable or impossible if the firms do not trust each other or if they are unable to agree on an appropriate strategy to meet the needs of the market.

Management problems of integration

Vertical integration may be counterproductive if it reduces the efficiency or flexibility of management. This could happen simply because integration involves an increase in the size of the firm. Large size will not necessarily cause a deterioration, but it may do so if the firm is unable to attract staff of the right quality, or if it continues with an organization structure that is no longer appropriate for its new strategy. Either of these is possible when top-class managers are generally in scarce supply. The resultant loss of control may lead to delays and errors in planning, which will ultimately affect the efficiency of the operating units. Further, if the cost or quality of the manufactured inputs should fall for any reason, top managers may be unable to control operating units, which adopt a bias in favor of internal sources of supply. The internal purchases may be suboptimal for the firm as a whole, but may be rational for the subunit taking the decision if they help to preserve existing social relationships or to establish internal support in subsequent interdivisional bargaining.

There are several reasons why integrated production may ultimately prove to be less effective than market coordination, and which may therefore counter the arguments in favor of integration which were developed in section 3.1, in the material on cost savings. First, it is clear that management may lack the skills required for joint operation of vertically related activities. In general, it may be inappropriate to impose a unified control over both stages when the complementary activities are dissimilar (see also 4.2). This seems to have been the major reason for the problems experienced by W. and J. B. Eastwood in the late 1960s after they took over Thompson, the established Smithfield meat traders (Foster 1976). Eastwood specialized in the factory-style production of broiler chickens and eggs, and had relied upon vertical integration and the development of specialized facilities to provide the tight cost control needed for their operations. The takeover of Thompson followed earlier cooperation, and seemed to offer a natural extension of their chosen strategy by providing integration of manufacturing and merchanting. However, in practice, full integration proved to be impossible. Eastwood-Thompson remained as an essentially separate operation, owned by Eastwood but very loosely linked with their other operations. The main problem seems to be that Smithfield trading demands flexibility in handling a range of meat products from different sources of supply, and it is simply not possible to combine successful market trading with concentration upon a single product.

Sometimes the problems of inflexibility only arise in the longer term. In particular, an integrated firm may find it increasingly difficult to keep up with technical progress in a number of different areas, or it may find that technical changes gradually erode the initial gains from integration. In some cases the fear, or uncertainty, of future changes in technology or markets will discourage integration from the outset, although in others, the risks may not be immediately obvious, and may appear only after a long period of integration. This may be exemplified by the early history of the Ford Motor Company in the United States. Ford's success in penetrating the mass market with the low-priced Model T has become legendary. The low price depended on the exploitation of mass production and on a closely integrated series of operations designed to control the costs and reliability of both suppliers and dealers. The policy was successful so long as the Model T retained its appeal, but eventually the market's increasing demand for more sophisticated products made a replacement essential, and the established vertical linkages were not always appropriate for the new model. Specifically, the changing styles left Ford underequipped to produce glass and body parts but overendowed with capacity to produce wooden structures.

Clearly, in cases like this, vertical integration may promote profitable growth for a considerable period of time, and yet may eventually prove to be a source of weakness as conditions change. In principle, the solution is simple: integration should be retained so long as it is beneficial, but no longer. However in practice, firms may be unable to foresee the future clearly enough, or to change their operations quickly enough, to avoid all the problems. An American study by Rumelt (1974) suggests that this may be generally true of the larger, raw-material-processing firms which are mostly vertically integrated and heavily dependent upon activities related to a single raw material. The main products of these firms are generally homogeneous, and although the total market demand may be inelastic, the market shares of different firms may be very sensitive to small differences in relative prices. In these conditions, long-run profitability depends primarily on ability to maintain or reduce costs, and firms have a strong incentive to pursue increases in scale or integration in the search for cost reductions. This sometimes results in a narrow-minded concentration on the technical requirements of a single product and absorbs managerial and financial resources which might otherwise be available to develop alternative strategies. As a result, many integrated firms appear to have become locked in mature slow-growing markets with relatively low profitability (Scott 1973).

Problems posed by indivisibilities and economies of scale

The second major barrier to integration reflects the problems that arise when linking different processes with different optimum scales. The discussion which follows owes much to Stigler (1951).

Let us first consider a formal model. Suppose that we are con-concerned with a product which requires one unit of a particular component for each unit of output. Suppose also that this relation cannot be varied, although there are no technological features to dictate that the product and the component must be manufactured in the same plant, and integration will not affect the cost of producing either the product or the component at any give rate of output. Our purpose is to see how scale economies in component manufacture may

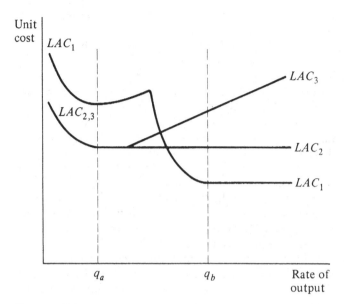

Figure 1. Alternative cost curves

discourage integration. Consider Figure 1, which contains three long-run average-cost curves (*LACs*), which represent the way in which the unit costs of performing some activities change with the rate at which the activity is performed, given that there has been plenty of time to discover and achieve the least-cost way of operating at that rate.

LAC_1 records the changes in unit manufacturing costs of the component as the rate of output changes; and to illustrate some of the problems of integration, this curve has been drawn on the assumption that there are only two possible processes. At low rates of output in the region of q_a, the least-cost method of production involves a process (say, batch production) that gives few advantages of scale, whereas, at higher rates, it becomes more attractive to use an alternative process (say, flow production), which permits significant reductions in unit costs as the scale of output increases to q_b. We wish to see the effect of integrating the manufacture of this component with further processing to produce a finished product and shall consider two alternative cost curves for the additional processing. If the curve has the form represented by LAC_2, then further processing can be undertaken with virtually constant returns to scale, whereas curve LAC_3 represents the possibility of decreasing returns to scale beyond output q_a.

Initially, if the product market is relatively small with demand in the region of q_a, a single firm may operate efficiently in an integrated form. Indeed, if the expertise required for component manufacture is not widely available, the firm may have no choice. At this stage, the market is too small to allow the firm to use all the potential economies of scale in component manufacture; but as the market expands, the scope for continued integration will depend upon the cost characteristics of the final product.

If the product cost curve is of the type represented by LAC_2, with constant unit costs, then the firm may be able to expand with the market toward scale q_b. Initially, for small increases in output above q_a, the firm may find it cheaper to extend its existing plant in preference to building a completely new plant of optimum design. However, if demand continues to expand, and the firm is able to grow, it may achieve optimum rates of output both for components and for the final product. More generally, if the component cost curve is also of type LAC_2, then unit costs are largely independent of the scale of operation. A large firm may make its own components, or it may purchase them from outside suppliers, or it may use a hybrid policy, manufacturing some of its requirements and buying the rest.

However, a different pattern results if the product cost curve is of type LAC_3, with some diseconomies of scale, because in this case the firm is less likely to grow beyond q_a, and market expansion is more likely to be met by new entry. (Even if the product cost curve is of type LAC_2, the same results may obtain if oligopolistic competition restricts individual final-product firms to scales in the region of q_a). Initially, any new entrants may copy the established firm and manufacture their own components: Provided that they have the necessary know-how, they will be able to match the costs of the established firm. However, as the market expands, the savings to be obtained from the mass production of components become more attainable. Independent suppliers would be able to offer increasingly attractive prices for components, encouraging the integrated firms to abandon their own production and rely upon market coordination.

We have already seen that a sequence like this was followed in the United Kingdom in many of the industries which supply components to the car manufacturers. A similar end result appears in the pottery industry (Gay and Smyth 1974). The industry is considerably smaller than many of its supplying industries: For example, pottery takes only twenty percent of china-clay production, while over seventy percent is taken for paper manufacture. By relying upon independent material suppliers, pottery firms are able to benefit from the scale economies and technical improvements introduced by specialist firms which serve several different industries.

We can therefore see how initial integration may give way to market coordination. But we must also note that there are at least two obstacles in the way of a smooth transfer. First, it may be delayed by the fixity of existing plant. The integrated producers will have already sunk the capital costs of their component capacity. Its continued use will pose no opportunity cost so long as it remains in working order, and so the independent suppliers must either wait for it to wear out or ensure that their prices undercut the variable costs of the integrated producers.

Second, the original producers may acquire know-how for component manufacture that is not readily available to other firms. In some cases, this might suggest that the potential economies of scale for component manufacture could only be realized if their production were concentrated in the hands of one or two existing producers. This is unlikely to happen, because other product producers would be reluctant to rely upon competitors for their supplies, but competing firms may be encouraged to enter into joint ventures for the supply of particular components or services.

Such ventures are fairly common in the computer, oil, and chemical industries. For example, the Advanced Systems Laboratory in the United States was set up as a joint venture between NCR and the Control Data Corporation to develop software systems for their computers. The software has to be compatible with the hardware of both companies, but the hardware is not directly competitive inasmuch as Control Data concentrated on larger computer mainframes than NCR (Martin 1975). Similarly, in 1976 the oil companies Elf and Petrofina reached an agreement designed to reduce the imbalance between capacity and output in their European refineries. Under the agreement, Petrofina agreed to use its share of capacity in the Immingham refinery (jointly owned with Total) to process Elf's crude oil in the United Kingdom, while Elf offered reciprocal services for Petrofina in France (*The Times,* November 6, 1976). However, we must not assume that joint ventures like this are undertaken solely to reduce manufacturing costs. They may also help to preserve stability in oligopolistic markets. This arises partly because of the increased opportunity for informal collusion, but primarily because the alternative to the joint venture may be a significant increase in aggregate capacity which would increase the risk of cutthroat competition in periods of slack demand.

4

Diversification

The previous chapter concentrated on the strategic effects of integrating vertically related activities in a single organization. We turn now to consider the consequences of lateral growth, or diversification.

Diversification occurs whenever a firm combines two or more activities which are not vertically related to each other, although they may both use the same inputs or be sold through the same outlets. Diversified companies therefore have more than one product line on offer to potential customers, and would normally be found operating in two or more different industries. The definition of industry which is appropriate for this purpose has long plagued economists and statisticians. Clearly, diversification must imply that the firm is taking on different activities, but just how different is different?

Statistical measurement generally relies on data obtained from the Censuses of Production and classsified in accordance with the Standard Industrial Classification (S.I.C.). Different activities within manufacturing industry may be classified into 15 industrial orders, or into 120 or so "three digit" industries, or if data were available, into an even larger number of product groups. (For further details, see Shaw and Sutton 1976, Chap. 1, or Utton 1977, pp. 97–9).

Clearly a very fine classification scheme identifying a large number of industries might suggest a higher level of diversification than would a coarser classification, because individual firms would appear to offer more product lines in the former case. But the appearance could be misleading. In practice, the S.I.C. industries often group together a number of products that use a common technology or raw material but are otherwise unrelated. Further, even if we could establish an unambiguous product-classification scheme, we would still have to allow for the relative importance of each product line to the firm. Presumably, a firm which covers several lines but concentrates the bulk of its output on just one or two is less diversified than another firm which spreads its output more evenly over the same number of lines. As a result, diversified firms are rather like elephants or pretty girls: you cannot describe them to the uninitiated, but you always know one when you see it.

In spite of these difficulties, there seems to be no doubt that diversified firms are becoming increasingly important in most capitalist countries. For example, in 1963 nearly twenty-three percent of all U.K. manufacturing enterprises employing one hundred or more people owned establishments operating in more than one industry, and these diversified enterprises accounted for over seventy percent of the net output of the group. Comparable figures for 1958 were fifteen and fifty-six percent (Gorecki 1975). Similarly, Channon found that among the largest one hundred British companies as measured by sales in 1969–70, the largest single product line in each firm accounted for less than seventy percent of total sales in nearly two-thirds of the cases, whereas in the early 1950s the proportion had been well below one-third of the cases (Channon 1973). Similar long-term trends have been observed among the largest firms in the United States, France, Germany, and Italy (Scott 1973).

In this chapter, we start in 4.1 by looking at the strategic pressures for diversification, and then turn in 4.2 to emphasize the continuing benefits of specialization, and to consider the strategic problem of balancing specialization and diversity. Finally, in 4.3 we review the findings of some broad-based studies of diversification to see if any lessons can be learned from them for strategic planning.

4.1 Pressures and motives for diversification

It is trite but true to say that a firm will diversify if it believes this to be an appropriate way to achieve its objective of profit, growth, stability, or whatever. However, the statement is operationally valueless: As it stands, it does nothing to identify the circumstances in which diversification is most likely to be the preferred strategy. This requires a more general discussion of the nature of the benefits available from diversification, together with some indication of the contribution made to alternative objectives.

With this end in mind, we can divide the origins of diversification into two: Either the firm may identify specific assets which could be exploited more fully, or it may first recognize a more general need for an improvement in performance without identifying the method by which the improvement is to be achieved. The two are related, and may pose a chicken-and-egg problem of identification if a general desire for improved performance encourages the firm to seek out specific assets as a basis for diversification. This is especially true of some larger firms, which have accepted diversification as a permanent strategic objective. Nevertheless, the distinction is valid, and may be useful. In one case, the incentive follows discovery of an underexploited asset. This asset may suggest the product lines which are to be used for diversification and these must compete directly with the alternative of specialized growth. In the second case, however, the incentive only comes after the firm has realized that it cannot achieve its overall objectives with its existing activities. Diversification is then established as a general strategy before the alternative projects are identified (Sutton 1972). The criteria which are used in practice to evaluate alternatives may be less rigorous in the second case, because the firm has already committed itself to find new product lines.

The development of specific assets

Changes in a firm's assets may provide a basis for diversification. These changes may come about as the value of the assets responds to alterations in the environment. Alternatively, the changes may arise as a by-product of planned growth, partly because the process of growth and diversification generates new skills and hence new capacity for further growth, and partly because each growth project will temporarily absorb management or other capacity which is then freed for further use once the project has been completed. As a result, some assets are constantly being regenerated in a new form as growth continues, and this may provide recurring opportunities for diversification (Penrose 1959). In all cases, however, our analysis must cover both the opportunity and the incentive. A firm may be able to realize the potential value of some assets by selling them rather than by using them internally for diversification, unless the market value understates their true potential. We shall therefore start by considering the ways in which a firm's asset base may change so as to provide an opportunity for diversification, and then look at the conditions in which diversification may seem to be the best way of exploiting this opportunity.

The opportunity. From one point of view, a firm may be defined as a collection under single control of a number of complementary assets, including materials, men, machines, and market contacts.

Many of these assets will be capable of adaptation for a range of alternative uses, while others, especially the materials, may generate joint products. The value of such assets in any one use depends upon the profit which can be earned in that use, but this must be compared with the profit available from alternative uses. The value therefore depends upon the market prices of the various products, the supply prices of complementary inputs, and perhaps also the scale of operation. Changes in market prices or in scale will alter the relative attractiveness of different uses of the inputs, and may therefore provoke some change in their use.

No firm will respond to every variation in market value because of the costs of change. Small or transient variations would not cover the costs of the changes in the firm's strategy or structure that would be needed to translate the potential values into realized gains. However, longer-term variations may encourage firms to redirect some of their assets to more profitable areas, without necessarily abandoning their old areas. Perhaps the clearest examples of this type of development occurred when firms which acquired skills or physical assets by developing military equipment in wartime, sought to develop civilian uses for those assets when peace broke out.

Prolonged changes in external conditions may therefore encourage firms to diversify in an attempt to exploit changes in the value of their assets. But underexploited assets may also emerge as a result of the firm's continuing growth. For example, a specific asset developed for internal use, such as computer software, may be seen to have a wide range of marketable uses. Alternatively, development programs geared to existing needs may produce unexpected by-products. Research and development may thus provide a basis for diversification even though this was not their primary function. Similarly, from time to time, a firm may develop excess capacity, which is available for alternative products. This could happen if it installed specific capacity for an intermediate input and then found that the forecast demand for the end product did not materialize. Alternatively, it may be that the optimum scale of production for the intermediate is greater than the scale required for the firm's own needs. As we saw in the previous chapter, this will often encourage the firm to rely on market coordination rather than integration. However, if integrated production is otherwise desirable, it may be achieved more cheaply if additional uses can be found for the input.

In general, it seems highly unlikely that a very specialized firm would ever be able to exploit the full capacities of all its different assets, especially when we recognize that these assets include such things as management and market contacts. Most firms will therefore operate with some underused assets, and they are more likely to do so as their activities become more complicated and so involve a greater range of skills or a greater variety of physical inputs. Diversification allows them to realize some of the value of these assets. The potential value will be small if the assets can be duplicated by many firms, but will be increased if they have some scarcity value. Further, in practice, the incentive may be reinforced by pressure from individual managers, whose professional pride may make them reluctant to see their own or their department's services underused, regardless of their potential profitability.

On the other hand, diversification will not necessarily eliminate excess capacity. Indeed, it is not clear that it should be intended to do so. For one thing, it will almost certainly require the addition of new resources to complement the old, and the objective must be to find the most effective use for all the resources involved. The utilization of existing assets is not of overriding importance, and although it is clearly one factor influencing the effectiveness of resource use, its apparent promise may sometimes prove to be illusory. This is especially true if the new activities are not viable on their own, and cannot cover the full cost of continued operation, because in this case their positive contribution to profits would disappear if other activities changed so that the internal services were no longer available at incremental cost. In general, the safest strategy is to try to ensure that new activities can stand on their own feet if necessary, but simultaneously to take advantage of every opportunity to economize on overhead costs.

Further, it is unlikely that the elimination of excess capacity could ever be more than a transitory achievement, even if it were appropriate. A firm's capacity is not static, and even if the physical components of capacity are fixed, its quality may change as a result of research or learning-by-doing. In consequence, a firm may continually generate underemployed capacity, even if market demands remain static. The strategic problem is not to eliminate such capacity, but to discover how and when it can be exploited most effectively.

The incentive. We have seen that a firm may find a ready opportunity for diversification if it develops or acquires specific assets that are not fully exploited by its existing specialism. However, this opportunity is not a sufficient reason for diversification. It may still be possible to realize the value of the asset without taking on more activities if the asset or its services can be sold to other firms for a reasonable price. Perhaps the simplest alternative is to use surplus capacity to undertake processing work on contract for other firms. This occurred, for example, in 1968, when the British Hovercraft Corporation undertook to produce the wings and fuselages of the Islander aircraft designed by Britten-Norman Ltd. The British Hovercraft Corporation was interested in the manufacture and sale of hovercraft and had no intention of diversifying into general aviation, but it did have surplus production capacity. Unfortunately however, in cases like this, the firm is unlikely to do a good job if it tries to load its capacity by taking on work for which it has no particular commitment. In other cases, the asset may be sold out-right, and this may be particularly attractive if other firms have easier access to complementary resources or can provide finance and management skills at a lower opportunity cost. Thus, when the first practicable polyester fiber for the textile industry was discov-ered by the Calico Printing Association, they chose to sell the patent rights to the product rather than attempt to manufacture it them-selves, because they were more interested in textile finishing than in the production of raw materials for the textile industry. ICI ac-quired the U.K. licence, and produced the product as Terylene, while in the United States the product was produced by Du Pont as Dacron.

Even when diversification appears as the preferred strategy, early cooperation with other specialists may be needed to give facilities or skills which would otherwise take too long to acquire – if they could be acquired at all. This may involve a joint venture with a more or less equal contribution from each party. For example, in 1940, ICI and Courtaulds established a jointly owned subsidiary, British Nylon Spinners, to manufacture nylon. ICI had acquired the manufacturing licence for the United Kingdom from du Pont, but Courtaulds could offer valuable technical know-how as a result of their long experience in the production and spinning of rayon. However, a joint venture of this sort is not the only way of combin-ing the complementary assets of independent firms. Less formal cooperation may provide a viable alternative if the complementary assets or services required for diversification can be purchased on the open market. This appeared to be true in 1976–7 when British Leyland were reported to be preparing to enter the general wholesale market for electrical components and fuel systems for motor vehicles, as an addition to their established role in providing a replacement service for their own customers (*The Times*, January 7, 1977). This was part of a general move to extend their activities in the component industries, and followed the reorganization of six existing subsidiaries to form SU/Butec. However, the distribution system could handle a wider product range than British Leyland were then able to supply, and the system probably needed the wider range to provide an acceptable standard of service to customers. Ultimately this may require more extensive diversification, but initially the additional components (contact sets, ignition coils, and so on) had to be bought out. British Leyland had to rely upon market contacts to provide the wider range of products needed to exploit the market potential of its established but limited skills as a component manufacturer.

Underused assets can therefore be exploited in several different ways. Independent diversification is only one of these alternatives. In some cases, a firm may choose diversification for what are essentially nonpecuniary reasons, much as a man may choose a difficult job out of a cussed desire to prove that he can do it. Edwards and Townsend have suggested that Sir Allan Gordon-Smith may have been partially influenced by such motives when he encouraged his engineering firm, S. Smith and Sons (England) Ltd., to diversify into the manufacture of watches. "Gordon-Smith had always wanted to make watches. He had been dissuaded hitherto by the heavy economic odds against success. The Government was now prepared to help. Gordon-Smith was a public figure with a strong sense of duty, so that his duty and his wishes coincided. Moreover he could rarely resist a challenge" (Edwards and Townsend 1962, p. 40). However, in general, we shall find that a firm is more likely to choose diversification if it believes that it cannot realize the full value of the underused assets by selling them, or if it believes that the sale would involve unacceptable transaction costs.

There are several reasons why this may happen. It may be that the value of the assets is depressed because the market is imperfect. This could occur if the market was dominated by a small number of buyers, who together can maintain enough monopsony power to hold down the price, although in such cases the potential seller of the assets might find it equally difficult to exploit the assets by diversification if this took it into competition with the established oligopsonists. More plausible, perhaps, is the possibility that the market may appear to undervalue the assets because potential buyers lack the information needed for a reasonable appraisal. Unless they are prepared to trust the seller, they may have no reliable source from which they can obtain such information. Alternatively, the firm possessing the assets may find that it cannot readily transfer its property rights in the assets to others. Knowledge, for example, may become a public good as soon as it is offered for general sale, and a firm can rarely claim property rights in the skills which have been acquired as a result of experience by its employees. Physical assets can be bought and sold, but people cannot. Similarly other intangible assets, such as goodwill, cannot be readily transferred as separate items from one owner to another.

A common example involves the results of scientific research and development by private firms. Unless effective patent protection allows the sale of exclusive use of the results to specified customers, the firm may be forced to exploit them internally so as to preserve secrecy. If it allowed the knowledge to become readily available, it might find that the resultant increase in competition made it impossible to appropriate the full potential value of the results. Even if exclusive use could be retained, potential buyers might lack the knowledge needed to exploit the results effectively, especially if the seller had not developed the initial discovery so as to establish its commercial value. These problems of innovation are discussed more fully in Chapter 8, but we should note here that it may sometimes happen that the value of an innovation cannot be appropriated by the developer unless it is used as a basis for diversification.

An alternative example can be seen in the early days of the computer-service industry. Large computer users often developed their own programming capacity to complement the hardware and basic software programs supplied by computer manufacturers. Sometimes this resulted in capacity in excess of their long-term requirements, and in turn, some users sought to capitalize on this opportunity. However, it was difficult to do so without setting up special facilities to sell computing services. The computers themselves were effectively an indivisible asset. In principle, unwanted computing time could be sold to other potential users, but they would typically require ancillary programming and data-preparation services if they were to buy the computing time. Similarly, the surplus programming capacity could not be sold off as a separate item. The capacity depended upon the skills of the programmers themselves, and while the individuals could and did exploit market shortages by transferring between firms, the only way in which the firms could exploit the capacity of their programming teams was by setting up software companies to sell programming services. Several large computer users therefore diversified to set up computer service bureaus alongside their existing business. By the end of the 1960s, the service bureaus in the United Kingdom included offshoots from nationalized industries such as the Coal Board or the Post Office and from private firms such as Laing or Wates in civil engineering. Some of these operations proved to be very successful and some bureaus eventually ceased to rely on their parent companies for any significant part of their turnover (Green 1971).

However, in this example, we should recognize that diversification was a necessary strategy only because the computer users wished to retain some part of the indivisible assets for their own use. Had it been possible for them to establish the service-bureaus as self-contained units from the outset, they could have been sold as going concerns. The same may also be true for parent companies whose subsidiaries may enjoy consumer loyalty or goodwill that remains underexploited because the parent lacks the resources to develop all opportunities simultaneously. In the United Kingdom, the relative importance of mergers which involve the transfer of quasifirms or separate subsidiaries from one parent to another has been increasing. This increase seems to reflect the firms' desire to find alternative ways of realizing the value of any surplus assets developed by the subsidiaries.

Improvements in corporate performance

The second general reason for diversification is a desire to improve performance. As we saw in our brief review of behavioral theories in Chapter 1, a firm may start to search for alternative policies if its achievements fail to match its aspirations. Its first choice will probably be to seek ways to improve its existing activities, but it may turn to diversification if it believes that it cannot reach its targets with its current specialisms alone.

The aspiration levels or targets may be measured in many different ways, but there are two main alternatives. First, they may cover the average performance of the firm. Alternatively, they may be concerned with the stability of that average and the certainty of its achievement. We shall consider the second alternative first.

Instability and uncertainty. At one extreme, diversification may be prompted by a desire to reduce the possibility of disaster by putting one's eggs into a variety of baskets. In military terms, it may be compared to "deploying forces so that, if there is an ambush round the next corner, total disaster is avoided" (Roy 1952, p. 432). This is the clearest motive for diversification, but it is probably an extreme case: A firm's survival is ultimately of overriding importance to its members but it does not dominate every decision. It is generally true, however, that diversification may help a firm to achieve greater security by giving a longer-term guarantee of performance and a more stable cash flow. Insofar as greater stability assists long-term planning, the security may go hand in hand with an improvement in average performance, but commonly the firm will be forced to accept a trade-off between the two, and may prefer to play safe even when a more risky strategy would offer some chance of a much better performance.

A firm's attitude to this trade-off will reflect the risk preferences of its decision takers, who may be owners or salaried managers. The two groups may well have different attitudes to the risks faced by the firm, even if their personal risk preferences are identical, because the owner-manager shares directly in all profits and losses while the salaried manager does not. However, in general, it is not easy to establish a priori how risk taking has been affected by the growth of large corporations and the emergence of a managerial class who do not own the firms they manage. The corporations offer limited liability to a large number of shareholders who can usually find a ready market for their shares. Individual shareholders can also adjust their own risks by varying the composition of their share portfolios, and in principle they can make themselves independent of the risks faced by individual firms. For these reasons we might expect that larger firms would be under less pressure to pursue risk-averse strategies.

However, in practice, shareholders are likely to lack the information required to assess objectively the risks faced by different firms. In a world of uncertainty, they may prefer to support those firms which can point to their past successes as "evidence" of their future potential, and they will be less inclined to support firms with a poor track record. Further, the managers will face a different range of options. They are more dependent upon a single firm for their security and can change jobs less easily than the shareholders can change their portfolios. If managers are able to impose their own objectives on a firm, they are more likely to seek an acceptable level of risk by varying the product mix of their existing firm than by moving between firms. As a result, managers may have a stronger incentive than shareholders to promote diversification.

Given the incentives, there are several ways in which diversification can increase a firm's stability or security. For example, a more stable cash flow may be obtained by linking products with different seasonal peaks, as with the combination of sausages and ice cream by Walls or of heating and gardening equipment by Valor. Similarly the firm of W. H. Smith & Son has been seeking to diversify from its base in newspaper and periodical distribution for some years. Its move in the early 1970s into the travel-agency business, which peaks in January and February, was influenced by the fact that cash inflow from its other retailing activities peaked very sharply in the last three months of the year with the Christmas sales boom (Tisdall 1977).

In cases like these, it is the stability of the aggregate cash flow that is significant. The relative stability of either business area in isolation may be irrelevant. Alternatively, a firm concerned by the instability of its existing business may wish to enter a new business area that is relatively stable and offers a more regular minimum cash flow, even though it does not offset the fluctuations of the original business. In this way firms manufacturing producer goods may attempt to reduce cyclical fluctuations by moving into consumer-goods markets which are less susceptible to stockcycles or accelerator-induced changes in demand. In practice, however, it may be that the most significant moves are dictated by longer-term secular changes in demand. "A firm's stability may be increased if it is able to operate products at differing stages of their life cycle and may be further increased if it follows the same policy with respect to industries" (Devine, Jones, Lee, and Tyson 1974, p. 243). The response to secular changes of this sort is taken up in the material on long-run trends.

So far, we have been concerned with instability rather than uncertainty. That is, we have assumed implicitly that the firm can estimate precisely the future pattern of profits or sales for the products concerned and then act on those estimates with full knowledge of the result. But similar arguments can be used when the future patterns are not known, because the chance of unforeseen fluctuations in performance can also be reduced by spreading resources over a number of different activities. This conclusion is often supported by reference to statistical sampling theory. It can be shown that if two activities are independent and are selected randomly from a single population in which each activity has a specified probability of failing, then the chance that both activities will fail simultaneously is less than the chance that either one will fail, and the dispersion of the average performance observed in such samples becomes smaller as the number of items in the sample increases. However, the simplicity of this argument can be misleading. The reduction of uncertainty is not simply an application of statistical sampling theory, and the reduction may not be realized if the performance of the different activities is affected by diversification, so that they cease to be independent. This seems probable, given that the activities are to be coordinated by a single management. As a consequence, a random sample of different projects could well produce highly unstable results and "if anything goes wrong, then there is a premium on knowing one's business, on understanding it, on being close to it" (Drucker 1974, p. 681).

On the other hand, there is no doubt that uncertainty can be reduced by *appropriate* combinations of activities. Further, a wider range of activities may give managers a wider range of strategic options. This can be particularly important in oligopolies. Unless their market is growing very rapidly, nondiversified firms must be prepared to respond to every competitive move made by their rivals, because if they do not, they may be unable to retain their market position. By contrast, more diversified firms are under less pressure to respond to every competitive move in every market. As a result, they may be more able to avoid ill-considered responses and/or to reduce the risk of destructive competition.

Long-run trends. The desire to improve expected trends in performance may be considered as the final motive for diversification. Existing or potential profits or growth may be unsatisfactory, and diversification may be the easiest way to improve performance, especially if existing product markets are limited or are becoming increasingly competitive. In principle, this may be thought of as a further case of the effects of changing supply and demand conditions which were considered at the start of the paragraphs on the development of specific assets: Changes in the market environment for existing specialisms may encourage diversification by changing the marginal return to investment in different areas. However, this interpretation may be misleading if it is taken to imply that the firm monitors all alternative investments before reaching a decision to diversify. In practice, it seems that the decision often comes first. It

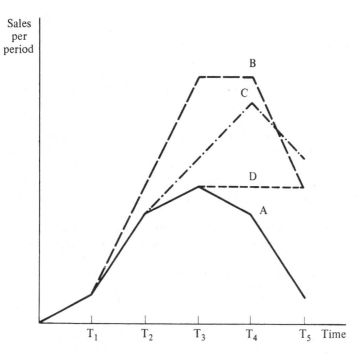

Figure 2. Product life cycles

may be encouraged if the firm observes that performance has fallen or will fall below the accepted targets, and the failure to achieve those targets acts as a stimulus triggering a search for new opportunities. In some cases it may even trigger a complete reappraisal of the firm's strategy.

Given that the purpose of such diversification is to fill the gap between aspiration and achievement, the timing may be critical. This may be shown by using the product life cycle, which assumes that all product markets pass through successive periods of growth, maturity, and decline. The general character of a life cycle is given by curve A in Figure 2. The curve is stylized and is drawn with straight lines rather than continuous curves representing the time path of sales growth during the introductory phase of slow growth up to time T_1, the rapid growth phase up to time T_2, and the phase of maturity which precedes the decline starting at time T_3. Nevertheless the curve is a fair approximation to the cycle of growth and decline which has been observed for many products and industries. We shall assume that the firm's objective is to find a new product to compensate for the decline of the old while maintaining a more or less constant rate of growth. We shall further assume that the firm has a monopoly of both products, so that it does not have to share the market with other firms; that the life cycle of the new product will follow exactly the same pattern as that of the old product no matter when the new product is introduced; and that the launch date chosen for the new product does not affect the development of any subsequent products. These are extreme assumptions, but will serve to illustrate the general problems involved. In practice we would need more precise estimates of the way in which the future pattern of sales by the firm may be effected by the timing of the product launch, after allowing for competitive activities.

In Figure 2, curves B, C, and D represent the time path of total sales of the firm, obtained by aggregating sales for the new and the old product, with the new product launched at the alternative times T_1, T_2, and T_3 for B, C, and D respectively. Given our assumed objective, it is clear that T_1 may be too soon: it implies an accelerated rate of growth which may be beyond the firm's financial or managerial resources. On the other hand T_3 is clearly too late, and involves a period of stagnation for the firm which could have been avoided if the new product had been introduced sooner. By comparison, an intermediate time, such as T_2, would seem to be about right in that it maintains fairly steady growth for a longer period.

In practice, however, it may be very difficult to ensure correct timing, because the future life cycles are not precisely predictable. If mistakes are likely to be made, then it may well be appropriate to try to err on the side of being too early rather than too late. This situation arises for two reasons. First, it is likely to be easier to restrict the rate of growth in a sellers' market, moving curve B towards curve C, than to accelerate the penetration of a new product in order to move D towards C. Secondly, if the launch of the new product is delayed to T_3, when the old product is already beginning its decline, the cash flow generated by existing sales may be inadequate to finance the new investment. The new product may promise good profits, but the firm may be unable to convince potential lenders of this if its own current performance is weak. It must therefore try to avoid the "Catch 22" situation where it cannot survive without new capital, but is unable to attract new capital because lenders believe that it cannot survive.

However, it is not only the declining products that cause financial problems. Profitable products for which demand is growing rapidly may prove to be a cash drain, absorbing finance for working capital, or for new production capacity to keep pace with expansion. This would inevitably pose financial problems for any firm whose product mix was made up entirely of products in the rapid-growth phase of the product life cycle. A satisfactory mix should include a few "cash cows" which may lack glamor, but which nevertheless provide a cash inflow from past investment, and can be used to provide finance for the new "calves" needed for diversification.

In general the best strategy for a large firm may be to prepare new product additions as *or before* they are needed at time T_2, even though this may mean that initially some projects are starved of the resources they need to realize their full potential. The logic of the argument may then take us back to the situation in which firms diversify in response to future uncertainty. Continual diversification becomes an integral component of the firm's strategy though, as a consequence, some projects may seem initially to be, and some may remain as, a diversion from the firm's main fields of interest.

Finally, we must note that a firm's diversification strategy is not concerned only with the addition of new activities, but should also consider the decline of the old. Company doctors cannot all specialize on midwifery, but some must turn to geriatrics and may have to consider euthanasia. In principle divestment decisions involve the same techniques as investment decisions. The benefits of continuing operation are given by the product's contribution: that is, by the surplus of sales revenue over variable cost. Conversely, the cost of obtaining that contribution is the opportunity cost involved in tying up production, marketing, or managerial capacity that could be sold or used elsewhere in the firm if the product line were discontinued. However, it is sometimes suggested that managers are reluctant to react quickly enough. "Usually there is also a great deal of organisational inertia and personal commitments to an old established product-market position. Managers typically tend to disregard the economists' sunk cost principle, which states that the decision to divest should be based entirely on comparison of future prospects, and not on how much money and resources were invested into the project in the past" (Ansoff 1969, p. 25). If this is true, old projects may continue to absorb resources which should have been released for more productive use, and therefore may unnecessarily increase the firm's diversification.

4.2 Specialization

In this chapter, we have concentrated on the advantages of diversification. It is now time to look at some of the problems. First, we consider some general constraints on the direction of diversification, and then we turn to the specific problems of management structure.

The benefits of "specialized diversification"

There will always be some diversification projects which succeed even when there is no logical reason for grafting the new activity onto the old. They will succeed because of the enthusiasm of the entrepreneur or because of the inherent merit of the new product. The two attributes coincided in 1907, when W. H. Hoover acquired the rights to the first "modern" upright vacuum cleaner developed, or rather, strung together out of bits and pieces by J. M. Spangler. The acquisition was completely unrelated to Hoover's existing business experience in harness making, and arose primarily because Hoover wished to diversify out of a declining industry whose prospects had been hit by the development of the motorcar. Yet Hoover's name has now become virtually synonymous with vacuum cleaner.

In spite of such an obvious exception, however, it is generally wise for a firm to accept some constraints, and to set a limit to the range of business areas in which it will seek opportunities for diversification. Indeed, we have already suggested in Chapter 2 that the recognition of these constraints is an essential feature of corporate strategy, which among other things, will allow the firm to exploit organizational learning as a defence against uncertainty. Without the constraints, any attempt to find profitable new business opportunities may mislead the firm into the worst form of what Levitt (1962) has called "blue skies diversification." Such action may lack any industrial logic. The danger is that firms may all rush from one prospect to another, like lemmings or Gadarene swine hell-bent on their own destruction. Some may survive, but even if the new business area fulfills its general promise, other firms will find that they cannot stand the pressure of competition. The firms which succeed will be those that have some comparative advantage to give them a competitive edge and/or restrict entry by potential competitors.

Successful diversification should be based upon such comparative advantages. In the jargon of some management literature, there should be some synergy between the firm and the new business area. However, we must also recognize that in spite of the arguments which can be made in favor of constrained or specialized diversification, there will always be some firms that find it difficult to identify an appropriate set of constraints that still leaves them with a reasonable range of alternatives. We return to this problem later, after looking at the potential advantages of specialized diversification in a little more detail.

Specialization and organizational learning. The comparative advantages upon which diversification should be based may reflect the possession of physical assets, but if these assets can be duplicated by competitors the advantage may prove to be short-lived. More significant benefits may flow from intangible assets, such as the goodwill of existing customers, experience of close cooperation with suppliers, technical knowledge, or the existence of a team of experienced people who are used to working together on complex problems. As we saw in section 4.1, it is often difficult to realize the value of such assets except by diversification.

These advantages are generally acquired as a result of continuing experience in a specific area – that is, they arise from learning-by-doing and take time to acquire. The reductions in cost which can be achieved as a result of learning-by-doing have been clearly established for many manufacturing processes and appear to extend to most of a firm's activities (see, for example, Pratten 1970, Abernethy and Wayne 1974). Just as skilled workers become more adept with experience, so managers become more able to evaluate a situation and take an appropriate decision.

The possible benefits may be illustrated by a simple example. Suppose that units costs are not affected by the rate of output at any one time but will fall as a result of experience accumulated over time. (Most learning depends upon cumulative output rather than time alone, but the distinction is not critical for our argument). Suppose, also, that price is set for all firms as a simple percentage markup over the units costs of the least-cost suppliers, so that price declines over time as early entrants learn by doing, whereas later entrants may have to accept smaller profit margins because of their higher unit costs. The results are portrayed in Figure 3a. Price falls continuously from an initial level of P_0. At time t_1, the unit costs of the most experienced supplier have fallen to C_1 and price is equal to P_1. Clearly P_1 is less than P_0: in this example $P_1 = C_0$. A new entrant

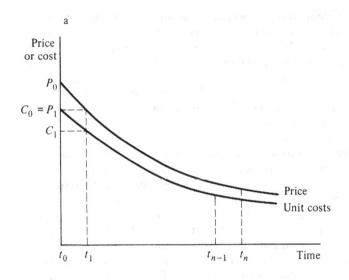

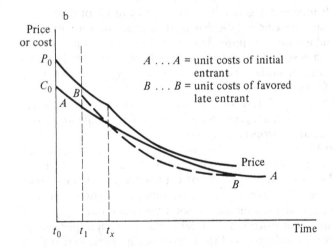

Figure 3. Learning curves

at time t_1 with no prior experience would have costs of C_0 and would be unable to make a profit at the existing market price, although his competitive disadvantage will become progressively less if he enters and eventually gains from experience. For example, a time lag of one period results in a significant disadvantage at time t_1, whereas by time t_n the disadvantage has virtually disappeared. The effect on late entrants clearly depends upon the time at which they enter, the rate at which unit costs decline with experience, and the time taken to reach minimum cost.

The disadvantage may be reduced if the entrant is able to carry over experience from some other industry so as to shorten the learning period and/or enter with initial unit costs of less than C_0. In some cases, the disadvantage could be eliminated or even reversed, so that the earlier entrants who had had no relevant experience to aid their entry could find themselves at a competitive disadvantage in facing later entrants. This possibility is illustrated in Figure 3b. Initial entrants follow learning curve A. Later entrants with relevant experience may follow learning curve B. By time t_r, the late entrants have made up for their early disadvantage, and subsequent prices are determined by their costs rather than by the higher costs of the earlier entrants.

This argument is not restricted to production costs. It may be extended to any feature which influences competitive success in the new area, so that a firm's learning-by-doing may give competitive advantages in some areas, which are not generally available to all firms. Diversification is likely to produce more favorable results if it builds on this expertise. Further, an entrepreneur will be less well qualified to judge opportunities in other areas. "As his special knowledge or advantages will inevitably be confined to certain particular spheres and capable of extension only through the expenditure of time and effort, the number of independent ventures offering profits greater than normal about which he is able to form reliable estimates will, therefore be small" (Richardson 1960, p. 209).

Even if a firm has expertise in several areas, it will still pay it to concentrate upon a narrower range where its comparative advantage is greatest. In part, this follows from the standard economic analysis of resource allocation: resources should not be spread over all areas which promise a positive net benefit, but priority should be given to those areas which yield the highest marginal net benefit. But diversity may also impair management control. A narrow range of specialisms makes it easier for managers to comprehend the problems of each activity. The same information channels may be used and managers can apply common standards in evaluating results. These economies permit a smaller managerial overhead and may be especially significant in times of rapid change because of the greater flexibility offered by a simpler management system.

Problems of transferability. Although diversification should aim to build on existing skills, firms will differ in their abilities to acquire skills which can be transferred to other business areas. This was suggested by Gort's major study of diversification in the United States. He found that the same firms were the most active diversifiers in each of a number of successive time periods, and that most of these firms came from an identifiable group of industries (Gort 1962, especially pp. 28 and 51). A similar conclusion appeared in Channon's study of the largest one hundred companies in U.K. manufacturing industry. Channon classified the firms as being fast, moderate, or reluctant diversifiers. This classification was found simultaneously to yield groups of firms classified to particular industries and therefore suggested that a firm's propensity to diversify depended upon it industrial origins (Channon 1973).

Channon's first group of early diversifiers covered firms in electrical and mechanical engineering, and in the chemical and pharmaceutical industries. These are science-based industries that require technologies and skills that can be used for a number of different markets. The science base encourages research, which often generates new opportunities for diversification, and is essential for entry to other science-based industries. These are usually among the fastest-growing sectors of the economy, and are often characterized by product differentiation, which enables new entrants with new products to attack specific segments of the total market without coming into direct conflict with the established firms. For the right firms, entry to such industries can be relatively easy. Further, the process of innovation and diversification is likely to be self-reinforcing. The initial steps will provide the firms with managerial skills that make it easier for them to identify, assess, and develop subsequent new opportunities.

By way of contrast, Channon identified a second group of late diversifiers, which included companies from the food, textile, and paper industries, among others. These are lower-technology industries, which offer fewer natural linkages to other product areas. For these firms, diversification appeared largely as a response to increased competition. Finally, there was a third group of firms whose activities are still dominated by a single product line. These firms are not homogeneous, but their characteristics are still interesting.

In some cases, the competition which promoted diversification among (say) the food processors was blunted by high concentration and rapid market growth. This appears to have been true until recently in the car industry. Some of the other specialized firms are highly integrated processors devoted to volume production of basic materials, and as we have seen vertical integration of this sort may inhibit diversification. Finally, the low diversification of aircraft manufacturers indicates that even high-technology firms may remain specialized if their technology is not readily transferable to other areas.

However, we must accept that transferability cannot be measured, and attempts to exploit the benefits of learning-by-doing are no guarantee of success. The learned skills are acquired by specialization, and all specialization implies a degree of risk if circumstances change in unpredicted ways.

Historical standards are good guides in repetitive situations: they are poor guides (and may be actively misleading) if essential elements in the new situation differ from those in the old – if, in other words, one is no longer sampling from the same population. . . So long as history does, in significant ways, repeat itself, experience is a good qualification for a decision maker; but when it ceases to repeat itself, experience is no qualification; indeed, if the experienced man should fail to recognize this (which is not always easy) then it is a disqualification. (Loasby 1976, p. 98)

This may explain why the same firm can succeed in some cases and yet fail in others which appear to require similar technological and marketing skills. For example in the United States, General Motors succeeded with diesel locomotives but not with aero-engines (Drucker 1974, p. 704). Even when the transfer of skills seems to be simple and straightforward, the apparent simplicity may reflect our ignorance of the true difficulties. In the 1950s, Eagle Picher, a leading U.S. producer of germanium metal, attempted to diversify into the production of high-purity silicon. The two metals are chemically similar, but the company found that its germanium technology was not readily transferable and silicon proved to be much more difficult to purify. In general, it seems that the direct transfer of technology has not been a very sound basis for diversification among metal producers (Brooks 1965, p. 99).

In some cases, the skills may prove to be irrelevant because the total system requirements change for reasons that were not foreseen. For example, when Singer, long established as a supplier of sewing machines, acquired Friden in 1963 and thus bought its way into the market for commercial calculators and accounting machines, the potential synergy seemed to be self-evident. At that time both sewing machines and accounting machines were electromechanical devices whose selling required customer demonstrations and reliable after-sales service. But Singer's established expertise in these areas rapidly became irrelevant for business machines, because the industry was transformed by the advent of the minicomputer. This involved the replacement of electromechanical by electronic technology, and required new marketing methods geared to computer systems rather than individual machines (*Fortune,* December 1975).

These examples demonstrate that there are major problems involved in estimating the positive benefits of learning-by-doing. The need to define an appropriate balance between specialization and diversity remains as a major problem for management, and it is not one that can be solved by formal model building. It seems that the balance of advantage will normally rest with a strategy which builds upon existing areas of specialization. However as George (1972) has suggested, the increasing professionalism of management may make it easier for firms to cope with diversity if it means that the managers can acquire general skills which are not dependent on their experience in existing business areas.

The importance of management structure

It is clear that the balance between specialization and diversity is a major strategic problem for large firms, and that organizational learning will have a significant impact on this balance. However, we must also recognize that the structure of an organization may affect the degree of diversity that it can tolerate without a significant loss of efficiency. It is possible to identify several alternative structures (see O. E. Williamson 1975) and each may be appropriate in context, but to simplify the exposition we shall here consider only the two polar alternatives represented schematically in Figure 4 (derived from O. E. Williamson 1971, pp. 345 and 351).

Type 1, the U-form firm, represents the traditional solution to the problem of coordinating separate specialist activities: Managerial responsibilities are separated into self-contained functional areas, which are coordinated by the chief executive. This structure may have originated with U.S. railroad companies and was fruitfully

Type 1, the unitary or U-form

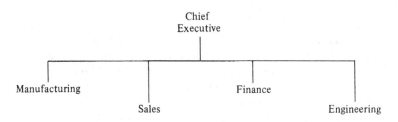

Type 2, the multidivision or M-form

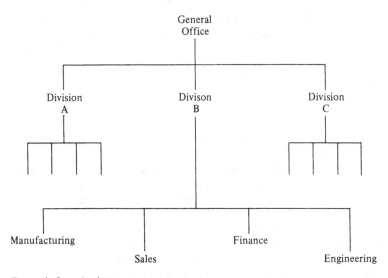

Figure 4. Organization structures

copied by other growing firms (Chandler 1961). It probably remains as the dominant structure for narrowly specialized firms or for firms of moderate size, and may also be appropriate for a larger firm if its products are interdependent, so that the manufacturing or sales functions must be closely coordinated across all products. In many cases, however, an increase in size means an increase in diversity: Different products require different policies, and the common control implied by the U-form structure becomes increasingly restrictive. Further, the communication channels feeding information up to the chief executive and decisions down to the ultimate point of action become longer and more complex. This leads to some loss in both the detail and the accuracy of information and to a longer time lag before the organization can devise an appropriate reaction to unforeseen changes in the environment. Centralized decision taking becomes less efficient, and is less able to constrain the pursuit of private goals or well meant suboptimization at lower levels.

These problems of the U-form firm led initially in the 1920s, and more generally after World War II, to the adoption of the alternative M-form. Similar trends favoring this alternative have been observed in the United States, the United Kingdom, France, Germany, and Italy, and in most cases it seems that firms changed their structure because increasing competition in the 1950s and 1960s highlighted the managerial problems caused by earlier increases in diversity (Scott 1973). In the M-form, the functions serving each distinct product area are grouped into separate divisions. Each division is structured as a U-form firm, which is intended to operate separately from the other divisions and communicate directly with independent suppliers and customers. So far as is possible, external spillovers from one division to another are minimized, so that the general office can avoid the detailed problems which would be involved in coordinating interdependent divisions. Instead it can concentrate on strategic decisions and try to use objective criteria to allocate resources between divisions, while leaving each division to identify the most beneficial use for the resources which are allocated to it.

Efficiency may be promoted if the divisions are forced to compete for resources in this way. O. E. Williamson (1975), in particular, has argued that the control over divisions exercised by the M-form firm can be more effective than the control which would be exercised by the capital market if the divisions existed as separate companies. The general office has more information and can make marginal reallocations or major strategic changes more readily than the capital market, which cannot easily reallocate undistributed profits from one firm to another. On the other hand, there may be occasions when the general office cannot rely solely on objective criteria when allocating resources between divisions. In conditions of uncertainty, subjective assessments may be unavoidable and will require detailed knowledge of the environment of each division. Greater diversity inevitably makes it more difficult to obtain the requisite knowledge, and so the M-form does not eliminate all pressures to avoid unnecessary diversity.

4.3 Diversification and performance: the empirical evidence

In recent years, industrial economists have undertaken several statistical studies of diversification. Clearly these are of potential interest to the corporate strategist, and we therefore end this chapter with a brief review of some of the findings, although unfortunately these are not very enlightening on the effects of diversification.

Empirical evidence tends to confirm that much industrial diversification occurs within areas of specialization insofar as these can be equated with the Orders of Industry (2-digit industries) used in the reports of the Census of Production. For example, Utton's study of the two hundred largest enterprises in U.K. manufacturing industry found that "if the engineering and vehicle Orders are treated as one unit and if some allowance is made for vertical integration, which could not systematically be isolated, then about two-thirds of the largest firms' diversification is probably into industries with close technical and marketing links with the primary industry" (Utton 1977, p. 111). Utton concluded that the largest firms typically concentrate their diversification into closely related industries, as had been observed in an earlier study relating to 1963 made by Gorecki (1975). Similar conclusions for U.S. firms have been suggested by Berry (1975).

On the other hand, the empirical studies also suggest that the average performance records achieved by diversified firms are no better than those of firms which remain more highly specialized. The most commonly cited evidence is Gort's finding for U.S. firms that profit rates in 1947–54 were neither correlated with diversification, measured as of 1954, nor with the change in diversification from 1947 to 1954 (Gort 1962, p. 65). A more recent survey of the effects of diversification concluded that "the advantages or disadvantages of the conglomerate have to be regarded as non-proven" (Gribbin 1976, p. 28).

In the light of this evidence, how are we to interpret our earlier arguments identifying the possible benefits of diversification? Do the results disprove our hypotheses? The answer must be no. The hypotheses suggest that a firm may be able to improve its performance by diversification. We are therefore looking for a comparison of the performance actually achieved with that which would have been realized if the firm had not diversified. One way or another, most studies attempt to do this by comparing the performance of separate groups of diversified and nondiversified companies, but this is not the same thing. Firms may wish to diversify either because they can see exceptional opportunities that will give them above-average profits, or because they are trying to avoid below-average profits. Conversely, the less-diversified firms may remain more specialized, either because their original specialisms continue to yield good profits, or because they are unable to find any successful diversification strategy to avoid low profitability. A priori, we simply cannot predict how the performance of a randomly chosen group of diversified firms will compare with that of a group of more specialized firms.

It may be that some further progress can be made with cross-section studies by a more careful specification of the type of diversification strategy that has been adopted. For example, Rumelt's study of larger U.S. firms reproduced the common finding that, in general, the more diversified firms perform neither better nor worse than the less diversified. However, he also suggested that for any given degree of diversification, the firms which retain clear linkages between their new activities, and between each new activity and the original business area, are likely to perform more satisfactorily than those whose diverse operations are less clearly linked together (Rumelt 1974). This confirms the benefits of specialization, but even in this case we cannot conclude that the more loosely knit firms have made a strategic mistake. It may be that they had no choice. As we have seen, it would be wrong to assume that all firms have equal access to good opportunities for diversification.

5

Strategy formulation in practice

This book is not intended to be a boardroom manual or handbook on strategy formulation but it must pay some attention to the process by which strategic decisions are reached. This may serve two purposes. It will show how strategic decision taking can exploit the conclusions of our general discussion of diversification and integration. It may also help to set the context for our later discussion of mergers and innovation.

There is no single set of universal rules for strategic decision taking, and the discussion which follows draws heavily on the sequence proposed by Cohen and Cyert (1973). In their scheme, the process is divided into three major stages: formulating the strategic program, implementing the program, and using appropriate information and control systems to monitor the progress of the program. The stages are not completely separable. For example, a program that includes too much diversity will prove to be more difficult to monitor. Nevertheless, it is appropriate for our purpose to concentrate on the formulation stage. This may be divided in turn into seven steps: (1) establishing goals; (2) analyzing the environment; (3) assigning quantitative values to the goals; (4) relating company-wide goals and assessments to plans made at divisional or department level; (5) "gap analysis" to compare forecasts and targets; (6) strategic search, to find means to fill the gap between forecast and target, if appropriate; and (7) selecting a portfolio of activities to define the strategic program for the firm's planning horizon.

These seven steps should not be thought of as a rigid chronological sequence, although they are most easily discussed in this form. Any one step may raise questions or identify problems which indicate that earlier steps should be retraced before any further decisions are made. Further, there is a sense in which the process is never complete: Management must remain sensitive to unforeseen changes which may affect the program, and must be prepared to change the program if necessary. One purpose of strategic planning is to ensure that the organization can cope with uncertainty without being diverted by every change in the environment. The strategy therefore restrains the firm's response to change, but it must not become a barrier preventing change. The firm must not attempt to follow narrowly defined programs after they have ceased to be appropriate.

Step 1: Establishing goals. An essential first step is to set the long-term objectives of the firm. Analytically, this may be equated with identifying the arguments to be included in the corporate utility function. It may include some attempt to determine an order of priority for the different objectives, but no attempt should be made at this stage to translate the general objectives into precise planning targets. For example, the firm may decide that growth of sales is a relevant objective, but will not yet set a target growth rate. (The role of objectives in corporate strategy was discussed in detail in Chapters 1 and 2.)

Step 2: Environmental and competitive audits. The second prerequisite is an appraisal of the general economic, and the narrower industrial environments in which the firm operates. This will certainly involve an assessment of the firm's competitive position. It should also involve an estimate of macroeconomic trends, including (say) likely changes in Government stabilization or trade policies, and it may involve some attention to longer-term social changes. These are not all equally important, and they should not be treated as such. For most firms, the process of monitoring changes in existing markets will be nearly continuous. It will make use of a variety of sources of information ranging from informal contacts, through trade associations or similar bodies to formal market appraisals undertaken by specialist staff or professional consultants. By contrast monitoring macroeconomic trends may be periodic rather than continuous, and except in very large firms the management will probably rely on the forecasts which are published in the national press. Finally, to monitor social trends may require no more than an informal watching brief. Changes in the birthrate, the age of retirement, or the age at which people leave full-time education may all affect the pattern of future consumer demand. Clearly a firm should try to anticipate such changes and, for example, it should be prepared to switch from prams to wheelchairs if the need arises. But the need in unlikely to arise overnight.

As part of their assessment of the competitive environment, or their "competitive audit" as it is sometimes called, the firms will need to appraise those features of each product market that determine the success or failure of alternative competitive moves. For this, they will need to consider substantially the same variables as those that are used by industrial economists to define market structure and to predict market conduct. The variables will not be the same in all markets.

Whether or not a particular characteristic is a relevant component of structure is an empirical question, not a matter of definition. However, there are some characteristics which are generally accepted as having a significant influence. These include (1) the degree of seller concentration; (2) the degree of buyer concentration; (3) the extent of product differentiation; and (4) the condition of entry . . . There is a long list of other potentially important variables which may affect market conduct and performance. The list includes: variables affecting demand conditions, such as price elasticity of demand, short-run income elasticity and long-run rate of growth; variables affecting supply conditions, such as economies of scale, cost flexibility, vertical integration and the underlying rate of technical advance; and forms of government intervention, such as specific taxes, hire-purchase controls, price and output regulations. (Shaw and Sutton 1976, pp. 2 and 3)

The appraisal should be completed for every product market in which the firm operates. The main objective is to ensure that the management can identify the factors relevant for competitive success in each market, so that they can appraise their own strengths and weaknesses and identify the major strengths and weaknesses of their competitors. These must be assessed in terms of the comparative advantages which are relevant for the industry.

Within each specific business, the real significance of a strengths and weaknesses analysis is what it says about the company's competitive posture. For example, having an unparalleled manufacturing capability may not be worth very much in an industry when competition is primarily on the basis of styling and distribution. Similarly, having a first-class marketing group scores no competitive points if many other people in the industry have a marketing group that is equally first class (Tilles, in Ansoff 1969, pp. 189–90).

Having identified its strengths and weaknesses, a firm must continue to monitor its competitors' actions, so that it can identify potential threats to its market standing, market outlets, or sources of supply. The information required for this purpose may differ for different firms. This has been highlighted by a survey of U.S. management undertaken by Wall (1974) by a nonrandom sample of readers of the *Harvard Business Review*. The objective of the survey was to identify the kind of information which, in the opinion of the respondents, managers need to know about competitors. Given the nature of the sample, the results are not statistically reliable, but they are provocative. For example, it seems that while pricing behavior was commonly stressed by relatively small firms, information about competitors' research activities was of most interest to larger firms. Similarly, the nature of the product market, and especially the degree of price and nonprice competition, may be reflected in the fact that data on competitors' costs were of more interest to industrial-goods manufacturers, whereas consumer goods manufacturers made more use of information about product styling.

Step 3: Fixing quantitative targets. Given that the environmental constraints have been identified and appraised in Step 2, the firm may realistically set quantitative target values for some of its objectives. At this stage, the purpose is not to set targets for comparison with future outcomes, but rather to set global targets for the firm as a whole, so as to assess the contribution that may be made by different product areas or operating divisions.

Step 4: Relating company targets to divisional plans. The next step is to assess the contribution that can be made by each division or product group within the corporation, and for this purpose, a provisional strategic plan must be developed for each subunit. These plans should be based upon the analysis of macroeconomic trends and upon the competitive audit specific to the subunit. They may be thought of as recommendations for future action by the division to further the objectives of the corporation. The recommendations may relate primarily to the development of existing products, and may involve proposals for changes in (say) sales promotion or in the scale or method of production. However, the plans may also cover changes in the range of activities, and may therefore include proposals to enter new product markets, to introduce new products, or to take on activities which are vertically related to existing products. These proposals will be included at this stage of strategic planning whenever they appear as a "natural" extension of existing activities or include steps which seem to be necessary to protect a division's competitive status (see sections 3.1 the material on risk, uncertainty, and integration, and 4.1, the material on pressures and motives for diversification).

Step 5: Gap analysis. Once the provisional plans have been drawn up for each subunit, the plans may be aggregated to obtain an initial forecast for the company as a whole. This forecast may be compared with the objectives and targets which were set in Steps 1 and 3, although care must be taken to ensure that the forecast is independent of the targets and is not distorted so as to appear to produce the sought-after result. If all the targets can be met, the firm may choose its strategic portfolio immediately (Step 7). On the other hand, if the targets cannot be met, the strategic plans must be revised. This may include some revision of the targets, but at least initially, it is likely to involve a search to discover new opportunities that were omitted from the original plan.

The search may take place even if the initial analysis suggests that existing targets can be met by existing specialisms, and firms may search for, and even introduce, new projects in advance of their real need, so as to preserve some flexibility in timing. However, the incentive to search will be stronger if the gap analysis indicates that the accepted targets cannot be reached without the help of new ideas.

Step 6: Strategic search. The strategic search may start with a reappraisal of existing products, their markets, and their sources of supply. A more careful definition of the existing business may show that marketing effort is inappropriate, or is misdirected to relatively unprofitable market segments. It may also lead to proposals for increased integration if (say) the existing distribution channels do not seem to be able to exploit the product's full potential. However, the existing products may still prove to be inadequate, even if it is found that they can be exploited more effectively than they have been in the past. The search must then be extended to include proposals for diversification. These should be related to existing specialisms, and the search may therefore build on the earlier assessment of strengths and weaknesses (Step 2).

For example, in 1959, the Singer Corporation was forced to reappraise its strategy in the face of a declining share of the market for sewing machines. The reappraisal included changes in its marketing strategy, which were designed, inter alia, to make more intensive use of its established retail outlets. It also aimed at diversification. To this end, it defined its main strengths as those of an operating rather than an investment company, skilled in manufacturing small electromechanical machines to high-quality standards, demonstrating these products to customers, and providing supportive after-sales services (*Fortune,* 1975). This definition helps to identify the type of product areas which should be included in the strategic search. It does not guarantee that opportunities will be discovered in those areas, nor that the firm can profitably exploit any opportunities which are discovered, but it does enable the firm to concentrate on those areas where it is likely to have a comparative advantage. The effect is similar to that on a racehorse wearing blinkers. The blinkered horse is less likely to be distracted from its main purpose. It may miss the occasional short-cut, but this hardly matters because there are very few shortcuts on race courses. There are also very few shortcuts in business.

Any business opportunities discovered by the strategic search must be appraised and related to the overall objectives of the firm. But the appraisal should not be restricted to the benefits of successful entry. It must also assess the likelihood of success. The firm should therefore undertake a competitive audit of the proposed new market area (see Step 2) and should pay particular attention to the conditions of entry. Economic analysis generally identifies three main types of entry barrier: economies of scale, product differentiation, and absolute-cost advantages. Economies of scale may limit entry if the most efficient plants can supply a large proportion of industry output, and unit costs rise significantly at suboptimal scales. Product differentiation implies that buyers may show a preference for the products of established firms, and an absolute-cost advantage occurs when established firms can expect lower unit costs than an entrant at any scale of output, because of (say) a favorable source of supply of inputs.

Barriers set by economies of scale become less significant if market demand is expanding rapidly enough to absorb significant increases in capacity, but otherwise they cannot be overcome unless the entrant can avoid a direct attack and concentrate instead on a limited market segment. By contrast, the two other barriers may be less significant if the entrant can carry over relevant attributes from other areas. The barriers imply that an entrant may have to accept an inferior technology and more restricted access to markets than the established firms, but these restrictions will be less significant if the entrant has an established reputation in a similar market area and/or has had some experience of similar technologies. This learning-by-doing may assist entry and may even give the entrant an advantage over some established firm. However, the possible advantages must be appraised carefully and related to the needs of the market. Without them, entry to some long-established markets may prove to be impossible even when there are no obvious entry barriers. Customers may develop ties of mutual respect and loyalty with established suppliers. From experience, they learn that some suppliers are more reliable than others: They meet their delivery dates and quality specifications, they help out at short notice to meet special orders, and they do their best to help their customers through the supply shortages of an occasional sellers' market. Customers are then reluctant to change from their established suppliers unless they are offered a specific incentive to do so. The incentive may be provided if the entrant offers an innovatory product or service, but more commonly entrants will rely upon mergers with established firms to provide the necessary market contacts. Even so, entry is unlikely to be profitable unless the entrant can offer some asset to complement the market contacts of the acquired firm (see Chapter 7).

Step 7: Portfolio selection. The final step in strategy formulation is to select the firm's portfolio of product and market areas, and to determine the priority to be given to each. Scarce managerial and financial resources must be allocated between them so as to promote the long-term performance of the firm as a whole. The firm will wish to identify and support its priority areas, or stars, and in consequence other areas may have to be starved of the resources that would be needed if they were to realize their full potential. Some of these other areas may have to be dropped altogether, but many will be retained, possibly as "cash cows" or as an insurance against the premature decline of a star.

The final assessment must make use of all the relevant information which is available for each product area, but often simple rules of thumb will help to identify the relevant alternatives. One set of rules is summarized in the Strategic Planning Matrix in Figure 5, which is based rather loosely on the Directional Policy Matrix (D.P.M.) developed for use by Shell International, part of the Royal Dutch/Shell group of oil and chemical companies. The D.P.M. has been used routinely by Shell's product divisions and was implicitly or explicitly used for corporate strategic planning (David 1976).

To use the matrix, it is necessary to identify two attributes for each product area. The first (measured horizontally) measures the general performance prospects of companies operating in that area.

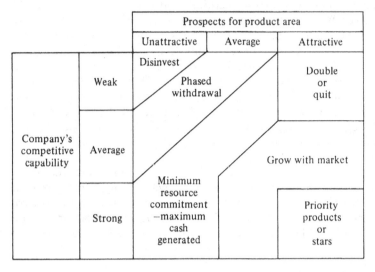

Figure 5. Strategic planning matrix

It therefore involves an attempt to identify the market structure and predict the resultant market performance. The second attribute (measured vertically) summarizes the company's present competitive strengths in the product area and hence measures its ability to share in that section's growth or profitability. Each product area may be classified by means of these two attributes. This determines its position in the matrix, and in turn the position suggests the role of the product area in the company's portfolio.

Stars, or priority products, are identified when a strong competitive position is established in an areas with generally attractive prospects. Conversely, the coincidence of a weak or declining competitive position and a weak market identifies the areas which are ripe for immediate or phased withdrawal. However, a weak competitive position in an attractive market area calls for a careful strategic decision. Continuing the current status could involve a cash drain with no offsetting prospect of reward in the long run. For this reason, unless the firm wishes to maintain a toehold for future expansion, it should either fight now to improve its competitive status or accept that it cannot share in the good prospects and should therefore leave the area. Hence the "double or quit" entry in the matrix.

The remaining areas in the matrix are likely to include the majority of the firm's products. Some will be more attractive than others and require a continuing commitment of resources to maintain competitive status, whereas the others will be slightly less attractive but worth retaining, so long as they do not call for any significant investment of new resources. In practice, however, the borderline between these two areas will be uncertain, and precise classification may very with the volume of resources available after priority needs have been met.

The matrix therefore assist the classification of individual product areas, but, on its own, this is not sufficient to determine the firm's strategic portfolio. The strategy must also consider the effects of interaction between different areas, and in particular it should consider the effects of instability and uncertainty. As emphasized in Chapter 4, the performance of the portfolio as a whole is what matters, not the performance of individual components. Finally, we must stress once more that strategy formulation must be an ongoing process. It must not lead the firm into a blind alley, and hence the portfolio should be consciously designed to include product areas that are expected to widen the range of future options in desirable ways, even though their inclusion would not be justified by their current performance on its own.

6
Multinational strategy

6.1 Introduction

No discussion of the direction of strategic growth can be complete without some reference to the increasing importance of multinational activities. The multinational enterprises (MNEs) which own and control income-generating assets in more than one country account for at least one-fifth of the world's output (excluding the centrally planned economies). In the United Kingdom, about one-third of company profits are derived from overseas operations, and about one-half of the one hundred largest manufacturing firms had a quarter or more of their output produced outside the United Kingdom (Dunning 1974, Stopford 1974).

The MNEs comprise a relatively small number of very large enterprises. The Comparative Multinational Enterprise Project run by the Harvard Business School covered those firms on *Fortune's* list of the 500 largest industrial companies in the United States in 1968 that had manufacturing subsidiaries in at least six foreign countries (187 U.S. companies in all), together with the 200 firms on *Fortune's* list of the largest non-American industrial companies in 1970. The project therefore surveyed approximately 400 MNEs. It estimated that in 1970 these enterprises operated nearly ten thousand wholly or partially owned foreign manufacturing subsidiaries. (For a convenient summary see Franko 1976, Chap. 1. For more detail see Vaupel and Curhan 1973). At the same time, some of the largest MNEs, such as General Motors or the Exxon Corporation (then Standard Oil of New Jersey), had annual sales which exceeded the gross national product of many countries, including Denmark and Norway (Tugendhat 1971).

At one time, multinational operation was thought to be an American prerogative, and was seen as the "American Challenge" which threatened the sovereignty of other countries (Servan-Schreiber 1967). It now seems that this was a distorted picture, which reflected the predominance of American data and research on the

MNEs. More recent evidence does not downgrade the significance of MNEs, but it does suggest that the U.S. predominance may have been exaggerated. For example, of the foreign subsidiaries operated by firms included in the comparative Multinational Enterprise Project, approximately forty-three percent had parent companies which originated in the United States, while twenty-six percent had Continental European parents, twenty-three percent had parents in the United Kingdom, and five percent had Japanese parents. Further it does not seem that the "American Challenge" is increasing. Franko (1976, p. 12) considered that by 1971 the large Continential European firms taken as a whole were expanding foreign manufacturing operations more rapidly than were the large U.S. firms. Similarly one study that deliberately set out to test the thesis of creeping American dominance in Europe, concluded:

Thus during 1962–7 the American firms grew faster than the European in electricals, and to a lesser extent in engineering. There are signs, therefore, of an "American Challenge" in these industries. Overall, however, the American and European firms grew at much the same rate 1962–7, and over the period 1957–67 the Continentals grew much faster. The larger size of American firms does not seem to have been an advantage. On the contrary, it was the smaller American firms with sales in the range $150 million to $500 million which grew fastest. (Rowthorn 1971, p. 85)

The growth of MNEs must be seen, therefore, as a genuine multinational activity which involves firms in many different countries, including especially the United States, the United Kingdom, France, West Germany, the Netherlands, Switzerland, and Japan. It will be clear from the discussion that follows that in many ways this growth is simply a logical extension of the growth and integration that may take place within national boundaries, and that has already been considered in previous chapters. To the extent that this is true, no separate treatment of MNEs is necessary. On the other hand, the simple fact that MNEs operate simultaneously in a number of different national environments must generate some problems for strategic planning that are different in degree, if not in kind, from the problems posed by operating in different markets within a single country. Further, though all MNEs have many features in common, there are some significant differences between the MNEs that originate in different countries. These differences reflect different national environments and must be recognized before the strategies adopted by the MNEs can be understood.

In order to provide a basic introduction to the problems of multinational strategy, the following paragraphs will concentrate on two features: first, the alternative patterns of growth; and second, the alternative methods of control. Throughout we shall refer to the MNE's country of origin as the "parent" economy and to the overseas economy as the "host."

6.2 Alternative patterns of growth

The most general explanation of multinational growth in manufacturing industry is provided by the product-cycle model, which seeks to explain how a product which was developed for a specific national market, such as the United States may provide a basis for overseas sales and, eventually, overseas manufacture (see especially Vernon 1971). The model assumes that all relevant products and technologies are developed initially to meet the needs of the parent economy, and it may therefore be less valid for the established MNEs, which base their new product strategies on worldwide considerations from the outset. However, the model does give an explanation of the past development of many MNEs, and therefore helps us to understand their current structure. It also provides a convenient framework for a discussion of strategic development in a multinational setting. Initially, we consider the historical sequence of developments by which firms were encouraged to set up overseas selling subsidiaries: Developments in U.S. manufacturing industry are contrasted with those in other countries and industries. Then we consider some of the strategic pressures encouraging firms to transfer their manufacturing operations overseas.

U.S. firms and the product-cycle model

The U.S. MNEs generally originated in the food processing, chemical, engineering, and transport industries. They owed their initial success to pioneering new products which were typically labor saving and/or highly income-elastic in demand, and were therefore appropriate for a labor-scarce economy with an increasingly wealthy mass market. In the course of this early growth, the firms not only acquired the technical expertise needed for specific products, but also developed comparative advantages in the research, production, marketing, and organizational skills needed to exploit new products and to penetrate new markets. The specific products then provided a basis for entry to international markets, and the more general skills have enabled the firms to establish and consolidate their early gains.

Once they had developed products specifically for the high-income American market, the firms found an expanding export demand as incomes increased in other countries, especially in Europe. Some of the sales arose spontaneously, in the sense that the initiative was taken by foreign buyers seeking imports rather than U.S. suppliers pressing for exports. When the sales were made to a few large customers who could be identified fairly easily, the firms could rely on direct selling. But when more local knowledge was needed to discover and develop market opportunities, the suppliers sometimes chose to rely upon overseas agencies. These were often satisfactory, but many suppliers were encouraged to set up their own selling subsidiaries in foreign markets because of the difficulty of finding agents who had the will and the resources to cope with significant increases in local demand. Further, in the longer term, the subsidiaries could often provide more usable market information than could an agent, because they would have a more intimate understanding of the parent company's operating procedures and, hence, its information requirements. Additional problems were caused by the legal complications of setting up agencies in different countries with unfamiliar legal systems. Some firms found that it was unexpectedly difficult and expensive to withdraw from an unsatisfactory agency agreement, especially if the agent could claim to have made a significant contribution to the product's goodwill in the local market (Brooke and Remmers 1977).

In the early stages, the pioneering firms generally relied upon their existing production facilities to meet the increasing overseas demands, but with time the pressures and opportunities for overseas manufacture increased. The causes and effects of these changes will be considered under the heading "The development of overseas manufacturing subsidiaries", but first we must ask whether the early growth of the U.S manufacturing firms is typical of all MNEs.

Growth in other countries and other industries

As with the U.S. firms, most Continental European MNEs began their international operations by exporting on the strength of comparative advantages derived from innovations. But generally they pursued different types of innovation. Whereas the pioneering products in the United States were developed to meet the needs of a labor-scarce economy, the innovations of the Continential European firms reflected an environment characterized by lower average incomes, a less even distribution of income, and a relative scarcity of land and raw materials rather than labor (see especially Franko 1976). This led to some bias in favor of material-saving processes, synthetic substitutes for natural materials, and goods developed specially for low-income consumers. The bias cannot be demonstrated rigorously, but the results have been well summarized by Vernon (1974, p. 93) as follows:

The U.S. firms do appear to specialise in innovations that are responsive to high incomes and high labour costs, such as frozen foods and the drip-dry shirt; the Europeans in innovations that are land- and material-saving, including synthetic fertilisers and rayon, or that represent cheaper versions of established consumer products, such as the Volkswagen; and the Japanese in innovations that are material-saving, such as synthetic paper, or that economise on living space, such as miniaturised electronic circuitry.

With a different pattern of innovations to build on, the Continental European MNEs also have a different geographical pattern of subsidiaries, which tend to be concentrated in host countries with similar cost environments. As a result, their subsidiaries are primarily in other European countries, although in the 1960s and 1970s there has been some slight trans-Atlantic movement by the European MNEs as the United States experienced increasing raw-material shortages (Franko 1976).

For a long time, the U.K. firms had less incentive than Continental European firms to develop material-saving technologies, because they had access to cheap raw materials from the Commonwealth. They could also develop tied export markets in the underdeveloped colonies, without relying on the stimulus of new innovations. As a result it seems that their initial moves towards multinational operation reflected the interests of specific firms rather than a general response to the environment (Stopford 1972). During the 1920s and 1930s, however, it became more common for U.K. firms to set up overseas manufacturing operations as they sought to defend export markets against increasing international competition. These pressures have continued during the postwar period, and although the earlier emphasis on Commonwealth trade has declined, it is still true that a majority of the subsidiaries of U.K. MNEs are in former colonies and dominions.

In general, it therefore seems that the overseas subsidiaries of the MNEs were set up initially to develop or protect existing export markets, and that in many cases they have profited from increasing demand for technical knowledge or other assets that are specific to individual firms. However, though the analysis applies to the early development of manufacturing subsidiaries, it may be less applicable to service or extractive industries. In practice, developments in the service industries have sometimes paralleled those in manufacturing as firms in (say) the financial or catering industries have established new branches to serve the increasing overseas activities of their established customers. But extractive industries often follow a different pattern. The MNEs will often have a comparative advantage in developing mineral deposits because of the technical knowledge and market outlets they have gained from earlier developments in their parent economy. The location of their overseas subsidiaries will depend upon the distribution of workable deposits, but the timing of their overseas moves has sometimes reflected their desire to prevent entry and to preserve established oligopolies, rather than any need to respond to existing demand.

The development of overseas manufacturing subsidiaries

We now turn to consider the strategic effect of developing manufacturing operations in foreign countries, given that the firm is already selling overseas, probably through its own subsidiaries. First, we discuss the reasons for manufacturing in the host country, and then we look at the question of the ownership of the facilities.

Manufacture in the host country. There are several reasons why firms with a profitable export business may choose to set up manufacturing facilities in foreign countries. These reasons may assume different importance for different firms or for the same firm in different countries, depending upon the characteristics of the product, the competitive strength of the firm, and the environment in each national market. Here we can simply provide a summary of the alternatives.

In some cases, the incentive to move overseas will reflect simple production economies. The firm's aggregate costs will be reduced if the total costs of setting up and operating a plant in the host country are less than the incremental costs of production in the parent country plus the transport costs and other expenses involved in moving the product across national boundaries. The incremental cost will be relatively low if there are significant unexploited economies of scale, or if the host economy is unable to supply the inputs needed for local manufacture at reasonable cost. Especially in the early stages of development, the hosts may lack the labor skills or component supplies needed for efficient production. On the other hand, manufacture in the host countries will be relatively more attractive if high transport and handling costs discourage centralized production; if tariffs or other trade barriers discourage imports to the host country; if host governments subsidize local facilities; if there are few economies of scale; if the host market is growing rapidly enough or is large enough to justify a plant of optimum size; or if the potential economies of centralized production are not obtainable because production has to be varied to meet the heterogeneous demands of different markets.

Overseas manufacture may also give some marketing advantages. Xenophobic consumers will develop more loyalty to a firm which has shed at least some of its foreign trappings. Further, for more purely commerical reasons, customers may expect better after-sales service and fewer delays in the supply of spare parts for durable goods if these goods are produced locally.

In some cases, these incentives will be reinforced by competition as the export sales are threatened by local sources of supply. Indigenous producers may be able to offer substitutes for the imported products as the host country develops and the production technology becomes more widely available. The original suppliers will then be encouraged to develop further product improvements or to set up overseas manufacturing facilities as a defensive reaction. Even if the indigenous producers cannot compete effectively, aggressive moves by other international suppliers may prompt a similar reaction. Many of the pioneering firms come from oligopolistic industries. As soon as one of the oligopolists chooses to set up a manufacturing subsidiary in a particular country, its rivals will be encouraged to reappraise their own strategies. In some cases, they will decide that no immediate action is necessary. But, in others, they may want to match their rival's move as soon as possible, in order to reduce any risk that he may establish a commanding lead in that market or acquire new skills to give him a competitive advantage in entering other markets. This risk will be greatest for firms which have a fairly narrow product line and which base their strategies on a combination of marketing skills and consumer loyalty, which could be eroded if rivals gain more experience of overseas operations. Such firms will have a strong incentive to match the overseas activities of their rivals. By contrast, firms which are more diversified, or more research intensive, have a wider range of strategic options and face less pressure to match their rivals' moves in any particular market (Knickerbocker 1973).

Under the right conditions, oligopolistic rivalry may therefore encourage multinational production as a defensive reaction designed to protect existing markets. Similar incentives may follow if the host governments attempt to protect indigenous manufacturers. These attempts are not confined to the less developed economies. For example, "Much of the rapid increase in the number of U.S. subsidiaries of Continental enterprises during the 1960s was a by-product of effort by high-cost American producers of price-elastic products to get the U.S. government to stop American imports of goods produced by European firms with more favorable cost structures" (Franko 1976, p. 175). On the other hand, the underdeveloped countries have sometimes taken more positive steps to attract the MNEs. Frequently, these attempts start with some pressure for local assembly and follow with increasing demands for local manufacture of components. The pressures are often backed by specific incentives, such as discriminatory taxes favoring local manufacture, although their significance will also depend upon the ease with which cash generated in the host country can be repatriated by the parent, either as profits or in the form of inflated transfer prices, royalty payments, and the like. The net incentive will also be affected by political instability, by the threat of nationalization, or by the exchange rate. For example, if the parent country's exchange rate is overvalued, its exports will be discouraged and the incentive for direct investment to protect overseas markets will be increased. This appears to have influenced some U.S. firms in the 1960s. By contrast, if a host country's currency is undervalued, it may seem particularly attractive as a location for exports to third countries.

Since the mid-1960s, it has become increasingly common for MNEs to establish labor-intensive manufacturing operations in the less-developed countries to supply exports to third countries or even to the parent economy.

Semiconductors, valves, tuners and other components are manufactured or assembled for a large number of Japanese and American electronic firms in

Hong Kong, Singapore, South Korea, Taiwan and Mexico. (The electronics industry is by far the most important industry in this field.) Garments, gloves, leather luggage and baseballs are sewn together in the West Indies, South-east Asia and Mexico for American and Japanese firms . . . Automobile parts are manufactured for British, American and Japanese firms in a wide variety of countries, e. g. radio antennae in Taiwan, piston rings and cylinder linings in South Korea and Taiwan, automobile lamps in Mexico, braking equipment in India, batteries and springs in Thailand etc. . . . Among other industries already engaged in these activities in less-developed countries are those producing electrical appliances (including television and radio, sewing machines, calculators and other office equipment), electrical machinery, power tools, machine tools and parts, motorcycle and bicycle parts, typewriters, cameras, optical equipment, watches, brass valves, aircraft parts, telecommunications equipment, chemicals and synthetic fibres, and musical instruments. (Helleiner 1973, p. 29)

These developments have been encouraged by improvements in transportation, including containerization, and by the fact that better education and health services in the less-developed countries have often improved the quality of unskilled and semiskilled labor without narrowing the wages gap between the developed and less-developed countries. The products are generally produced by nonautomated assembly or by manufacturing operations which use a mature technology. They are often high-value products with relatively low transport costs.

Ownership of manufacturing facilities. Given that a firm has decided that manufacturing facilities should be established in the host country, it must also decide how these facilities should be operated. There are several alternatives to the extreme of a wholly owned foreign subsidiary. One alternative is to license a manufacturer in the host country to use any patents required for efficient operation. This may give the licensor firm a more rapid return, which will be attractive if its own resources are limited or if (say) political instability in the host country suggests that it would be unwise to adopt a longer time horizon. Licensing may also be attractive in more developed economies, which offer better prospects for reciprocal licensing agreements. However, the licenses may help future competitors to develop more rapidly in the host country, and may weaken the developer's ability to control the subsequent exploitation of the technology. Further, it is often said that a new technology bears the generic code of its developer, and is therefore more difficult to transfer to other firms. By contrast, a mature technology may be more widely available. It may then be possible for a host country to exploit the rivalry among potential suppliers and so dictate the terms on which technology can be used. It may seek to obtain licences for indigenous manufacturers, or turn-key plants which are provided by the supplier complete and ready for operation by the user. Alternatively it may negotiate management contracts under which a plant is provided and managed by the supplier but remains under the ownership of the host.

Even when the multinational firm is able to retain some control of operations in the host country, it may try to develop a joint venture with a local partner (see especially Stopford and Wells 1972, Part II). In some countries, the host govenments apply very strong pressure to encourage local participation. This appears to be true in Japan, Spain, India, Mexico, and Pakistan; although even in these countries, the MNEs which can offer unique know-how or facilities are in a very strong bargaining position and may be able to retain complete control of their subsidiaries. On the other hand, some MNEs may prefer to cooperate with local partners even when they are not under any political pressure to do so. The local partners may contribute capital and can usually offer local expertise and more ready access to local markets. These advantages can be significant for small firms. They may also be important for larger firms that are trying to diversify and require additional marketing expertise in a number of different areas. For similar reasons, some raw material producers in the aluminum, copper, and oil industries have relied on joint ventures to provide downstream marketing outlets for their material, at the same time trying to retain close control of the main sources of supply in order to deter the growth of competition.

In general, the MNEs will be reluctant to rely upon joint ventures whenever their strategy requires detailed control that might conflict with the interests of the local partner. This might happen if the MNE wished to rationalize production and concentrate particular operations in particular countries, or if it wished to pursue a common international marketing policy, as do several firms in the food and detergent industries. Note, however, that this sort of control is only feasible if the product requirements can be standardized across national boundaries. Generally this implies a fairly mature stage in the product life cycle.

6.3 Alternative patterns of control

If the MNEs are to rationalize their operations and exploit the potential synergy between national subsidiaries, they must devise ways to coordinate their activities. They appear to have faced increasing competitive pressures to encourage rationalization as their products have matured and the necessary skills for multinational operation have been acquired by an increasing number of firms in different parent countries. At the same time, their ability to impose coordination has been enhanced by improvements in communications and changes in organizational structure, while the opportunity to gain by doing so has been improved as the demand in different host countries has become more standardized, and obstacles to transfer between national subsidiaries caused by tariffs or other barriers have declined. In all cases, however, the attempts at coordination may bring the MNEs into increasing conflict with the host governments.

In the early days of multinational operation, many firms adopted a fairly loose control system, which gave considerable autonomy to the overseas subsidiaries. Often there was little or no attempt to integrate the subsidiaries with the divisions operating in the parent economy, and negotiations over transfer prices or royalty payments by the subsidiaries were conducted at arm's length, as if between separate organizations. This looseness reflected the fact that the subsidiaries emerged as a defensive reaction, rather than as part of a preplanned strategy; but even if the parent firms had wished to impose a tighter control, it is unlikely that many of them would have been able to do so successfully, because they had no detailed experience of overseas operations. Similar problems may still face national companies that are moving towards multinational status, but they are now more likely to be able to recruit executives who have already gained experience in established MNEs. Obviously this was not possible for the pioneers.

Pressure for more central control generally increased within the parent organization as the subsidiaries grew to take an increasing share of the total activities and resources of the firm. In the United States, the typical response was to establish a separate division to coordinate the operations of the overseas subsidiaries, while retaining a clear distinction between domestic and overseas activities. In effect, this response introduced an additional international division alongside the product divisions of the typical M-form firm. By contrast, the U.K. and Continental European MNEs have generally preferred coordination by consensus. Typically, they have ignored the International Division structure and have relied upon less formal structures based upon mutual trust between individuals. These are often based on what have been called "mother-daughter" relationships between the chief executives of the parent and subsidiary companies: The subsidiaries enjoy considerable autonomy, while acting within precise but unwritten constraints set by a common "family" background of long experience in the same organization (Franko 1976).

Whether firms initially adopt the U.S. International Division structure or prefer the feudal structure of the European firms, they are, however, likely to face increasing competitive pressures to avoid suboptimization by their subsidiaries. The coordination will generally be easier to achieve in the more specialized MNEs, whereas increasingly precise coordination will be needed to rationalize the activities of interdependent subsidiaries as the number of subsidiaries or the range of activities increases. The reaction has generally taken one of two alternative firms (see especially Stopford and Wells 1972). One alternative is to emphasize coordination for individual products and to place the appropriate activities of the overseas subsidiaries directly under the product divisions of the parent organization. This structure seems to be particularly appropriate for innovative products, because it eases the communication of technical information. The alternative is to adopt a geographical structure, in which each division of the M-form is responsible for all activities within its assigned area, and the parent country appears as no more than a single division with the same bargaining strength as the others. This structure seems to suit MNEs that produce a narrow range of mature products, whose marketing requirements have become standardized within broad regions, such as the E.E.C. or Latin America. Thus, for example, the Area Structure may be appropriate for food manufacturing while the Product Structure may suit some chemical firms.

Clearly the Area Structure can strengthen coordination between the subsidiaries and the parent organization, but it may weaken coordination between product groups in any host country. Similarly an Area Structure facilitates coordination within, but not between, different areas. If a choice has to be made, it should reflect the type of coordination and the types of information flow that have to be given priority within the MNE. However, increasingly, some MNEs have been trying to retain the benefits of both structures by developing a "grid" or "matrix" structure, in which subsidiaries report to more than one parent division. One example has been discussed by Stopford and Wells (1972, pp. 88–9) as follows:

In Dow Chemicals in the late 1960s, area divisions had prime responsibility for all the products in their territories, whereas corporate product departments took a long-term view of product planning, capital investment, and the meeting of production schedules for the worldwide markets for each product line. The product departments, despite their apparent lack of direct involvement in the global operations of each product line, had full responsibility for product competitiveness and success in world markets. Two major functional groups in the central office provided co-ordination of interdivisional transactions: one group co-ordinated prices, schedules of investment plans for production, and made forecasts; the other group co-ordinated economic planning and evaluation. In addition, there were strong central financial control and research groups. Dow was attempting by means of this structure to develop a flexible system that could provide a pooling of product expertise to respond rapidly to changes in its global environment without muddling the clear lines of responsibility for profits in the area divisions.

As we have already implied, however, while the MNEs have sought to tighten their control over their subsidiaries, they have increasingly come into conflict with the governments of the host countries. Initially, host countries that were starved for capital and technology welcomed the contribution offered by the MNEs, as they did, for example, in Europe during the 1950s. Later, the Continental European MNEs were welcomed by some less-developed countries as an alternative to the established dominance of American and British firms. But inevitably the sources of conflict have increased. The MNEs search for control and rationalization has reduced the autonomy of the overseas subsidiaries just as the host governments have become increasingly involved in the management and planning of economic growth on a national basis. There is no ready solution to the conflict. In general, any attempt at rationalization is likely to offend the national self-interest of at least one host government, which fears the consequential loss of exports or employment. Ultimately, any strategic decision by an MNE must represent a compromise between the desire to exploit the full potential of multinational operation and the need to coexist with a number of separate host governments.

Part III
Strategy and growth

Introduction

The previous part was concerned with the range of a firm's activities; this one will concentrate on the means by which the range can be modified or extended. Specifically, it is concerned with the choice between mergers and internal expansion in Chapter 7, and with innovation in Chapter 8. Our main purpose is to examine the contribution which mergers and innovation can make to the growth of different firms in different circumstances, and to pick out the major characteristics that might affect any strategic assessment. As in the previous chapters, the treatment draws on a variety of published work by economists and management scientists. Much of this work has been done in the United States, and so American experience is used frequently to emphasize, or contrast with, experience in the United Kingdom, which remains as the main focal point of the analysis.

Each chapter starts with an extended discussion of the nature of the activity in question. In the case of mergers, this discussion seeks to identify the various steps involved in a merger and to give some indication of the laws and codes which affect each step. Similarly, Chapter 8 starts with an overview of the total innovation process and of the possible role of such things as patents and licences in that process. It also seeks to explain why innovation is so much more important in some industries than in others, and why its nature and importance may gradually change with time within a single industry.

In each case, the strategic problems depend upon both the internal operations of the firm and upon its external relations with other firms or institutions. In the case of innovations, it is convenient to discuss these problems sequentially, starting with the use of resources within a firm and turning subsequently to consider the effects of competition and the complex reactions of potential customers. Clearly, any strategic assessment must include all these factors, but the sequential treatment is convenient for exposition. By contrast, the internal and external aspects are inseparable in any analysis of mergers, because any merger involves at least two separate organizations and will probably involve decisions by many other outsiders, who have an active interest as (say) shareholders or alternative merger partners. Our main objective in discussing mergers is to explain why one particular firm may expect to gain by merging with another, but if we are to do so, we cannot avoid looking at the simultaneous assessments made by shareholders, and at the prevailing attitude to mergers of the Government and of the general industrial and commercial community.

7
Mergers

A merger or takeover occurs when two or more firms are combined under common ownership. Sometimes a merger is distinguished from a takeover. A "takeover" is then said to occur when one dominant firm acquires the assets of another, whereas a "merger" produces a new firm from a marriage of two more-or-less equal partners. But, in practice, this distinction may be difficult to maintain, as would happen, for example, if a merger were actually effected by means of a takeover bid in which one of the firms offers to buy the assets of the other. We shall therefore use the terms "merger" and "takeover" interchangeably; and when appropriate, we shall refer to the actual, or potential, buying firm as Beta and to the potential victim, or seller, as Sigma.

Our major purpose is to investigate the contribution which mergers can make to the strategic development of a firm. But if we are to do this satisfactorily, we must have some understanding of the institutional constraints that affect merger activity and of the various factors which influence the costs of a takeover. It may also help to have some background knowledge of the history of mergers. With this in mind, our discussion starts in 7.1 with a general review of the procedures involved in a merger, and follows this in 7.2 with a brief historical survey. We then turn more directly to consider merger strategy, starting with a discussion of the general choice between mergers and internal growth in 7.3, and continuing with a simple model of share-price determination in 7.4, which is used as a framework for discussing a wide variety of merger motives in 7.5. The chapter then continues with some comments on the timing of mergers and concludes with a discussion of the results of empirical studies of merger activity.

7.1 Mergers: general procedures

In principle, we may distinguish two alternative methods of acquisition: Either Beta can use cash to purchase Sigma from its original

101

owners, or it can offer them a share-exchange deal in which they receive new shares in Beta in exchange for their original holdings in Sigma. After a cash purchase, the original shareholders of Sigma have no continuing interest in the firm, and Beta will simply have acquired an income-earning asset in exchange for cash, as in any other investment transaction. By contrast, after a share-exchange deal, Sigma's original shareholders will share the total equity of the enlarged firm with Beta's original shareholders, and the relative shares of the two groups will depend upon the terms of the merger. In practice, these terms may not give Sigma's shareholders the same class of shares in Beta, and the latter may have different voting rights, or represent a fixed-interest loan which may or may not offer the right of conversion to equity status at a later date. The choice between these alternatives may have a significant impact upon the gains made by different shareholders, but a comprehensive treatment would require specialist analysis that is beyond the scope of this book.

Many takeover bids involve a combination of cash and shares, or offer a choice between the two. Historically, the relative importance of cash deals declined over a long period until, in 1972, they accounted for less than twenty percent of the value of all acquisitions, while fixed-interest securities were used for another twenty percent and ordinary shares accounted for the remainder. After 1972, however, the relative importance of cash deals increased considerably, while the proportion of acquisition expenditure covered by issues of fixed-interest securities declined to insignificance during a period of very high interest rates (*Trade and Industry*, May 13, 1977; pp. 294–5).

Casual reading of newspaper reports may sometimes give the impression that most mergers are fiercely contested by the parties involved. This impression would be misleading. Takeover battles do sometimes occur, and the maneuvers by which the managers of one firm struggle to retain their independence, or by which two buyers compete to acquire the same victim, may be newsworthy. They may also be costly: it is reported that Watneys spent nearly £.5 million in an abortive attempt to avoid takeover by Grand Metropolitan (Caulkin 1975). But the battles are not representative of the majority of mergers, which appear to be relatively amicable. Newbould (1970) estimated that over ninety-five percent of the mergers reported by the financial press in 1967–8 were not opposed by the directors of the victim: of 2,600 recorded mergers, 2,181 were deals which had been previously agreed on by the directors of the firms concerned, while a further 296 involved unexpected, but uncontested, offers. Further, although the initiative is probably taken by the buyer in most cases, it is always possible for a willing seller to search for a potential buyer, either by a direct approach or more probably through some intermediary, such as a merchant bank.

How do the deals normally occur? Whether or not the initial approach is made by Sigma, Beta should first decide on the direction of expansion required to meet its strategic objectives, and should make some appraisal of the relative merits of internal and external expansion, a topic which we shall discuss later. If external expansion seems to be appropriate, Beta should draw up a short list of possible takeover candidates with a profile of each candidate to identify its possible strengths and weaknesses. Hopefully, this profile will give advance warning of possible problem areas, as well as identifying the benefits that might be derived from a merger. It may possibly serve to eliminate all but one of the candidates, or suggest that further search is needed to identify a viable candidate; but if this does not happen, Beta will have to select the most preferred candidate from its list. Its choice will depend upon the price it is likely to have to pay to acquire Sigma, as well as the possible benefits of the acquisition; but the choice cannot be made simply on the basis of relative cost, because no two candidates are alike. Further, the uncertainty surrounding many of the estimates may preclude formal quantitative analysis: As one finance director is reported to have said, "You can't do a d.c.f. [discounted cash-flow calculation] for faith" (Pickering 1974, p. 121). Nevertheless estimates of cash flow are still essential, if only to identify the performance that will be needed to justify the costs of the merger. It is always desirable to know the extent of one's ignorance before leaping into the dark.

Once Beta has identified a potential takeover victim, it must assess the terms that it would be prepared to offer. This may be done by Beta's own staff, but it will almost certainly make use of the advice of outside consultants, especially the specialist departments which have been built up for this purpose by merchant banks or similar institutions. The remaining stages in a takeover bid have been well described by Weinberg (1971, Chap. 10) and may be summarized as follows.

As a first step, Beta is likely to make an informal approach to Sigma's directors in order to seek their support for a bid. In turn,

Sigma's directors should seek advice from bankers or from specialist consultants in the interests of their shareholders; they may also seek to satisfy themselves that Beta has the resources to make a bona fide offer, unless Beta's existing reputation makes further information redundant; and once they are satisfied, they may agree to provide Beta with up-to-date trading figures, so that a fair offer can be agreed upon. Whether or not it obtains Sigma's cooperation, Beta may decide to make a formal offer; and in the first instance, this is made to Sigma's directors. One or both of the firms should make a preliminary public announcement as soon as it is clear that a firm offer will be forthcoming, and as soon as possible thereafter the full text of the offer should be sent to Sigma's shareholders. The offer will then be kept open for a specified period of at least twenty-one days, but will normally be conditional upon Beta's acquiring a set percentage of the shares bid for. Until the preliminary announcement has been made, all parties to the discussions are under an obligation to preserve secrecy (in an attempt to discourage ill-informed speculation) and to refrain from share dealings designed to profit from their inside knowledge. However, in practice, the control of insider dealings in shares has posed a perennial problem for the authorities.

When the formal offer is made, Sigma's directors will advise shareholders of their own attitude to it and will provide formal arguments to support their view. If they believe that the offer should be rejected, there are several things they can do to reinforce their view. Especially if the offer involves a share exchange, so that Sigma's shareholders retain an interest in Beta, Sigma's directors may try to disparage Beta's prospects. This course was pursued vigorously by Courtaulds in 1961 as part of a successful campaign to throw off an unwanted offer from I.C.I. (see, for example, Davis 1970, pp. 45–6). More commonly, the directors will try to suggest that the offer undervalues Sigma's shares; and to support their arguments, they may seek to revise estimates of future profitability. Alternatively, they may introduce proposals to change the capital gearing (that is, the ratio of fixed-interest securities to equities) so as to benefit the ordinary shareholders (see 7.5, the material on uncertainty). However there are limits, and once it has become clear that a bid is in the offing, the directors should allow the shareholders to decide on its merits and should not try to rearrange the affairs of the firm so as to impede a genuine offer. The City Code on Take-overs and Mergers states that during the course of an offer, or even before the date of the offer if the board of the offeree company has reason to believe that a bona fide offer might be imminent, the board must not, except in pursuance of a contract entered into earlier, without the approval of the shareholders in general meeting, issue any authorised but unissued shares, or issue or grant options in respect of any unissued shares, create or issue or permit the creation or issue of any securities carrying rights of conversion into or subscription for shares of the company, or sell, dispose of or acquire or agree to sell, dispose of or acquire assets of material amount or enter into contracts otherwise than in the ordinary course of business. (City Code 1976, rule 38)

If Sigma's directors do oppose the bid, Beta's directors may publish a rejoinder and may improve the terms of their offer; in which case, they must extend the period during which the offer is open for acceptance so as to give Sigma's shareholders time to consider the terms and the arguments (City Code 1976, rule 22). Once the offer period is over, Beta may withdraw the offer if it has received too few acceptances. Otherwise, it must make the offer unconditional, giving any uncommitted shareholders an additional fourteen days to accept. If Beta receives acceptances in respect of ninety percent of the shares bid for, it may in most cases compulsorily acquire the remaining shares under section 209(1) of the Companies Act of 1948.

Clearly, this sequence may involve considerable legal and financial costs. In the United Kingdom, it has been suggested that each concluded acquisition absorbs between three thousand and five thousand executive man-hours (Kitching 1974), while Steiner (1975) recorded that "as the roughest of estimates" the out-of-pocket costs for routine acquisitions in the United States may be between three and five percent of the market value of shares acquired, with even greater costs for contested acquisitions. Further, in both countries, the procedures are circumscribed by externally imposed regulations, and though these are not intended to deter mergers as such, they may affect the administrative costs or influence the types of merger which are undertaken. (A convenient summary of the regulations affecting mergers in the United Kingdom has been provided by Davies 1976)

In the United Kingdom, the regulations are a mixture of legal requirements and informal codes of conduct. The legal requirements are designed primarily to discourage fraud and to encourage the disclosure of information relating to such things as directors' shareholdings and dealings in the firm's shares, whereas the informal rules set out in the City Code on Take-overs and Mergers are designed to establish standards of good business practice so as to guide the steps taken by the parties involved in a merger and to ensure the equitable treatment of all shareholders. The code is sponsored by a number of institutions such as the Issuing Houses Association or the Unit Trust Association, whose members have an active interest in the workings of the securities markets. It is administered and enforced by the City Panel, whose executives are ready to give advice before or during a takeover, or to give rulings on points of interpretation. If at any time there appears to have been a breach of the code, the panel will consider the case with the parties involved, and if appropriate "it may have recourse to private reprimand or public censure or, in a more flagrant case, to further action designed to deprive the offender temporarily or permanently of his ability to enjoy the facilities of the securities markets" (City Code 1976, p. 6).

However, the code does not have the force of law, and indeed its authors argue explicitly that the concept of equity between one shareholder and another is not amenable to legislation (see City Code 1976, p. 4). As a result, the panel can guide those who wish to conform but may have little control over deliberate offenders: "individual officers (of the Panel) have been known to admit, privately, that it has no effective ultimate sanction against those with no good name to lose" (*The Accountant,* May 6, 1976; p. 522). This status of the panel may be contrasted with that of the Securities and Exchange Commission in the United States. Like the panel, the commission has set up a framework of rules relating to mergers, but unlike the City Code, the commission's rules may be enforced by the courts. Anyone who suffers as a result of a breach of the commission's rules may bring a civil action for redress against the offender, while the commission itself may apply to the federal courts for an order against any acts which break its rules.

The costs and hazards of merger activity may be further increased by official antitrust policies. In the United Kingdom, there was no effective action against mergers before the Monopolies and Mergers Act of 1965, which was subsequently replaced by the Fair Trading Act of 1973. This act makes it possible, but not mandatory, for the Secretary of State at the Department of Prices and Consumer Protection (formerly the Department of Trade and Industry or the Board of Trade) to refer certain types of merger to the Monopolies and Mergers Commission to determine whether they are likely to operate against the public interest. The mergers concerned are those involving the acquisition of assets of more than £5 million or where the acquisition would create or intensify a monopoly, which is defined for this purpose as the control of twenty-five percent of the supply of a commodity. The commission must report within six months and a proposed merger can be held in abeyance during this period. If the commission's report is adverse, a completed merger may be reversed, and a proposed merger may be prohibited or made subject to specified conditions.

In principle, these provisions could present a significant deterrent to large horizontal mergers. However, until recently, the impact has probably been relatively slight. Up to the end of 1972, there had been over seven-hundred merger proposals that were subject to the 1965 act and reviewed by the Government departments concerned. Excluding newspaper mergers, which must be referred automatically, only sixteen of these proposals were referred to the commission, although an unknown number may have been abandoned before a proposed reference was made public. After 1973, the work of the commission was intensified. In two years (1973 and 1974) the number of references was nearly as great as in the previous eight years, and represented nearly five percent of the mergers covered by the act. In 1975 and 1976, however, the proportion of eligible mergers referred to the commission fell again to about two-and-a-half percent, similar to the pre-1973 proportion. During 1973 and 1974, almost half of the proposals were abandoned before the commission submitted its report. This represents a higher proportion than in earlier or later years, and may reflect a belief that the commission was hardening its attitude to mergers at this time, although in the event, the proportion of critical reports proved to be substantially the same before and after 1973.

In general, there are several other reasons why a reference to the commission may deter a proposed merger. It may give Sigma's directors more time to contest a bid if they wish to do so, whereas in other cases, the intervening changes in stock-market prices, or in the economic environment, may change Beta's assessment of the benefit to be obtained from the merger. Even if the merger eventually goes ahead, the delay caused by the reference may have adverse consequences. For example, the merger between Wilkinson Sword and British Match which was referred in 1973 was ultimately approved by the commission. However the firms observed that the information required by the commission during the four months of investigation had diverted managerial effort from other activities, and so had delayed the reorganization needed to equip the merged firms to meet the difficult trading conditions of 1973–4 (Caulkin 1974).

In contrast to the United Kingdom, the United States introduced its antitrust policies at a very much earlier date. Action against mergers was embodied in the Clayton Act of 1914 and made more effective by the Celler-Kefauver "antimerger amendment" of 1950, which extended the Clayton Act to cover transfers of a firm's assets, as well as its stocks and shares. The effectiveness of the legislation has been criticized, for example, by Reid (1976), who refers to the "regulatory sham" and emphasizes that less than one percent of the reported mergers have been challenged by the antitrust agencies since the passage of the Clayton Act. On the other hand, the legislation does seem to have deterred the more obviously monopolistic mergers, and in the late 1950s and early 1960s, the Anti-trust Division of the Department of Justice successfully challenged a number of proposed horizontal and vertical mergers, including for example, a proposed merger between Bethlehem and Youngstown steel companies, whose combined market share was less than that needed to justify a "monopoly" reference to the commission in the United Kingdom (Blair 1972, p. 592–3).

Antitrust reaction to diversification mergers is less clear. Following the antimerger judgment in the Procter and Gamble–Clorox case in 1967, it appears that if pursued aggressively, existing legislation could be effective against mergers between one of the potential entrants to an industry and one of the existing market leaders. It may thus deter some product-extension mergers between firms producing commodities that are related but not directly competing. (In the case cited, Procter and Gamble dominated in soaps and detergents, while Clorox – though relatively small – dominated the market for household liquid bleach.) On the other hand, it appears that pure conglomerate mergers are less likely to be challenged successfully (see, for example, Boyle 1974).

7.2 Mergers: history

Casual observation of the late 1960s and early 1970s might well give the impression that mergers are inevitable and pervasive features of all business growth. However this would be a distorted view of reality. To provide a more balanced perspective, we shall review the historical development of mergers before we consider their motivation. This perspective should also assist our later discussion of the timing of merger activity.

Merger movements in the United Kingdom

Until recently, there were no official statistics of mergers in the United Kingdom, and details of early merger movements have been built up by the painstaking collection of scraps of data recorded in the financial press of past periods, supplemented by historical surveys of individual businesses and industries (see especially Hannah 1974, 1976). The results are almost certainly less comprehensive and less reliable than the current official statistics, but the general pattern that emerges is too clear to be suspect, even if the precise details are less certain.

The first period of significant merger activity occurred at the end of the nineteenth century, with a peak in 1898–1900. Many of these mergers appear to have been born out of a faith in large units as sources of economies of scale or market power, and were probably facilitated by the extension of limited liability and by the increasing tendency for firms to seek a stock-exchange quotation. The first allowed shareholders to limit their risk of loss to the sums they had directly invested in a firm, whereas the later offered them a more ready market for their shares. The two therefore combined to offer less risk and greater liquidity to shareholders and reduced some of the financial obstacles to the growth of large units.

These early mergers were often multifirm amalgamations and were primarily horizontal: According to Hannah (1974), at least eighty-seven percent of the mergers were horizontal, with twelve percent vertical, and less than one percent involving diversification. However, they were concentrated in a relatively small number of industries, including textiles and brewing, and left many industries untouched. Although some of the firms which were formed at this time, such as Watneys or Imperial Tobacco, have remained to become household names, the movement did not transform the Victorian economy as a whole nor did it establish the general predominance of large units: The financial obstacles to large firms had been reduced but formidable managerial obstacles remained.

After this peak at the turn of the century, multifirm amalgamations declined progressively. Merger activity in general fluctuated at a relatively low level until the end of World War I when it rose again to a minor peak in 1919–20 and a more significant peak in 1926–9. This second wave of merger activity was of considerably more importance than the first. During the 1920s as a whole, mergers accounted for a larger share of total investment spending by firms than at any time before the 1960s, and it caused a doubling in the average size of firm during the decade. Concentration increased in many industries, and several of today's market leaders, including I.C.I. and Unilever, can trace their current form to mergers completed during this period (Hannah and Kay 1977). The activity so impressed at least one contemporary that in the early 1930s Mark Spade (né Nigel Balchin) could write tongue-in-cheek that "nowadays, if one gets to a position were there is no obvious move to be made, one merges at once, exactly like castling at Chess."

Subsequently, there were occasional flurries, but merger activity in general remained fairly low throughout the 1930s and 1940s. It grew slowly during the 1950s and then accelerated through the 1960s to reach a peak at the end of the decade and again in 1972–3. This was followed by a sharp drop in 1974–6, which may well prove to be the start of a fairly long period of decline.

During the 1950s, mergers accounted for an insignificant share of total investment spending (Hannah 1976), although they did have a significant impact on specific manufacturing industries, such as paints, or in some retail and service trades. In the latter, changing property values left many firms with real assets that were underexploited and undervalued, and therefore ripe for acquisition and development by specialists like Clore, Cotton, or Fraser (see, for example, Davis 1970). By contrast, during the 1960s, mergers were generally the dominant influence on industrial structure, leading to significant increases in concentration in most industries, and especially in brewing, electrical engineering (led by G.E.C.), and textiles (led by Courtaulds) (Hannah and Kay 1977). More than one-third of the firms quoted on the London stock exchange in 1960 had lost their independent existence as a result of mergers by the end of the decade, and one estimate suggests that approximately ten percent of the United Kingdom total of nonnationalized industrial assets changed hands during the merger boom of 1967–8 (Newbould 1970).

Throughout this period, it seems that the greater proportion of mergers has been horizontal, although there has been some increase in the relative importance of diversification mergers since 1965–7, possibly as a result of the Monopolies and Mergers Act of 1965.

Using a sample of quoted companies, Utton (1969) estimated that horizontal mergers accounted for eighty-one percent of the assets acquired in all mergers between 1954 and 1965, whereas diversification mergers accounted for only nine percent. By contrast, of the total assets involved in mergers between 1965 and 1973 covered by the 1965 act, seventy-one percent were in horizontal mergers and twenty-four percent in diversification mergers (Gribbin 1974). On an annual basis, the diversification mergers' share of assets increased from ten percent or less in 1965–7 to between thirty-five and fifty percent in 1971–2, although there was an unexplained drop in 1973.

Merger movements in the United States

Like the United Kingdom, the United States has experienced three significant periods of intensified merger activity, or merger waves (Markham 1955, Nelson 1959, Reid 1976). The first of these developed from 1887 to 1905 with a peak in 1899–1900; the second from 1916 to 1929 with a peak in the late 1920s; and the third in the 1960s with a peak in 1968. The first wave was dominated by multifirm amalgamations: mergers involving at least five firms absorbed about three-quarters of the firms which lost their identities in mergers during this period. By the 1920s, however, this proportion had fallen significantly, and in the post–World War II period, multifirm amalgamations have been almost completely replaced by acquisitions in which a large firm takes over a smaller firm.

We can therefore observe close parallels between the merger movements in the United Kingdom and the United States so far as these are concerned with the timing of mergers or the trend of multifirm amalgamations. However, there are at least two significant differences. First, the early merger movement was undoubtedly more pervasive in the United States than it was in the United Kingdom. It affected a wider range of industries and established the large corporate enterprise much earlier and more firmly as the typical organizational structure for manufacturing industry. In part, this difference reflected a greater readiness in the United States to develop or accept new management methods in the larger units (Hannah 1974), but the differing official attitudes to cartels and restrictive practices were also important and provided a stronger incentive for mergers to reduce competition in the United States.

Concentration generally increased as many industries came to be dominated by the quasimonopolies that resulted from the amalgamations. Subsequently, in the 1920s mergers between the smaller competitors provided further reorganization in these dominant-firm industries. For example, mergers helped Bethlehem Steel to provide a more effective challenge to the United States Steel Corporation; while in the tin-can market, Continental Can grew to challenge the dominance of American Can. Both U.S. Steel and American Can had been products of the earlier merger boom in 1901.

Subsequently, the significance of horizontal mergers declined, especially after the antitrust provisions against horizontal mergers were tightened by the Celler-Kefauver amendment in 1950. At the beginning of the 1950s, diversification mergers were already much more significant than they were in the United Kingdom, and their significance increased through the 1960s. According to the classification made by the Federal Trade Commission, in 1952–55 mergers involving firms producing completely unrelated products ("other conglomerate" mergers) or products that are related but not directly competing ("product extension" mergers) represented about fifty percent of all mergers. By the late 1960s, this proportion had increased to around seventy to eighty percent. The comparable figures for the United Kingdom were less than ten percent for the earlier period and certainly under fifty percent for the latter. The definitions may not be directly comparable, but the differences are too great to be explained as simple statistical errors.

Merger movements in other countries

It seems that many industrial countries experienced an upsurge of merger activity at the end of the 1960s, although often this lagged a little behind the movement in the United States. In Canada, the movement seems to have followed a very similar pattern to that of the United States. In Australia, mergers rose sharply after World War II to peak in 1959–61 and again in 1968–72; and on the continent of Europe several countries experienced a sharp rise at the end of the 1960s, typically leading to peaks around 1970–2 (George and Silberston 1975, Reid 1976). Generally the mergers have had some impact on a wide range of industries, but it seems that in nearly all countries, the industries most affected in terms of the number of mergers or the resultant increase in concentration include food, fabricated metals, textiles, and (except in the United Kingdom) chemicals.

These similarities in the patterns of merger activity experienced by different countries suggest that the more significant determinants of activity will also be common to all countries. Examples might include, say, international trade cycles or secular changes in the intensity of international competition. By contrast, local tax incentives or Government plans for the reorganization of industry are more likely to be specific to particular national economies. They may have a considerable impact on some firms or industries, and may provide the major incentive for individual mergers, but they are unlikely to explain the international trends of activity.

This distinction between the particular and the general explanation must be borne in mind throughout the following discussion of merger motivation.

7.3 Internal versus external growth

Given the background sketched in the last two sections, we can now turn to consider the possible strategic advantages which a firm may gain from a merger. Frequently, Beta will be able to choose between internal and external growth as alternative means of expansion. That is, it may compare the costs and benefits of growing internally, providing its own ideas and facilities, recruiting new staff and developing new market contacts, against the benefits of growing externally by merger and acquiring a ready-made solution – along with a new set of ready-made problems. Few firms grow entirely by either method alone, and to this extent the two are not pure substitutes. Further, they may sometimes appear to be complementary. A firm with good profits and a record of rapid internal growth may acquire a good image on the stock market, which makes it easier to expand externally by means of share-exchange deals. Nevertheless, internal and external growth may appear as alternative ways of extending production or marketing facilities once Beta has chosen the direction in which to expand; and to see mergers in perspective, we must therefore look at the main features of each alternative.

The case for internal growth

When there is a real choice, it is usually true that internal growth can be controlled more easily to meet a firm's individual needs. Provided that Beta has unrestricted access to the appropriate know-how and physical facilities, internal growth will allow it to select the most efficient technology, plan the new production and marketing arrangements so as to complement its existing range, and subject each stage of the expansion to repetitive reappraisal to ensure that modifications may be made when needed to meet changing requirements. By contrast, a merger may sometimes involve a discontinuous change in scale that is beyond the capacity of existing management and inevitably lacks the precise fit of a custom-built expansion. For example, if Beta needs additional marketing facilities to balance a current excess of production capacity, it may be able to obtain facilities by taking over Sigma. But in so doing, it may also have to take over unwanted production capacity, or it may find that Sigma's distribution channels are designed to handle a different product range and therefore require different systems of transport or warehousing, or offer a different set of incentives to salesmen.

A further reason for internal growth is that, in some cases, external growth may be virtually impossible. This is most obviously true if antitrust laws provide an effective veto against certain types of merger. But even if a merger would be permissible, suitable partners may simply not exist, because all existing firms operate with capacity that is out of date or otherwise irrelevant for the proposed expansion. This may happen, for example, in new industries, or in old industries after a revolutionary change in technology. However, even in these cases, the irrelevance of mergers is easily exaggerated.

In new industries, the rapid entry of new firms, many of which are long on technical expertise but short on managerial competence, may provide a number of early opportunities for fairly cheap entry by acquisition. This appears to have happened in the early days of the computer industry (Freeman 1965, Harman 1971). Alternatively, in an old industry confronted by a change in technology, acquisitions may prove to be a less painful way of eliminating old capacity than a protracted war of attrition. It was this desire to smooth the introduction of new technology that prompted Sir William Firth of Richard Thomas and Company to start on a series of amalgamations in the U.K. tinplate industry in the 1930s. The intention was to acquire and ultimately to eliminate enough of the older pack mills to make room for a new strip mill, which operated at very much higher capacity. However, in the event, the plan strained Richard Thomas's resources beyond their limit and the firm was only saved by a rescue operation financed by the Bank of England and other commercial banks (Minchington 1957, Chap. 7).

The role of mergers

So far, the discussion has suggested that internal growth may often be the only possible method of expansion, although external growth may sometimes offer a relevant but imperfect substitute. It therefore implies that Beta's strategy should normally give priority to internal growth. This is correct for a wide range of expansion plans, and especially for those which build on a new technology or involve a simple extension of existing activities to meet increased market demand, but it does not give a complete picture of the role of mergers in the growth of a firm.

This is reflected in Newbould's study. After investigating a small sample of mergers which occurred at the peak of the merger boom in the United Kingdom in 1967–8, he concluded that managers had rarely considered internal expansion as a serious alternative (Newbould 1970). In these cases, the usual objective was either to make a rapid response to competitive threats or to achieve an immediate change in scale (possibly to reduce the risk of takeover), which would not have been possible by internal growth. In general, it will often be true that mergers can offer real advantages of greater speed and (less certainly) lower risk than internal growth. Horizontal mergers may reduce competition between firms and therefore increase their security, whereas internal growth could only achieve the same result, if at all, if some rivals were eliminated after a costly period of cutthroat competition. Alternatively, if Beta is intent on diversification, acquisition of Sigma may enable it to acquire an experienced management team, technical know-how, product-differentiation advantages and distribution outlets more rapidly than through internal expansion. Even if the merger involves relatively high costs, it may accelerate entry to the new area and thus reduce the period during which the unestablished entrant is exposed to the risk of a preemptive strike by established firms. Further, Beta may be able to offset its own ignorance of the new area by acquiring firms which already have a proven track record.

These advantages of speed and risk may provide very good reasons why Beta may wish to acquire Sigma, but they do not explain why Sigma may be prepared to sell at a price which is favorable to Beta. If Beta is to gain from a merger, its demand price must be greater than Sigma's supply price. The latter will depend partly upon the benefit which Sigma expected to gain if it retained the assets for its own use, and partly upon the other buyers who may compete for the assets if Sigma chooses to sell. If the assets are of a type which is readily available, Sigma's assets will have no scarcity value and are unlikely to provide a strong motive for merger. On the other hand, if Sigma's assets are unique, Sigma's ability to exploit their value through merger will be greater if there are several buyers competing for the same assets and thus forcing up their price. Sigma is then more likely to obtain the full value of the assets, leaving the successful buyer with no more than a normal return on his investment after allowing for the transaction costs of the merger.

However, if Sigma is the only source of the assets concerned, and Beta is the only potential buyer, there may be a large margin between Sigma's supply price and Beta's demand price. The actual price may then lie anywhere within this range, depending upon the skill of the managers and their advisers and/or upon their sense of urgency.

This situation appears to be fairly common, and it is difficult or impossible to lay down precise rules to determine the acquisition price that will result from the bargaining process in such cases. The best that we can do is to identify possible reasons why Sigma may appear to have a higher value when combined with Beta than it would if it retained its independence. There are several reasons why this may be so, and we shall consider them at length in due course. First, however, we shall note that Beta will normally acquire control of Sigma by buying shares from shareholders, rather than by direct purchase of Sigma's assets, and if we are to consider the factors which may justify Beta's acquisition of Sigma, we must start with some understanding of the way in which the market may value Sigma's shares, in order to see how this may differ from Beta's valuation.

7.4 A simple model of share valuation

In this section we seek to identify the main factors that will affect the market price of a company's shares. We start with a formal model, and then turn to consider more general implications. The model is very simple (compare, for example, Solow 1971, or Steiner 1975) but it will serve to bring out the most significant features of the market. Throughout, we shall use the following

symbols. They are given here solely for convenience. Further definitions are given as they arise in the text.

P Recorded profits

K Capital employed

p Rate of profit on capital $= P/K$

g Growth rate of assets and profits (note that if p is
constant, K and P will grow at the same rate)

r Proportion of profits retained by the firm and not
distributed to shareholders

D Total dividends paid to shareholders

S Number of shares outstanding

d Dividends per share $= D/S$

m Price per share

M Total market value of shares $= m \cdot S$

The model

We may assume that although shareholders will buy shares for a
variety of reasons, including a romantic desire to be associated with
their favorite company or the desire to attend an occasional shareholders' meeting for the pleasure of arguing with the chairman, the
majority of them will be motivated primarily by the prospect of
financial gain. In the absence of a takeover bid, this gain depends
upon the firm's ability to earn profits; that is, it requires a surplus of
revenue over cost. The measurement of cost is never simple, but in
this context, we may concentrate on one particular complication. In
a growing firm, "costs" will include not only the operating costs
needed to produce current output, but also some of the expansion
costs which were incurred in order to change that output. The latter
include the cost of developing and appraising new opportunities, of
planning expansion, and of developing new markets. Strictly they
should be distinguished from the current operating costs but in
most cases this is not possible, so that the expansion costs are included in the firm's marketing or administrative overhead. It is
therefore convenient to assume that recorded profits (P) are measured net of all expansion costs other than direct expenditure on
capital investment.

These monetary profits may also be expressed as a rate of return
p, such that $p = P/K$ where K is the capital employed in producing
the current output. There is no empirical evidence to suggest that

the rate of profit is any greater or smaller in large firms than it is in small firms, and we may therefore assume that p is independent of K. On the other hand, it is clear that for a given size of firm, P (and hence p) will vary with the expansion costs incurred and will therefore vary with the growth rate. In principle, p might also vary with changes in the firm's operating efficiency or in the business environment, but for the formal model, we shall assume that the firm operates in an unchanging environment and always achieves the highest level of recorded profits consistent with its growth rate. With these assumptions, the profit rate for a particular firm will only change if the growth rate is varied, and we may write $p = f(g)$ where g is the growth rate.

What is the probable form of this relationship? How would we expect changes in the growth rate to affect profitability? In general, an increase in the growth rate will need higher expansion costs, which will tend to reduce profitability, but there are other effects to be considered, and these may well increase profitability so long as the change occurs at some fairly low initial growth rate. An organization may well be stimulated by growth. New managers may be attracted with new ideas, new market contacts may offer expanding opportunities, and existing managers may be catalyzed into rethinking established procedures. However, the growth rate cannot go on increasing indefinitely. The existing managerial resources are clearly limited, and the organizational structure cannot absorb an unlimited number of new tasks in a limited period of time without some loss of efficiency. Further, more rapid growth may eventually force the firm to look further afield for less-profitable opportunities and to appraise those opportunities less carefully. The net effect of these arguments is that maximum current profitability may well require a positive growth rate. A firm which grows very slowly may find that the stimulus of faster growth would raise its profitability, but ultimately profitability will decline as growth becomes too rapid. Technically we may say that given $p = f(g)$, we expect f' to be positive for small values of g and negative for higher values.

The profit function $p = f(g)$ for a given state of the environment is graphed in Figure 6. In principle, a firm may try to achieve a profit–growth combination lying on *or below* the curve, but we are assuming that it will always seek the highest profitability consistent with any chosen growth rate, and will therefore choose a combination which lies somewhere on the curve. However, its choice must also be constrained by the need to finance the chosen growth rate,

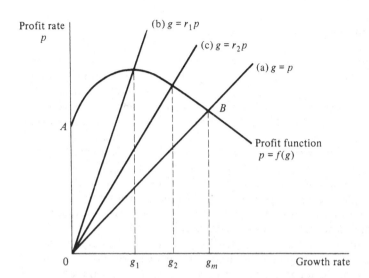

Figure 6. Profit rates and growth rates

and to see how this comes about we must ask what happens to the recorded profits.

The profits (P) may be distributed to shareholders as dividends (D), or a proportion (r) may be retained for internal use. In practice a firm may hold its retentions for future investment, and must ensure that it has adequate liquid reserves to support its current operations, but in the long term, it will not wish to hold idle resources unnecessarily. Further, it seems that a firm will normally seek to exploit its acquired advantages as an operating unit, and will avoid portfolio investment in other firms in which it has no controlling interest. We may therefore assume that the retained profits (rP) will be used to finance investment to increase the capital employed by the firm. If we also assume that all investment is financed out of retained profits (which is true for most firms for most of the time) then the increase in capital employed (ΔK) will be equal to retained profits. We have

$$\Delta K = rP$$

whence

$$g = \frac{\Delta K}{K} = \frac{rP}{K} = rp \tag{1}$$

That is, the maximum growth rate which the firm can achieve will be determined as the product of the retention ratio (r) and the profit rate (p).

This must constrain the firm's choice of profit–growth combination from the alternatives given by the profit function in Figure 6. Three of many possible feasible choices are illustrated in the diagram: (a) Clearly a firm cannot retain more than one hundred percent of its profits, and so the maximum growth rate must occur when $r = 1$ and $g = p$. In the diagram, this occurs at a growth rate of g_m, and implies that the firm must choose a profit–growth combination along the segment AB of the profit function. (We assume that the firm will not deliberately choose a negative growth rate. In principle, it could still choose any combination within the area OAB, but any point below the frontier AB is ruled out by assumption, because it would involve some slack resources.) g_m is clearly a feasible growth rate, but as we shall see, a firm could never sustain a policy of retaining one hundred percent of its profits indefinitely, and so in the long run it must select a growth rate less than g_m. (b) One possibility would be for the firm to seek the highest attainable profitability. In the diagram, this occurs at a growth rate of g_1 which requires a retention ratio of r_1. (c) Alternatively, the firm may choose an intermediate growth rate such as g_2, lying between g_1 and g_m and requiring a retention ratio of r_2, where $r_1 < r_2 < 1.0$. Growth rates less than g_1 are less plausible, because then it would always be possible for the firm to change to a higher growth rate without any loss of profitability.

We may therefore think of the firm as if it selected a profit target from a range of feasible values and then adopted the appropriate retention ratio to give the growth rate required to achieve the target. Alternatively, we may imagine that the firm chooses its growth rate, which then dictates the profits which can be achieved and, hence, the retention ratio needed to finance the growth. Either of these behavioral assumptions is feasible, or it may be more plausible to assume that the firm has preferences for both profits and growth, but in any event we must recognize that the firm in our model cannot set growth and profit targets independently of each other.

The choice of retention ratio implied by a particular profit or growth target will also determine the dividends which can be distributed to shareholders, because profits which are not retained for investment will be distributed. We can see that total dividend payments (D) will be given by

$$D = P(1 - r) = pK(1 - r) \tag{2}$$

If there are S shares outstanding the dividend per share is

$$d = \frac{D}{S} \doteq \frac{P(1 - r)}{S} = \frac{pK(1 - r)}{S} \tag{3}$$

Our objective is to see how the shareholders will value their shares, given the dividend function in (3) and the firm's choice of growth rate. We shall assume that the firm operates in an unchanging environment, and that it has chosen a growth rate which will be kept unchanged in the future, so that the corresponding profit rate and retention ratio will also remain unchanged. We also assume that shareholders know that the chosen values of p, g, and r will not be changed, and that they are interested in the present value of future dividends discounted at a rate (i) which is the same for all shareholders and for all time periods. These are restrictive assumptions, but they are necessary to produce a tractable model. Later we shall look at the effects of relaxing some of them.

Suppose that shareholders expect to receive dividends per share of d_1 at the end of the current time period. The present value of d_1 is $d_1/(1 + i)$. The dividend (d_2) to be received at the end of the next time period will be higher than d_1 because the firm's profits and dividends will have grown at a rate g during the intervening period, so that $d_2 = d_1(1 + g)$. The present value of d_2 discounted for two time periods is therefore $d_2/(1 + i)^2$ or $d_1(1 + g)/(1 + i)^2$. Given our assumptions, in equilibrium the shareholders must be indifferent between the price paid for a share and the present value of the future dividends anticipated for each share. If we assume that shareholders are interested in the dividends to be received over the next N time periods, then the equilibrium price per share, m, will be given by

$$m = \frac{d_1}{(1 + i)} + \frac{d_1(1 + g)}{(1 + i)^2} + \frac{d_1(1 + g)^2}{(1 + i)^3}$$
$$+ \cdots + \frac{d_1(1 + g)^{N-1}}{(1 + i)^N} \tag{4}$$

or

$$m = d_1 \left[\frac{1}{(1 + i)} + \frac{(1 + g)}{(1 + i)^2} + \frac{(1 + g)^2}{(1 + i)^3} \right.$$
$$\left. + \cdots + \frac{(1 + g)^{N-1}}{(1 + i)^N} \right] \tag{5}$$

If we then multiply both sides of (5) by $(1 + i)/(1 + g)$ we obtain

$$m \left[\frac{(1 + i)}{(1 + g)} \right] = d_1 \left[\frac{1}{(1 + g)} + \frac{1}{(1 + i)} + \frac{(1 + g)}{(1 + i)^2} \right.$$
$$\left. + \cdots + \frac{(1 + g)^{N-2}}{(1 + i)^{N-1}} \right] \quad (6)$$

Subtracting (5) from (6) gives

$$m \left[\frac{(1 + i)}{(1 + g)} - 1 \right] = d_1 \left[\frac{1}{(1 + g)} - \frac{(1 + g)^{N-1}}{(1 + i)^N} \right] \quad (7)$$

For the moment, we shall assume that shareholders have an infinite time horizon. It is then immediately obvious from (4) that if g were greater than i, shares would have an infinite value. This is clearly impossible, and so, although a firm may grow very rapidly for a limited period, it cannot be expected to grow indefinitely at a rate greater than the shareholders discount rate. Given then that i is greater than g, it is also clear that as N becomes very large the value of the fraction $(1 + g)^{N-1}/(1 + i)^N$ will become smaller and smaller and will eventually approach zero. Hence in the limit as N approaches infinity, (7) approaches

$$m \left[\frac{(1 + i)}{(1 + g)} - 1 \right] = d_1 \left[\frac{1}{(1 + g)} \right] \quad (8)$$

The price per share, m, can be derived from (8) as

$$m = \frac{d_1}{(i - g)} \quad (9)$$

The total market value, M, may then be expressed in several alternative ways. First it is clear that

$$M = mS = \frac{d_1 S}{(i - g)} \quad (10)$$

Alternatively by substituting (3) for d_1 in (10) we obtain

$$M = \frac{K(p - rp)}{(i - g)} \quad (11)$$

Finally given that $p = f(g)$ and $g = rp$ we may also express the market value as

$$M = \frac{K(f(g) - g)}{(i - g)} \quad (12)$$

Implications of the model

The alternative formulas given in equations (10), (11), and (12) may be used to see how a firm's market value may be affected by changes in, say, its dividend policy or its growth rate, but in order to do so we shall have to relax some of the assumptions which we introduced to keep the formulas simple, and we shall therefore discuss some of the changes in less formal terms at this stage.

Dividend policy. An immediate increase in dividends is often used by Sigma's directors in an attempt to raise the market valuation of its shares so as to combat a takeover bid. However, the desired result is not inevitable.

A superficial glance at equation (10) may suggest that M necessarily increases as d_1 increases. This is valid so long as there is no offsetting change in i or g, which would be possible if the increased dividends resulted from increased profits following an improvement in efficiency or a favorable change in the competitive environment. This was ruled out in our formal model, but would clearly be possible in practice. However, in many cases an increase in d_1 will imply a lower retention ratio, and unless the retentions were previously used to build excessive reserves, this must result in a lower growth rate. It is clear from (10) that a reduction in g may offset the effect of an increase in d_1, so that the market valuation may or may not increase. We must therefore consider the effect of changes in g more carefully, which we shall do in the paragraphs on profit and growth rates.

Discount rates. It is clear that the market valuation will vary inversely with i, and will be lower if shareholders have a higher discount rate. In building the model we assumed that all potential shareholders used the same discount rate to determine the current value of anticipated dividends, but in practice there may be substantial differences between shareholders. These could reflect differences in shareholders' time preferences. For example, shareholders with a stronger preference for immediate consumption would be inclined to discount the future more heavily. Alternatively, the higher discount rate may include a risk premium, reflecting the shareholders' aversion to the risks faced by the firm. Strictly, the use of a single risk-inflated discount rate is suspect, because it assumes that the risk premium is the same in all time periods, regardless of year-to-year variations in the risk or in the expected payoff. This is hardly plausible, but the argument may also be unnecessarily pedantic. Given the high cost of using more refined techniques to value risky outcomes, the simple risk premium may be justified as a rough-and-ready rule of thumb in many cases.

However, we should note immediately that if we wish to use the resulting differences in share valuations to explain takeover bids, we must be very careful to specify whose discount rates we are interested in. We would not expect to find that Beta's shareholders persistently valued Sigma's shares more highly than their present holders if any differences that did arise could be eliminated fairly rapidly by the purchase and sale of small blocks of shares on the open market. The trauma of a takeover bid would then be unnecessary. On the other hand, differences in time or risk preferences may lead to takeovers if the market for Sigma's shares is imperfect, or if the decisions are influenced by managers who are less able to profit from marginal share transactions.

Time horizons. Instead of raising discount rates, shareholders may react to uncertainty by using a shorter time horizon to value their shares. That is, they may simply assess the value of dividends anticipated for a fairly short period in the future during which they have reasonable confidence in their forecasts, and ignore the less certain "guesstimates" for future periods. The effects are qualitatively the same as those of an increase in discount rates, as is readily apparent from our simple model.

Recall that in deriving our market valuation formulas, we were able to proceed from equation (7) to equation (8) only because the value of $(1 + g)^{N-1}/(1 + i)^N$ approached zero as N became very large. If we use a shorter time horizon, then we must put a relatively small value for N, and the fraction will then have a positive value which increases as N becomes smaller. It then follows from equation (7) that the share price, m, will be greater the longer is the time horizon over which dividends are valued.

Profit and growth rates. The market value of shares will be improved by any policy which allows simultaneous increases in profitability and growth, or allows one to be increased without changing the other. This is clearly possible if the environment improves or if the firm is able to raise its operating efficiency. The market value would also increase if these improvements were anticipated at some future date, provided that this came within the shareholders' time horizons.

On the other hand, if improvements in profitability can be achieved only by cutting expansion costs, growth will be reduced and the apparent gain will involve an opportunity loss of profits in future time periods. To complete our discussion, we must therefore pursue the relationship between growth and profitability in more detail, and we shall do so by asking whether the growth rate that maximizes the market value of shares will also imply the maximum possible profitability. It is convenient to focus our analysis in this way on the effect of changing the growth rate, but as we have seen already, if the firm is operating as efficiently as possible, the choice of growth rate simultaneously determines the profit rate and the retention ratio. Unfortunately we cannot get very far in our analysis without the aid of a little calculus, but hopefully for the non-mathematician the results should be intuitively acceptable if not intuitively obvious. We have already argued that the profit rate will normally achieve its maximum value at some positive growth rate. That is, given $p = f(g)$ we may identify $g^* > 0$ such that $f'(g^*) = 0$. However we may also show that g^* will not yield the maximum market value, M^*, which occurs at a growth rate g^{**} such that $g^{**} > g^*$.

Equation (12) above may be rewritten as

$$M = M(g) = K(f(g) - g)(i - g)^{-1} \qquad (13)$$

whence

$$M'(g) = K\{[f'(g) - 1](i - g)^{-1} - [f(g) - g](i - g)^{-2}\} \qquad (14)$$

The first-order condition for a maximum at g^{**} is that $M'(g^{**}) = 0$. Given $K \neq 0$, this implies

$$[f'(g^{**}) - 1](i - g^{**})^{-1} = [f(g^{**}) - g^{**}](i - g^{**})^{-2} \qquad (15)$$

which may be rearranged to yield

$$f'(g^{**}) = \frac{i - f(g^{**})}{i - g^{**}} \qquad (16)$$

or, given that $p = f(g)$

$$f'(g^{**}) = \frac{i - p^{**}}{i - g^{**}} \qquad (17)$$

where p^{**} is the profit rate which results when the growth rate is selected to maximize the market value of the shares.

How can we interpret equation (17)? We know that $i > g$, and so the denominator of the fraction must be positive. Further it is clear that if the firm is to remain in business in the long run it must achieve a profit rate which is equal to or greater than the shareholders' discount rate. This requires $p \geq i$. If $p^{**} = i$ then $f'(g^{**}) = 0$ which means that the growth rate (g^{**}) which maximizes the market value of shares also satisfies the condition $f'(g) = 0$ which is required for maximum profitability. However if $p^{**} > i$ then $f'(g^{**}) < 0$, and given that $f'(g)$ is assumed to be less than zero only if $g > g^*$ it follows that $g^{**} > g^*$. That is, the maximum market value, M^*, requires a growth rate which is greater than that needed to maximize profitability.

This result simply reflects the fact that current profits may be sacrificed to obtain future profits. If a firm diverts additional resources to expansion, its current profits will fall, but the immediate loss to shareholders may be more than offset by the higher profits and dividends which result in the future. Even if the profit rate (P/K) does not increase in the future, a higher absolute level of profits (P) will eventually follow from the increase in capital employed. It follows that a very conservative management may offend shareholders either by paying inadequate attention to opportunities to increase current profits or by overemphasizing current profits at the expense of long-run growth.

The firm may therefore grow too slowly for its shareholders. But it may also grow too quickly, especially if managers are more strongly motivated by growth or size than by profits. Shareholders may then lack the direct control needed to prevent an increase in the growth rate above g^{**}, but they have an indirect control through their ability to "vote with their feet." As the growth rate increases, shareholders become increasingly reluctant to retain their shares. The share price falls and the market valuation increasingly understates the potential earning power of the assets. The firm therefore becomes more attractive as a potential takeover victim.

Market values and share premiums

Before leaving the discussion of our simple model, we must note one further point. The model gives a reasonable picture of some of the factors which influence share prices, but the total valuation obtained by multiplying the share price by the number of shares as in equation (10) will normally understate the price that would have to be paid to acquire all the shares in a takeover bid. The structure of the model makes it fairly easy to see why this may be so.

We have seen that the valuation of a share will vary with changes in interest rates or in future profitability, but in drawing up the model we assumed explicitly that all shareholders used the same discount rate, and that they all had the same expectations of future profits and dividends. In practice, these assumptions may be misleading except as a first approximation. Different shareholders will have different wealth holdings, different attitudes to risk, and different expectations, and will therefore value their shares by applying different discount rates to different estimates of future dividends. In equilibrium, the market price would be such that the *marginal* shareholder would be indifferent between retaining and selling his shares, but other shareholders with (say) longer time horizons or greater faith in the firms future prospects would put a value on their shares which was greater than the current market price.[1]

To persuade these intramarginal shareholders to part with their holdings, a takeover bid must offer a premium over the market price, and because the bidder cannot discriminate between different sellers, the same share premium must be offered to all shareholders. This premium will normally be greater in a cash purchase than in a share-exchange deal, given that the share-exchange premium is measured as the difference between the market price of Sigma's shares and the market price of the package of Beta's shares offered in exchange. The lower premium in a share-exchange deal occurs because Sigma's intramarginal shareholders may also value Beta's shares above the ruling market price, and may therefore accept a lower apparent premium than they would in a cash deal.

In general, the need for share premiums inevitably increases the uncertainty surrounding the outcome of any takeover bid. The market price is generally known by the bidder, but it is more difficult to predict the minimum share premium which must be offered to shareholders to secure a controlling interest.

Further, it is not true that the share premium is always positive. In exceptional cases, the bidder may acquire control at a price which is less than the previous market price of the shares. This could happen, for example, if a single individual or organization held a very large block of shares which could not be sold quickly without a very marked reduction in the market price. This large shareholder might well have a valuation below the market price and yet be

---

[1] The extra value attached to their holdings by these intramarginal shareholders is clearly akin but not identical to the Marshallian concept of consumers' surplus.

unable to sell significant numbers of shares on the market at a price above that valuation. An offer to buy all the shares for something less than the market price could therefore be very attractive to such a shareholder. Alternatively, shareholders may be willing to sell at prices below the original market price if they are persuaded that the price was based upon naively optimistic expectations. This is certainly possible if shareholders initially rely upon information which is inferior to that available to potential bidders, and which only becomes available to them after the bid has been made. It happened from time to time in the United Kingdom during the 1930s, but has become less plausible as shareholders have become increasingly well informed as a result of the firms' legal obligations to provide more information and the more sophisticated advice offered by independent analysts.

7.5 Merger motivation

The major implications of the previous section, shorn of the rigid assumptions needed for the formal model, may be summarized as follows.

Except for short-term speculation over, say, the prospects of a takeover bid, share prices will be strongly influenced, if not determined, by the present value of anticipated future dividends. The present value will be lower if shareholders use a higher discount rate or a shorter time horizon in valuing dividends. It will also vary directly with the value of anticipated profits. These may reflect expectations about the opportunities facing the firm or the efficiency with which opportunities are exploited, and the latter may include changes in the growth rate as well as changes in technical efficiency.

From this simple structure, it is quite clear that there are two main reasons why Beta may value Sigma's assets more highly than Sigma's current owners. Either Beta may anticipate increases in profitability or it may value the same profits differently from Sigma's shareholders. These alternatives must now be considered in detail. We shall start by discussing a range of factors which may influence anticipated profitability, including monopoly, economies of scale, synergy, and management efficiency. We shall then consider differences in discount rates, and finally, some aspects of uncertainty, which were not formally included in our simple model but which are fully consistent with its spirit.

Monopoly

Mergers and concentration. The combined profits of Beta and Sigma after a merger may be greater than their aggregate profits before the merger, because their combination reduces competition and enhances Beta's monopoly power. The drop in competition may reduce the elasticity of demand for Beta's products and enable it to raise prices relative to costs. Alternatively, it may allow Beta to avoid some of the costs of rivalry by cutting expenditure on sales promotion, reducing the number of product lines, or otherwise saving expenditure that was previously needed to counter competitive moves by Sigma. Any of these alternatives might encourage Beta to expect that it could get increased profits to cover the cost of acquiring Sigma.

Monopolies are rarely popular among nonmonopolists, and therefore it is unlikely that managers would readily admit to potential monopoly profits in trying to justify mergers. As Scherer (1970) argues, however, monopoly power has resulted from mergers so often that it would be ludicrous to claim that it was always an unintended result. The effect on monopoly was seen clearly in the early horizontal merger movement in the United States. Similarly, in the United Kingdom, the merger waves of the 1920s and 1960s caused significant increases in national concentration, although the effect on monopoly is less certain because of the simultaneous changes which occurred in international competition. Utton (1971) estimated that mergers were responsible for at least half of the increased concentration in manufacturing industry which occurred between 1954 and 1965, while Hannah and Kay (1977) suggested an even higher estimate for 1957–69. The mergers seem to have affected concentration in most industries but Hart, Utton, and Walshe (1973) suggested that the desire to eliminate competition provided a particularly clear motive for mergers between manufacturers of electric cables, caravans, or wallpaper.

Mergers and restrictive practices. Some of this increase in concentration appears to have been a perverse reaction to Government antitrust policies, especially when these policies have been more successful against collusive agreements and restrictive practices than they have been against single-firm monopolies. In the United Kingdom, there was no policy against either monopolies or restrictive practices before the Monopolies and Restrictive Practices (Inquiry and Control) Act of 1948, whose primary effect was to establish a commission to investigate selected cases. Following these investigations, the Restrictive Practices Act (1956) retained the pragmatic approach of separate investigation for single-firm monopolies but established the principle that collusive agreements were generally undesirable and unlawful unless proven innocent before the Restrictive Practices Court. The court took a fairly jaundiced view of most of the agreements, and many were abandoned voluntarily once the full implications of the act became clear. In some cases, and especially in the electric-cables industry, firms then turned to merger as an alternative route to the security offered by a quasimonopoly.

A similar impact had been observed much earlier in the United States, where the Sherman Act of 1890 also tended to discriminate against restrictive practices rather than monopolies. The more aggressive attitude to restrictive practices in the United States compared with the United Kingdom partly explains why large firms came to predominate much earlier in the United States. In the United Kingdom at the turn of the century, the problems of managing large organizations were a stronger deterrent to mergers because collusive agreements were more often available as a partially effective alternative.

It would clearly be wrong to suppose that monopolies and restrictive practices are perfect substitutes from the point of view of the firms concerned. If several firms have different objectives and different expectations for the future development of their industry, restrictive agreements will be difficult to establish and are unlikely to be stable. Mergers to eliminate dissent may then be a necessary prerequisite for effective agreement. On the other hand, if firms can readily identify common interests, the formality of a restrictive agreement may be unnecessary, especially if the exchange of information ensures that each knows what the other is doing and that all operate with similar knowledge of market and technical conditions.

This appears to have been true of many of the information agreements or open price agreements which replaced restrictive agreements in the 1960s and were ultimately made registrable under the Restrictive Trade Practices Act of 1968. Nevertheless, it is clear that even if a restrictive agreement is less effective than a monopoly, it will reduce the gains to be made from a merger if it gives its members any quasimonopoly profits which would not otherwise be available to them as independent firms. In turn the prohibition of such an agreement would increase the incentive for firms to merge because it would increase the margin between pre- and postmerger profits.

Even if Sigma would be unable to survive without the protection offered by the restrictive agreement, acquisition may still be more profitable to Beta. The alternative is to rely upon competition to eliminate the smaller rivals, but these may retain their nuisance value for some considerable time, especially if their assets are durable and cannot be transferred to other uses. The longer this competition is expected to survive, the greater is the incentive to eliminate it by acquisition. As many writers of detective fiction have observed, murder is more plausible if the suspect would otherwise have had to wait a long time for his inheritance.

Other competitive effects. Since 1965, horizontal mergers in the United Kingdom have had to face the possibility of Government intervention. This has probably discouraged some horizontal mergers and encouraged mergers aimed at diversification, thus following the historical pattern which was set earlier in the United States. However, the threat of intervention has not killed the monopoly motive, even though it may have blunted it. In the United Kingdom, in contrast to the United States, the antitrust authorities must balance the anticompetitive effects of a merger against possible benefits to the public, and may accept assurances or undertakings from the firms concerned as effective offsets for potential detriments. For example, in 1965 when the British Motor Corporation (subsequently part of British Leyland) sought to acquire Pressed Steel, which was the largest independent manufacturer of stampings for car bodies, the authorities accepted assurances from B.M.C. that outside customers, who then accounted for forty percent of Pressed Steel's business, would continue to be supplied on a nondiscriminatory basis. Further, our reference to a "monopoly" motive need not imply that the firm seeks increased control of the market for a single product in order to restrict output in the classic textbook manner. General considerations of monopoly and of the suppression of competition may enter into decision-taking processes in more subtle ways, which are probably of greater strategic importance.

First, the increase in market power may be sought to offset the domination of established monopolists or the increased threat of attack from new sources of competition. Such mergers may have the statistical effect of raising concentration in that they involve an increase in the market share of any given number of firms, but they will not necessarily give rise to an increase in exploitable market power and hence (at least in the United Kingdom) are less likely to be condemned by the antitrust authorities. Mergers of this type were fairly common during the 1920s merger wave in the United States, which has been characterized as creating oligopolies in place of earlier dominant firm quasimonopolies (Stigler 1950). More recently, in the United Kingdom, mergers in the food and electrical engineering industries may have been undertaken in part as a response to the growth of United States direct investment in these sectors, which often involved substantial new entry by potentially more powerful competitors. Similarly, merger activity in France in the 1960s, which was generally fairly sluggish, was intensified in those industries such as primary metals, chemicals, and electrical machinery in which the established French suppliers lost a significant share of their domestic market through competition with other members of the European Economic Community (McGowan 1971).

Anticompetitive motives may also lead to vertical or diversification mergers (see also Chapter 3). Mergers between large firms may still be investigated by the antitrust authorities, as in the case of the B.M.C./Pressed Steel merger already considered, but in general the effects on market power will be less obvious and less direct than in the case of horizontal mergers. The search for market power may influence diversification mergers if Beta believes that its greater absolute size would enable it to organize a more disciplined oligopoly in Sigma's industry, or if it believes that Sigma already possesses latent market power that it has failed to exploit (Steiner 1975). Alternatively, market power may be affected by vertical integration if this raises entry barriers against potential entrants or discourages aggressive moves by existing rivals. The potential gains may often be overrated, but anticipated gains may still strengthen the incentive for vertical mergers. For example in the United Kingdom, the acquisition of independent bakeries by flour millers appears to have been strongly influenced by the millers' attempts to secure outlets so as to safeguard the relatively high returns realized in flour milling (Hart, Utton, and Walshe 1973).

Economies of scale

Even if there are no monopoly profits, Beta and Sigma may both gain from a merger if it enables them to realize economies of scale. The economies may be denied to them as independent firms because of market imperfections: because internal growth is inhibited by a limited market, because oligopolistic competition deters specialization by encouraging product heterogeneity, or because it involves increased marketing overheads which can be covered more easily by a large firm. This dependence on market imperfections may have implications for economic welfare (see especially Scherer 1970) but need not affect the private motivation of the firms concerned.

The potential economies are sometimes subdivided into real and pecuniary economies. Real economies arise as a result of improved operations within the firm, whereas pecuniary economies depend upon lower input costs resulting from the advantages of bulk buying, including a lower cost of capital. In turn, the pecuniary advantages may reflect real economies achieved by suppliers when dealing with larger customers, or they may reflect market imperfections by which larger firms are able to exploit some monopsonistic power.

Scale economies are most likely to arise in horizontal mergers that bring together a number of similar activities. The combination of separate outputs for a single product, or range of related products, may permit technical economies at the plant level if work can be reallocated to give higher output rates for specific plants, or longer production runs for specific products, possibly coupled with the adoption of more specialized equipment. Further benefits may be realized at the firm level if some administrative or marketing activities are more or less indivisible, and the merger allows firms to avoid duplication, or to introduce activities which could not be justified by smaller firms. These activities might include, say, distribution, research and development, data processing, or fund raising, and the benefits in this case need not be restricted to horizontal mergers: diversification mergers may also benefit from the spread of overheads if the activities are not specific to one industry.

We may therefore identify a number of ways in which economies of scale may result from a merger. But it seems wise to be sceptical about the extent to which they can be realized in practice. This is especially true of real economies at the plant level. There is no doubt that economies can be significant for many products, especially in the oil and chemical industries (Pratten 1971), and that several firms have successfully rationalized their production after a merger. An example is given by the case of television-set production in the United Kingdom in the mid-1960s. After a series of deals to acquire the television interests of other firms, Thorn Electrical Industries concentrated the manufacture of specific products at specific locations (including those acquired from Philco and Ultra, among others) and concentrated designs on a narrower range so as to assist the exploitation of advanced manufacturing techniques (Hart, Utton, and Walshe, 1973). However, the scope for such rationalization may be limited. In most United Kingdom industries the leading firms already operate several plants, and the extent of multiplant operation is typically greater than it is in comparable industries in Germany or France (George and Ward 1975). This suggests that mergers between such firms would rarely be justified by the need to combine the output of two firms in order to load the capacity of a single plant of efficient size. Indeed, after a series of interviews with managers who had been involved in mergers, Newbould (1970) concluded that firms rarely pursued the reorganization which would have been necessary to achieve such economies of scale.

Some studies have suggested that postmerger improvements are more commonly achieved in the nonmanufacturing activities, such as finance, marketing, or research, than they are in production (see, for example, Kitching 1967), and this may indicate that mergers are more concerned with scale economies at the firm rather than the plant level. It may be that such economies are inevitably more significant. Alternatively, it is possible that the costs of rationalizing nonmanufacturing activities are lower than those for manufacturing because the nonmanufacturing activities involve less specific assets, concern fewer people, and can be changed with less union negotiation and with less risk of disruption of supplies to customers. Nonmanufacturing scale economies have been important for the relative success of the United Kingdom's major computer manufacturer, International Computers Ltd. (I.C.L.). I.C.L. was formed in 1968 by a merger between International Computers and Tabulators (I.C.T.) and English Electric Computers, after a series of mergers in which I.C.T. acquired the data processing computer activities of G.E.C., E.M.I., and Ferranti, while English Electric absorbed the computer interests of Leo Computers, Marconi, and Elliott Automation. Before this series of mergers, the separate suppliers were undoubtedly too small to continue with major research programs, to finance the leasing of computers to customers, or to give customers the service and software support which they needed. These activities are essential in the computer industry, and especially in the section of the market dealing with commercial data processing, which is dominated by the IBM Corporation of America (see Shaw and Sutton 1976, Chap. 4.3).

On the other hand, the attempt to use nonmanufacturing economies in the pharmaceutical industry to justify a proposed merger between Beecham and Glaxo was rejected by the Monopolies Commission (1972). The pharmaceutical market is characterized by strong international competition and offers significant advantages to large firms in the development and marketing of new drugs (Shaw and Sutton 1976, Chap. 4.2), but Beecham and Glaxo are two of the largest British-owned suppliers of ethical drugs and may well be large enough to realize any scale economies without losing their independence.

More generally, Steiner has observed that in the United States, many of the firms involved in mergers are already large enough to realize most or all of the observable pecuniary advantages of size (Steiner 1975, p. 65). It seems that economies of scale may provide a relevant motive for medium-sized firms, who hope to grow by merger to challenge the market leaders. Such medium-sized firms need an increase in size to cover the cost of the range of services or products needed for an effective challenge, but economies of scale will rarely justify mergers by firms that are established already among the market leaders.

Synergy

Synergy may provide a profitable basis for merger if Beta and Sigma possess complementary assets that they cannot develop fully as separate units. The cost of the merger may be justified if Beta cannot obtain the use of the assets more cheaply by any other means, and this is quite likely to be true if the assets are nonreproducible, if they cannot be separated from the parent organization, and/or if their sale or rental would involve very high transaction costs.

The nature of these underexploited assets and the barriers to their transfer by normal market transactions were discussed in

Chapter 4 in the context of diversification. But their significance is not confined to the case of diversification. Underexploited assets may also influence horizontal mergers, in which case the search for synergy may be indistinguishable from the exploitation of quasimonopoly power. The most common alternative probably arises when Sigma is well established in a segment of the total market, is possibly protected by long-standing consumer loyalty, but lacks the financial or managerial resources to exploit its full potential. If Beta can provide these resources, it may exploit the potential synergy by acquiring Sigma, but at the same time the acquisition clearly removes a competitive barrier to Beta's growth. Similar results could follow if Sigma possessed unexploited patent rights or had access to restricted sources of supply.

In principle, financial synergy may also occur if Sigma has substantial accumulated losses which can be carried forward to set against taxes on future profits. Such provisions are of no value to Sigma's shareholders unless Sigma starts to make a profit, whereas they *may* be available to Beta if Sigma's profitability can be restored after a takeover. However in the United Kingdom, especially after the 1969 Fnance Act, Beta's ability to realize the gain is closely circumscribed. The tax losses cannot be carried forward if it appears that Sigma's loss of independence was followed by a change in the type of business undertaken (see for example, Weinberg 1971, paragraphs 1727-9). This seems to restrict the gains to cases where Sigma's existing business can be made profitable by the injection of financial or managerial resources from Beta. However, if Sigma can restore its profitability without Beta's help, the gains are available equally to Sigma's present and future owners and cannot by themselves justify a change of ownership. Similar tax incentives exist in the United States, where a tax loss carry-over may create "a net incentive to a merger that might not have any other justification" (Steiner 1975, p. 80). However, the U.S. statistics suggest that this is not a significant incentive: Acquired firms are typically no less profitable than their acquirers (see for example, Conn 1976, Melicher and Rush 1974).

The incentive to exploit complementary assets was exemplified in 1976 by the offer for the Swiss-based Juvena Cosmetics by British American Cosmetics, a subsidiary of BAT Industries (formerly British American Tobacco). British American Cosmetics wished to increase its penetration in European markets but was forced to consider entry by merger with an established firm because of the strong brand loyalty which exists for cosmetics. At the same time, Juvena's parent appeared to be short of cash after a number of expensive new ventures and suffered from the extended recession in this market (*The Times,* Oct. 13, 1976).

The same type of motivation influenced some of the mergers between insurance brokers in the United Kingdom during 1976. The brokers must find underwriters to carry the insurance risks of their clients if they are to provide a continuing service. But the underwriters' capacity to accept risks is limited by their financial reserves, and in 1976 a rapid expansion of insurance business, especially from the United States, meant that the demand for underwriting capacity outstripped the supply. One way by which some large brokers sought to avoid this restriction was by the acquisition of smaller brokers who had long-established links with particular underwriters and could thus offer "captive" sources of supply. These smaller brokers were often willing to sell because they believed that the wide range of management services available to the larger groups would be essential for longer-term competition (Rowley 1976).

However, although mergers are often justified in this way, it will sometimes make better commerical sense to develop the complementary assets by cooperation between independent firms rather than by merger. There are several reasons for preferring cooperation in specific cases. First, it may be that the venture is expected to be temporary as, for example, to meet a single civil-engineering contract. Secondly, it may be that mergers are ruled out for political reasons: Many international cooperative ventures have been prompted because takeover was discouraged by one country's desire to avoid foreign control of its domestic assets. For example, in the computer industry, the Japanese government has allowed relatively little direct foreign investment, and has encouraged licensing agreements or other joint ventures to provide access to technical know-how (see for example, Harman 1971). Such agreements may be the only way by which the licensor can obtain access to the overseas market, although in the long run they may encourage competition from a successful licensee. Thirdly, as in the case of the early cooperation between I.C.I. and Courtaulds to exploit nylon patents (see Chapter 4 above), a joint venture may prove more attractive if it affects only a small part of the total activities of two firms that are not otherwise complementary. However, as with vertical integration (Chapter 3 above) it may often prove to be difficult to maintain a cooperative agreement. As conditions change, the agreement may prove to be unworkable. Alternatively, it may prove to be an intermediate step toward a merger, especially if the firms become increasingly dependent upon their cooperation and are no longer able to pursue independent strategies. In the case of nylon, the growing significance of man-made fibers encouraged I.C.I. to seek complete control of Courtaulds in 1961. But its approaches were rejected. Subsequent disagreements over strategy led the two firms to separate, and in 1964 Courtaulds opted to manufacture its own nylon and sold its share in British Nylon Spinners to I.C.I.

Managerial efficiency

General management. It is clear that if Sigma is managed inefficiently, Beta may be able to effect a significant improvement in its long-run performance by injecting new management. The increased profits would enable Beta to recover the transaction costs of the merger, including any share premium paid to Sigma's shareholders, but the gains are by no means automatic. In practice, the potential benefits must be set against the costs of changing the performance, and these costs may be very high if past inefficiency has become embodied in the structure of the firm as a result of misguided investment decisions or faulty management structure. Further, the merger may often produce intractable new problems for Beta's management. This is especially likely if Beta's management are not familiar with Sigma's operating problems, or if the management structure has to change so that Beta and Sigma can be rationalized to take advantage of potential synergy or economies of scale. For example, the merger between Plessey, Ericsson Telephones, and Automatic Telephone and Electric in 1961 appears to have allowed improved efficiency in the production and installation of telephone apparatus, but was followed by frequent changes in management structure as the company sought to devise an effective control system for the enlarged operations. It seems that the management problems had still not been resolved satisfactorily by the end of the decade (Hart, Utton, and Walshe 1973, pp. 109–13).

In spite of these difficulties, however, there are many cases in which the cost of effecting a turnaround in efficiency is relatively low, and significant gains can be made from relatively small changes in, say, the planning and control procedures already used by Sigma.

Indeed Lynch (1971) appears to suggest that this may be one of the most significant consequences of many conglomerate acquisitions in the United States.

An example for the United Kingdom is given by Pratten's detailed study of the acquisition of Greengate and Irwell (G. & I.) by Slater Walker Securities (S.W.S.) in 1969 (Pratten 1970). The acquisition was followed by an increase in G. & I.'s profits. This included a notional improvement reflecting a change in the method used to account for depreciation: G. & I. had used a reducing balance method, whereas S.W.S. adopted the straight-line method, which spreads depreciation more evenly over the life of an asset with less concentration on the early years. But the increased profitability also reflected some real gains, and Pratten considered that

neither SWS's conglomerate holdings, nor its size, appear to have been important factors enabling it to improve the performance of B. & I. The ability of SWS to increase profits was attributable to its financial and management expertise. The management of independent firms could perhaps achieve similar increases in profitability in similar circumstances if they took a *fresh and realistic* look at the assumptions and the methods they use, if they obtained advice from consultants and/or if they recruited and gave responsibility to outside managers. (Pratten 1970, p. 52)

The improvement seems to have required a very small input of managerial time from S.W.S., although it did involve the recruitment of new staff and the use of consultants.

The valuation of assets. In other cases, the acquiring firm, Beta, may be able to make a fairly ready profit by selling real assets that were underexploited or undervalued by Sigma. For example, in 1971, Sterling Guarantee Trust acquired Wharf Holdings for a price of £6.3 million, which was almost double the value of the equity assets recorded in the firm's books

but with property potential for redevelopment at Beagle House (in Leman Street, London E1), which received planning permission for office development shortly before the bid (and was subsequently sold for £4.5 million) plus 10 acres on London's South Bank, 2 acres at Wapping and 19 acres at Avonmouth, to say nothing of a tea warehousing and shipping business, the price paid was substantially below real asset value." (Buckley 1972, p. 252)

The exploitation of such asset situations is sometimes criticized, implying that it is wrong for some managers to exploit the inefficiency of others. But in most cases, it is the earlier inefficiency rather than the subsequent exploitation which is to be condemned, and although Sigma's shareholders may not get the full benefit of the improvement they are usually left better off than they had previously thought themselves to be. The criticism may have more point if the asset stripping leaves Sigma in a nonviable trading position and therefore threatens the livelihood of its employees, but even in this case it must not be forgotten that the previous apparent viability concealed a failure to cover the true opportunity cost of the assets employed by the firm. In principle, Sigma's directors are supposed to draw attention to any significant differences between the market value and the book value of the firm's real property. However, a genuinely inefficient management is unlikely to recognize such a discrepancy, and even a relatively efficient management may genuinely disagree about the relevant market value when this depends upon unforeseen developments in unfamiliar markets.

It is sometimes suggested that the valuation ratio, which measures the market valuation of a firm as a ratio of the book value of its equity assets, may be used as an index of the efficiency with which those assets are used for the benefit of shareholders. Strictly, we would be more interested in the maximum possible value of the assets rather than the book value, but the latter has the merit of being readily available even if the figures are sometimes suspect. If anything, the evidence available for the United Kingdom supports the view that the acquired firms generally had a below-average valuation ratio (see Singh 1971, Buckley 1972, Kuehn 1975, but compare Newbould 1970). However, the ratio is rarely a good discriminator: Many firms with low ratios are able to maintain their independence and many victims appear to have had quite respectable ratios.

Discount rates

We have been concerned with the circumstances in which Beta may try to take over Sigma because it expects to be able to increase the aggregate profits by combining the two firms. Now we shall look at various reasons why Beta may value the same profits differently from Sigma's shareholders. We start with the effects of different discount rates.

Share valuations depend on the rate of discount or the time horizon which is used to assess future profits, as well as on the year-to-year values of the profits themselves. A merger, like any other share transaction, may therefore be desired by both buyers and sellers even when neither of them expects it to produce any change in future profits. The earlier discussion of the share-valuation model stressed that individual shareholders would often be able to satisfy their preferences by marginal transactions which do not involve any change in the control of Sigma, whereas a merger may sometimes be the only way to satisfy the preferences of managers or of shareholders owning large blocks of shares.

Owner-managers often become more willing to sell their shares as they approach retirement simply because their time horizon changes. An owner-manager who wishes to end his active participation in the firm may find it more difficult to appoint a successor to take over from him as manager. He may therefore be forced to choose between staying in harness and selling out to a firm with a greater reserve of managerial talent. But even if he can find a successor, he may still have a strong incentive to sell if he wants immediate cash to enjoy the future profits during his own lifetime: Jam today is inevitably more attractive than jam tomorrow if tomorrow is likely to be canceled at short notice. At the same time he may become increasingly reluctant to face the financial risks involved in ownership of a small firm and may prefer the greater liquidity he would get by exchanging his ownership for a more marketable block of shares in a larger firm. In either case, he may be prepared to discount the future earning power of his firm fairly heavily and may therefore accept a price which allows Beta an attractive return on its investment.

Differences in valuation may also arise if Beta is more interested in growth than profitability and so, implicitly or explicitly, uses a lower discount rate to value Sigma's income-earning assets. This is more likely to be true of Beta's managers than its shareholders, but even if the shareholders are less interested in growth, their control over the managers is likely to be less than perfect. We argued in Chapter 2 that the managers of a firm will rarely, if ever, be able to know for certain that they have chosen the optimum strategy. Given that shareholders will typically have even less-perfect information than the managers, they are even less likely to be able to assess the firm's true profit potential and accordingly they are not likely to become actively dissatisfied so long as their firm does about as well as other firms in comparable circumstances. Further, even if some shareholders would prefer other policies, the dispersion of share ownership may make it difficult for them to organize an effective challenge to the management. If the feeling becomes widespread, it may eventually have an adverse effect on the firm's market value. This may constrain the behavior of those firms which raise new capital from the stock market, but in practice this effect seems to be small and uncertain (Whittington 1971), and for the majority of firms the ultimate constraint is probably imposed by the threat of takeover (Marris 1964).

There are several reasons why managers may prefer to emphasize growth. First, it may be a source of managerial prestige. Secondly, it may provide better opportunities for internal promotion and/or immediate increases in salary. It seems that among large firms, the financial rewards of senior executives are more strongly influenced by the size of the firm than by its profitability (Cosh 1975, Meeks and Whittington 1975), and although the changes in size that are needed to have much effect may not be readily achieved through internal growth, they may be approached by merger. Finally, growth may lead to significant gains in security. An increase in size may help to stabilize earnings. More significantly, perhaps, it may help to protect the existing managers from the risk of a takeover bid: Medium-sized or large firms appear to be able to reduce the risk of takeover more effectively by growth than by improvements in profitability.

Empirical attempts to show that a reduction in shareholder control leads to a greater emphasis on growth have generally been unconvincing, and justify the Scottish verdict of "not proven" (see for example Radice 1971, or Holl 1975). However this does not mean that all firms pursue the same objectives, but simply that the differences in performance do not correlate closely with differences in ownership. It is still possible that the different emphasis placed on growth by different managers may account for specific mergers, or may explain why some firms adopt a long-term policy of growth by acquisition. This has been argued most forcefully by Mueller (1969) and Kuehn (1975). Further, although the evidence on the effects of mergers is seldom clear-cut, there is some suggestion that acquisitive firms do commonly achieve a higher growth rate at some cost to their original shareholders both in the United States (Reid 1968) and in the United Kingdom (Newbould 1970).

The emphasis on external growth may be further justified if the managers identify their comparative advantages as those that are most readily suited to growth by merger. These might include the ability to identify business opportunities that have been overlooked by other managers, and the ability to restructure an organization in order to introduce improved operating methods. These are the skills of the consultant, but they may often be exploited more profitably by a strategy of acquisition than by the sale of consultancy services, because consultants can only work *after* existing management has recognized the need for change and has decided to seek specialist advice, and even then the consultants cannot appropriate for themselves all the gains to be achieved by reorganization. Neither of these problems need deter effective takeovers.

Uncertainty (I): access to information

So far, we have assumed that the potential earning power of both firms is known by Beta and, unless its management is inefficient, also by Sigma. This was convenient for exposition but was clearly unrealistic. In practice, the forecasts of future income will be clouded by uncertainty.

The introduction of uncertainty into the argument does not require any substantial modification to the preceeding discussion. Monopoly, scale, synergy, and efficiency will still influence the outcome of a merger even if their precise effects are not predictable. But uncertainty does introduce additional reasons for mergers, because if Beta and Sigma have imperfect information they may well form different estimates of their future income streams and associated risks, and a merger becomes possible whenever Beta's estimate of Sigma's current value exceeds its current market price. Unfortunately, this observation is not very useful as it stands if all that it does is to introduce a subjective and haphazard element into the explanation of mergers. It explains why some mergers fail, but that is all. If is it to assist our understanding of why mergers take place, it must help us to identify specific types of merger which would be unlikely to take place in conditions of perfect certainty.

We shall now discuss some effects of access to information: first, the results of unequal access; and second, the results of a general change in the quality of information available. We shall then add some further financial considerations.

Unequal access to information. Different firms may form different estimates of Sigma's future profitability if they start with different information. In most cases, Sigma's existing management will have access to the most accurate information, and provided that they can convince shareholders that they are right, their estimates should be reflected in the current market value. In this case, unless there are some other reasons for a merger, a takeover bid by Beta would imply that its inferior information had encouraged it to overestimate Sigma's prospects. However, Sigma's management will not always have the best information. Beta may sometimes learn about new opportunities for Sigma before Sigma is aware of them, because Beta is more diversified, has a wider range of market contacts, or can more readily cover the fixed costs of a good data-collection system, simply because it is large. By moving before the information becomes more readily available, Beta may be able to obtain control of Sigma for less than its true value. Even if Sigma's managers obtain new information and revise their estimates before the merger is completed, it may be too late for them to persuade shareholders that the deal is undesirable: Especially if Beta's profits are good whereas Sigma's have been relatively depressed, Beta's management may seem to be more farsighted, and may be welcomed by Sigma's shareholders as the new broom needed to sweep out their managerial cobwebs.

A similar situation may arise if prior cooperation between Beta and Sigma enables Beta to identify opportunities for synergy or market exploitation before they are recognized by other firms. In this case, Sigma's management should also know of the possible benefits, but Beta may gain if previous contacts make it easier to obtain the cooperation of Sigma's management and to avoid the higher costs which would follow if the bid were contested by another potential buyer.

General changes in uncertainty. Mergers may also be encouraged if rapid environmental change increases uncertainty by reducing the value of past experience as a guide to future prospects. Possible changes in the competitive environment would include new entry, the development of new products or technologies, and the opening of new markets. The increases in uncertainty that result from these changes would widen the range between the expectations formed by different people and hence lead to a wider range of asset valuations.

A priori, unless there are differences in the access to information, we cannot say that any general increase in uncertainty will necessarily increase Beta's valuation of Sigma by more, or decrease it by less, than it changes Sigma's market value. Hence, the impact on individual firms is not predictable. However, it is possible that changes in uncertainty will influence the timing of mergers. The expectations of managers and of shareholders with inside knowledge of a firm are likely to be less volatile than the expectations of other investors with more limited or superficial knowledge of the firm's prospects. Their estimate of the firm's value should therefore be more stable than that of the marginal shareholder, and they are likely to feel that the firm is more heavily undervalued by the market in times of general recession than it is in times of boom. In consequence, they will be more reluctant to sell during a recession, and will look for a higher share premium before they will agree to a takeover bid. This question of the timing of mergers will be considered more fully in section 7.6 below.

Uncertainty (II): some additional financial points

The shareholders' perception of uncertainty and their reaction to it may vary systematically between firms of different size or between firms operating in different industries. These variations may allow simple financial gains to be made from a merger, especially when they result in significant differences in gearing or in price–earnings ratios between Beta and Sigma.

Gearing. If Beta is larger or more diversified than Sigma, it is likely to be able to maintain a more consistent performance and will therefore be able to adopt a higher financial gearing or a higher leverage: that is, it can raise a greater proportion of its capital by fixed-interest borrowing. The cost of fixed-interest borrowing is generally less than the potential return on assets and provided that it does not involve an unacceptable increase in risk, higher gearing may allow a higher return to the equity shareholders for a given level of profitability.

This result can be demonstrated by a simple numerical example. Assume that firms can earn twenty percent on assets employed but can borrow at ten percent. Ignore taxation. A firm with assets of £1 million, which is all financed by equities, will earn £200,000 and give a return to shareholders of twenty percent. However if the same firm had used equity capital of £.5 million and borrowed £.5 million it would have to pay £50,000 of its earnings in interest, while retaining £150,000 for its shareholders, who would therefore receive a return of thirty percent on the total equity capital of £.5 million. Higher gearing can therefore raise the return received by ordinary shareholders. But it may also increase their risks. For example, suppose that the return on assets employed fell to five percent. With no fixed interest debt, the firm would still be able to offer a positive return to its shareholders; but if it had borrowed £.5 million at ten percent, it would find that all its current earnings were needed to meet the fixed interest charges. The shareholders will therefore receive a more steady flow of dividends from the firm that has a lower gearing. It follows that a firm whose earnings do not fluctuate markedly from year to year can exploit a higher gearing with less risk to shareholders.

When Beta is able to employ a higher gearing than Sigma, it may be able to raise additional capital by increasing Sigma's gearing after the takeover, or it may be able to finance the acquisition of Sigma's shares partly by the issue of fixed-interest securities. Changes in capital gearing can therefore affect the profitability of mergers. Examples include Slater Walker Securities' exploitation of the overdraft facilities available to Greengate and Irwell, which had been hesitant to use loan finance before its takeover (Pratten 1970), or Cornwall Properties' acquisition of Edward Webb and Sons (Stourbridge), which had virtually no gearing in spite of its properties, which later provided security for considerable mortgage debt (Buckley 1972).

Further, Meeks and Whittington (1975) have suggested that the higher gearing permitted by their more stable performance record has enabled the gaint companies in the United Kingdom to issue equities fairly readily in share-exchange deals to acquire subsidiaries in spite of the giants' relatively poor profitability. However it does not follow that acquisitive firms are necessarily highly geared, and in the United Kingdom empirical observations of the actual gearing of Beta-type firms do not produce consistent results for different time periods (compare for example, Singh 1971 and Tzoannos and Samuels 1972). By contrast, results for the United States seem less ambiguous. There the data suggest that the acquisitive firms are typically more highly geared than their victims, and that conglomerates, in particular, have often included fixed-interest shares or convertible shares in the "packages" offered to the shareholders of their victims (Melicher and Hempel 1971, Melicher and Rush 1973, 1974).

Price–earnings ratios and the "p/e game." If there were no uncertainty, and if it were known that each firm's earnings per share
would grow in the future at a rate which was the same for all firms,
then each firm's share price would be a fixed multiple of its current
earnings per share. That is, all firms would have the same price-
earnings ratio, or p/e ratio. However, in practice, different firms will
have different p/e ratios, partly because of real differences in future
earning capacity but also because these differences cannot be foreseen perfectly by shareholders. As a result, a firm whose recent
performance has appeared to be promising may have a higher p/e
ratio than a declining firm, even though the promise may prove to
be exaggerated and the decline may prove to be temporary. Similarly a low p/e ratio may be given to a firm in an unglamorous
industry, or to a firm whose performance lags behind the standard
set by other firms in its industry.

If Beta has a better p/e ratio than Sigma, its shares will have a
higher relative value, which may be exploited in a share-exchange
deal. In effect, Beta's shares have a favorable exchange rate which
makes Sigma's current earnings relatively cheap. The immediate
effect of the takeover will then be an increase in Beta's current
earnings per share, and although the current earnings are really less
relevant than anticipated future earnings, the short term improvement may be interpreted as an indication of an improvement in
management efficiency. Shareholders may therefore continue to
award Beta a favorable p/e ratio, so that the price of its shares rises
after the merger even if there is no improvement in the return on
capital employed.

The mechanics of the "p/e game" may be illustrated as follows.
Assume that Beta and Sigma are of equal size, that each has one
million shares outstanding, and that each has current profits of £1
million. In each case the earnings per share are therefore £1. Assume further that for one of the reasons given above, Beta has a p/e
ratio of 20 and Sigma a p/e ratio of 12. Beta therefore has a total
market value of £20 million, or £20 per share, while Sigma has a
value of £12 million, or £12 per share. If Beta could take over
Sigma for its market valuation of £12 million, it would offer three of
its own shares (valued at £60) for every five of Sigma's shares (valued at £60) and would need to issue 600,000 shares in exchange for
Sigma's one million. After the merger, the enlarged Beta has
1,600,000 shares outstanding, while the aggregate profits will be

unchanged at £2 million. Earnings per share are now £1.25 (that is 2,000,000/1,600,000) compared with the earnings of £1 per share recorded by each company before the merger, and if the market continues to apply Beta's p/e ratio of 20 to the combined earnings, Beta's share price will rise to £25 and its market value to £40 million. Even if the p/e ratio were to fall after the merger, Beta's share price would still rise provided that the ratio did not fall below 16.

In practice, this simple calculation must overstate the probable gain, because even if we ignore further complications such as the legal costs of the merger, Beta will have to pay a premium over Sigma's premerger market price. However, Beta will still experience an increase in earnings per share, provided that it can obtain Sigma for less than one million of its own shares. Such a one-for-one share exchange would imply the same value for Sigma's shares as for Beta's: that is, £20 per share. While this is not impossible, it implies a share premium of sixty-seven percent of Sigma's prebid share price.

It would be misleading to claim that many firms base their merger strategies solely on p/e ratios, but changes in the ratios may often influence the timing of mergers which are otherwise desirable. Newbould (1970) considered that in the United Kingdom in the late 1960s, the market generally responded favorably to acquisitions in which the bidder had a higher p/e ratio than the victim, and both Buckley (1972) and Tzoannos and Samuels (1972) found that acquired firms were typically characterized by below average p/e ratios.

In general, similar results are indicated by studies of U.S. mergers (see for example, Conn 1973, or Melicher and Rush 1974). However the U.S. studies have paid particular attention to the use of p/e strategies by conglomerates. This interest generally follows from the observation that share prices and p/e ratios are more volatile for the conglomerates than for other industrial firms. For example, Steiner compared the average annual ratio for a sample of industrial firms and a sample of conglomerates (Steiner 1975, Table 5.1). The ratios were approximately the same in 1964 (18.1 for the industrials and 17.6 for the conglomerates). By 1967 the conglomerates had increased to 22.0, nearly four points above the industrials, but by 1971 when the industrials stood at 18.1 the conglomerates had dropped back to 14.6. It is therefore clear that the conglomerates were given a particularly favorable stock market rating in 1967–8, which encouraged them to play the "p/e game" (Mead 1969). But it is equally clear that the conglomerates subsequently lost some of their glamour-stock rating, and in general it seems that they have certainly not been the only firms to consider p/e ratios as an important component of their merger strategies (Melicher and Hempel 1971, Melicher and Rush 1974).

7.6 Timing

Although it is possible to identify a number of alternative reasons why one firm may wish to take over another, these reasons are not all equally good predictors of the timing of mergers. As we saw in section 7.2, mergers have occurred in waves, with alternating periods of frenetic activity and apparent disinterest. Further, the waves occurring in different countries have often been synchronized, if somewhat loosely, and appear to have been more or less in phase with general economic cycles of boom and recession, with merger activity typically declining during the recessions. The mechanism determining these cycles is imperfectly understood, but there appear to be two main factors. The first is financial and depends primarily on stock-market behavior, whereas the second stresses the response to changes in the market environment. The stock-market effects have generally been emphasized more strongly in the United States, while the effects of environmental change are more commonly discussed in the United Kingdom, especially in relation to the mergers of the 1960s. However, the two are almost certainly complementary. They are considered very briefly in the discussion which follows, because most of the steps in the argument have already been discussed individually in the earlier sections of this chapter.

Financial factors

Acquisitions have often increased during a stock-market boom, and there are several reasons why a general increase in share prices may help to encourage mergers. First, the effect may be partly psychological, reflecting changes in business expectations. If expectations are influenced by share prices, firms may feel more optimistic in a bullish stock market, and may therefore take a more favorable view of the potential gains to be made from a merger. On the other hand, if the industrial and financial communities disagree about future prospects, as they appear to have done in the United Kingdom in 1973 (Hannah and Kay 1977, p. 87), takeovers may flourish in spite of a weakening stock market.

Secondly, a stock-market boom will not affect all shares equally. The shares of some firms will increase in value more rapidly than others, and the more fortunate firms will find that takeovers using share-exchange deals will require fewer new shares and can be accomplished with less dilution of the interests of existing share-holders (see 7.5, the material on uncertainty).

Thirdly, the long-term investors in Sigma may feel that the firm is less undervalued (or more overvalued) when share prices are high, and may therefore require a smaller premium over the existing market price. Thus the average share-premium in takeover bids in the United Kingdom was higher in 1971, when the stock market was relatively depressed, than it was in the takeover boom of 1967–8 (Buckley 1972, Newbould 1970). The share premium may also influence the buyer, because although Beta is primarily influenced by the total price paid for Sigma, its future stock-market rating may be stronger if it can acquire subsidiaries at relatively low premiums.

Environmental factors

Although changes in share prices can influence the ease with which firms can undertake mergers, their incentive to do so may also respond to changes in the general economic environment. Both favorable and unfavorable changes will force firms to reappraise their opportunities, and may well lead to different appraisals of the same opportunities by different firms or individuals. Such valuation discrepancies may sometimes provide a basis for mergers (Gort 1969; see also 7.5, the material on uncertainty). If the changes involve increased domestic or international competition, they may promote mergers which are designed to change the market structure and restore more orderly competitive relations between the remaining firms, especially if the alternative of a restrictive trading agreement is ruled out for legal or other reasons (George and Silberston 1975; see also 7.5, the material on monopoly).

More generally, the mergers may represent a response to any changes which cause greater uncertainty. These changes need not be restricted to increases in rivalry (Newbould 1970, Aaronovitch and Sawyer 1975b). A change in market structure brought about by merger may then enable firms to control their environment more effectively by internalizing decisions which were previously beyond their control; it may enable them to exploit any scale economies in the collection of information; and it may facilitate tacit collusion among the larger firms that retain their independence. Once the merger movement has begun, it further increases the uncertainty felt by other firms and therefore encourages them to plunge into the takeover wave.

7.7 Empirical research on mergers

The last decade has seen a flurry of empirical research on mergers, and especially on the characteristics of the firms involved, and on the consequences of mergers. This section summarizes some aspects of this research, but concentrates on those aspects which throw some light on the relationship between mergers and strategic behavior. This has rarely been the main focus of the research. Typically, the investigators have been more concerned with the implications for government policy than with strategic management, and have sought answers to such questions as "Does the market for the control of firms operate effectively?" or "Do conglomerate mergers differ from other mergers?" Any strategic lesson drawn from this research must therefore be treated cautiously. First we look at the risks of being taken over, and then turn to postmerger performance.

The probability of being taken over

Especially in the United Kingdom, several studies have sought to discriminate between the firms that have been taken over and those that have retained their independence. These studies identify some characteristics of the acquired firms, surviving firms, and (possibly) acquisitive firms, and then seek to identify significant differences between the groups. The results rarely provide very good discrimination: they may identify characteristics such as profitability for which the *average* value is significantly higher in one group than in another, but there is usually so much variation within each group that any two groups will overlap to a considerable extent. As a result it is difficult to use the results to predict the probability that a firm will be taken over, because firms with the same observed characteristics often end up in different groups.

Typically, the results suggest that the clearest discrimination is obtained by comparing size or simple performance measures such as growth and profitability (or the related valuation ratio), rather than with more narrow details of financial structure. Variables reflecting a firm's gearing, its liquidity, or the proportion of retained profits, are either insignificant as general explanations of mergers, or appear to be significant at some times but not at others.[2] This is generally consistent with the spirit of our original valuation model (section 7.4), which did not include gearing or liquidity but did show that the effects of changes in retentions or dividends were uncertain, depending on the consequential effects on growth and profitability. In general, it also suggests that strategic management should concentrate on identifying and exploiting opportunities for growth and profitability, without which time spent on the refinements of financial structure would appear to be misplaced.

Several studies have confirmed that the probability of being taken over declines as a firm grows larger (see especially Singh 1971, 1975, or Aaronovitch and Sawyer 1975a. In contrast, Kuehn 1975 reported that the effect was rarely significant within each industry, although the direction of the effect was generally observed to be the same as in other studies.) Presumably this reflects the fact that the cost of managerial resources and (possibly) the finance needed for the takeover increase disproportionately as Sigma becomes large relative to Beta, and as a result the number of firms which can afford a takeover declines as Sigma grows larger. This immunity appears to increase with size even among the largest one hundred quoted manufacturing firms (Whittington 1972), but given that most mergers in the United Kingdom are horizontal, a firm's absolute size will generally be less important than its size relative to others in the same industry.

Singh's estimates are summarized in Table 1, which gives the probability of acquisition within one year for firms in different size categories. The categories relate to the range of sizes within the firms own industry, and are identified as size quintiles, containing the smallest twenty percent of firms, the next smallest twenty percent, and so on.

---

[2] Some of these differences may be provocative. For example Singh (1975) reported that retention ratios appeared to be significant in 1955–60 but not in the later 1960s. In the earlier period, takeover victims typically retained a smaller proportion of profits. This might imply that in the 1950s some firms paid too little attention to growth, but that by the 1960s takeovers had absorbed some of these and forced others to change their priorities.

Table 1. *Relative size and probability (percentage) of acquisition*

	Size quintile					
	Q_1 (smallest)	Q_2	Q_3	Q_4	Q_5 (largest)	All
1955–60	3.6	4.2	3.5	3.1	2.5	3.4
1967–70	3.0	10.1	9.7	6.5	4.5	6.7

Source: Singh 1975

For both periods, the probability declines consistently with size from Q2 through Q5, but is lower in Q1 than Q2. This runs counter to our preceding argument, but the conflict is more apparent than real: Q1 contains many firms which are closely controlled by a small number of shareholders, such as a family group, and are therefore less open to unsolicited bids than the firms in larger size classes, whose shares are more widely held.

The other fairly clear result under this section relates to the effect of prior performance on takeover activity. The acquiring firms typically grow more rapidly than their victims (Kuehn 1975, Aaronovitch and Sawyer 1975a) suggesting that they are not using mergers simply to buy themselves out of a slow-growth situation. (A contrary view has been taken by Weston and Mansinghka 1971 but their study relates specifically to U.S. conglomerates.) Instead they appear to be more strongly motivated by growth and/or they are gaining from the favorable market valuation conferred by a growth-stock image which enables them to acquire other firms on favorable terms. Conversely, the acquired firms are not only slower growing but are also typically less profitable (Singh 1971, 1975) and/or have experienced an inferior trend of profits (Tzoannos and Samuels 1972, Buckley 1972).

Comparable results have been found in the United States, where the firms acquired in mergers are typically "perhaps slightly below average in their premerger profitability but certainly not generally on the brink of financial disaster" (Steiner 1975, p. 188). Some of the firms in this category will have exhausted their profit opportunities and offer little prospect for postmerger improvement. These will hardly be attractive takeover candidates. But, in many cases, the poor profit record will be evidence that management has failed to control current operations, has retained aging products that ought to have been discontinued, or has otherwise failed to exploit its opportunities to the full. These opportunities provide an incentive for acquisition, whereas the risk of takeover would have been reduced if the original management had taken steps to improve profitability. However, Singh (1975) suggested that although this incentive is valid for the least profitable firms, the risk of takeover may remain the same in the face of quite large changes in profitability. The least profitable thirty percent of the firms he studied might have reduced the probability of being taken-over by increasing their profitability, but this was not true for the remaining seventy percent of firms. Further, although smaller firms may increase their security by trying to increase profitability, this may not be true of the larger firms: Large unprofitable firms may experience a greater increase in security by devoting resources to growth rather than by improving profits, and hence may seek to acquire others in an attempt to reduce their own susceptibility to takeover. A similar point is made by Aaronovitch and Sawyer (1975b, p. 190): "One way of summarising the results might be that a firm which has a dip in its fortune, reduces its rate of dividend increase, performs poorly on the share market and hence also in VR (valuation ratio) and p/e ratios, becomes a target for acquisition. If such a firm were big enough, it could become an acquiring firm!"

The impact on performance

Attempts to assess the impact of mergers on performance face many problems. The measurement of performance is inevitably difficult, especially if it includes measures of profits or assets and the merger is followed by accounting changes involving the revision of depreciation policy or the revaluation of capital. Further, the conclusions may be dependent on the time period chosen for analysis – if, for example, the performance of merger-intensive firms is more volatile than that of internal growers. This possibility does not appear to have been tested directly, but it is certainly true that the market valuation of U.S. conglomerates in the late 1960s was more volatile than the price of "blue chip" industrial stocks (Vance 1971).

But even if we could find unambiguous measures of performance, we still have the problem of isolating the effect of mergers. It is rarely possible to observe Sigma's postmerger results, because these are incorporated with Beta's. We are therefore forced to look for changes in the total performance of the combined firms. This may be acceptable if the combination involves only a single merger, although we would still face the problem of allowing for, say, spontaneous changes in demand conditions which affect before-and-after performance comparisons. More commonly, however, we find that firms engage in a series of mergers, so that it is simply not possible to identify the long-term effects of a single merger. We are then forced to concentrate on "significant" mergers, hoping that the rest, even in combination, are insignificant; or to make broader comparisons between merger-intensive and internal-growth firms, although the former do not grow solely by merger and the latter rarely abstain from merger altogether.

In a brief review of this sort, it is simply not possible to provide a detailed critique of the steps which different studies have taken, or have not taken, to minimize these problems. For the most part, the studies produce similar conclusions, and we shall simply concentrate on the broad generalizations with some reference to the occasional points of dissent but without reference to the many refinements which embellish the best of the studies.

United Kingdom studies of postmerger performance have typically used some index of return on assets to measure performance. The results do not favor mergers. Singh (1971) found that in a marginal majority of cases, relative profitability declined after the merger, and Meeks (1977) suggested that this decline typically persisted for several years. Newbould (1970) suggested that merger-intensive firms had an inferior gain in profitability, whereas Utton (1974, p. 24) concluded that "companies heavily dependent on external expansion may, in a subsequent period of largely internal growth, pay the price of lower overall efficiency (to the extent that this is reflected in their rate of return on net assets) than companies whose long term growth is slower but whose internal efficiency can be sustained." When available, U.S. data also suggest that mergers are followed by declines in operating profitability, although these may not be significantly different from the changes experienced by other firms in the acquired firms' industries (Conn 1976).

By contrast, most U.S. studies have concentrated on the return to the stockholders of the acquisitive firms. Generally, the results are fairly negative. For the 1950s and early 1960s, Kelly (1967) and Reid (1968) suggested that merger-intensive firms typically grew faster than average, but did not generate exceptional share-price gains for their original shareholders, whereas Hogarty (1970) confirmed that the total gain to stockholders of merger-intensive firms was often worse than the average for other firms in the same industries. Subsequently, Mandelker (1974) stressed that the return to shareholders should allow for any reduction in the risks that they faced after the mergers, and suggested that the stockholders did in fact receive a normal return, equal to that offered by other activities of similar risk. However, Haugen and Langetieg (1975) found that mergers typically failed to produce economically significant changes in the risk attributes of the distribution of rates of return to shareholders: the risk attributes were no different from those in a less formal purchase of both Sigma's and Beta's shares by a portfolio investor. On balance, therefore, these studies suggest that the shareholders of acquisitive firms have not gained, but may have lost, as a result of firms' merger activities.

A dissenting view was voiced by Lev and Mandelker (1972) who used a paired-sample technique to compare the performance of acquisitive firms before and after a major merger against the continuing performance of nonmerging firms. They concluded that the return to stockholders was probably higher in acquisitive firms, although they could detect no change in risk. However, their results may reflect the empirical problems of identifying paired samples. Using a subsample selected in accordance with more stringent criteria, Honeycutt (1975) reversed Lev and Mandelker's original conclusion on postmerger profitability.

Results which were more favorable to mergers were suggested by studies concentrating on the effects of conglomerate mergers in the United States in the 1960s. Weston and Mansinghka (1971), supported by Melicher and Rush (1973), suggested that conglomerates may have been able to exploit mergers to improve their profitability relative to nonconglomerates. However, the market standing of the conglomerates declined markedly after 1968–70 and Mason and Goudzwaard (1976) suggested that even during the conglomerate heyday of 1962–7 the shareholders in conglomerates could have gained more from a randomly selected portfolio of shares with the same industrial composition as their conglomerate, in spite of the higher transaction costs involved in managing the portfolio. In general, therefore, these statistical comparisons of performance suggest that shareholders have not benefited significantly, if at all, from the higher growth rates generated by mergers.

Aware of the problems of measuring performance, some studies have simply reported the postmerger appraisals made by the managers themselves. These suggest a failure rate of about one-third of all mergers, although the studies are hardly comprehensive and cannot guarantee a consistent definition of failure. In the United States, Kitching (1967) suggested that 22 of 69 acquisitions were rated as failures by the 21 acquisitive companies involved, and Reid (1968) reported an unpublished study made by the management consultants Booz, Allen, and Hamilton, which found that eleven percent of 120 acquisitions made between 1960 and 1965 were subsequently sold or liquidated, while a further twenty-five percent were judged to be of doubtful worth. In the United Kingdom, the failure rate may be even higher. Kitching's (1974) study of 145 acquisitions reported thirty percent classified as failures and a further seventeen percent as not worth repeating.

The evidence is extremely thin, but there is some suggestion that this high failure rate may be a consequence of inadequate preparation by the management of the acquiring firms. On the basis of a questionnaire survey, Newbould (1970, p. 84) concluded that bidders rarely used formal techniques to assess the value of their victims, whereas Birley's (1976) interviews with company executives suggested that acquisitive firms with more formal planning proceedures, who sought for acquisitions systematically and established some financial criteria to appraise potential acquisitions, also tended to be more satisfied with the eventual outcome of their bids. Similarly Ansoff, Brandenburg, Portner, and Radosevich (1972) have shown that in the United States "the systematic planning, search, and evaluation approach not only produced better results on the average, but also produced more predictable results" (p. 99).

The relatively high failure rate may indicate that many victims are initially overvalued by their buyers. Newbould's estimates suggest that the price paid for Sigma would often require an unrealistically large increase in earnings to give a fair return to the buyer. It may be that "having taken the initial step, executives appeared too emotionally involved to consider not acquiring" (Birley 1976, p. 70). It is perhaps for this reason that victims which are undervalued before the takeover bid, and hence appear as genuine bargains, are often overvalued by the acquisition price (Samuels and Tzoannos 1969). Using U.S. data, Gort and Hogarty (1970) suggested that a merger is often a zero-sum game in which buyers lose and sellers gain: that is, on average, the stockholders of Sigma gain from a merger, but they do so at the expense of Beta's stockholders, because the mergers generally produce few real gains for the stockholders. Similarly, although Franks, Broyles, and Hecht (1977) suggest that mergers in the U.K. breweries and distilleries sector have produced gains for shareholders, they also suggest that most if not all of these gains were enjoyed by the shareholders of the victim, not the acquiring firm. On the other hand, some acquirers do make significant gains, indicating that mergers may be a form of high-risk activity offering a low probability of a high payoff. Gort and Hogarty also suggested that the correlation between real gains and share premiums was negative: Mergers offering real gains were less likely to be overpriced. They concluded that the more effective managers also tended to pay below-average premiums. This is not surprising. Managers who select their merger partners with care and avoid competitive bids likely to lead to overvaluation are more likely to produce successful mergers than those who react to events without prior planning.

This brief summary is not encouraging. After summarizing results covering the period up to the mid-1960s, Reid (1968, p. 95) suggested that "the common thread revealed in an examination of the relative success of mergers is that they have been less successful than 'conventional wisdom' would lead one to believe . . . The highly publicised success of a few mergers tends to obscure the more important empirical findings." Today, following the changing environment of the 1970s the "conventional wisdom" may be a little less optimistic than Reid suggested, but otherwise his rather negative conclusion is still valid. However, we must be careful to avoid an overreaction against mergers. The results should not be taken as demonstrating that the managers who promote mergers are naive, nor that they necessarily pursue their own security or prestige at the expense of shareholder or national interest.

In a world of imperfect knowledge, some mergers necessarily involve risks, and inevitably some of these risky ventures will be observed after the event to have resulted in failure. Careful planning may reduce the risks, but it cannot eliminate them altogether, and perversely it is probably true that the risks are greatest in those firms which make a positive attempt to achieve synergy in mergers, because the adjustments necessary to achieve that synergy will require operating changes that are quite likely to generate internal conflict. Further, the performance tests normally assume that if the merger had not taken place, the firms would have continued with their premerger profitability, or would have followed the same trend as other firms in their industrial sector. But as we have seen, many mergers take place because the firms anticipate a future decline in performance: For example, they may be trying to offset a worsening competitive situation, or to counter emerging weaknesses which might otherwise, in due course, have led to a gradual deterioration in performance. The statistical studies cannot allow for these anticipated but unobservable changes, and so remain as an imperfect test of the consequences of those mergers that are undertaken for strategic reasons.

8

Innovation

8.1 Introduction: The nature of innovation

Innovation is a process which involves the adoption of procedures or products which are perceived as being new by the adopter. It is therefore concerned with changes in the established ways of doing things. In many cases, it will result from progress in science and technology, which permits new methods of production, new designs for existing products, or completely new products or services. But innovation is not necessarily tied to prior technical change. It may also reflect changes in (say) marketing techniques or management procedures. Perhaps the clearest example is the growth of self-service retailing, which is a significant innovation with a widespread social impact but very low technological content.

In other cases, the technological input may be significant but invisible, as in the spread of credit-card trading, which has been made possible by advances in electronic data processing to handle the centralized accounts. Conversely, even when the innovation has followed from a technical breakthrough, its successful use will depend upon the social and economic environment as well as upon the technical specifications of the product. Further, although technical change sometimes requires significant preinvestment in research and development, this is not always the case. Many innovations occur as the aggregate result of a series of improvements which individually have a minor impact and require little research, whereas other innovations may involve the adoption of new products or new ideas which have been developed by someone else, and may or may not require further research by the adopter. In general, it is therefore clear that the link between research, technical progress, and innovation is often loose and indistinct.

Major innovations are fairly rare. Most of the time, most firms concentrate on continuing to do the things they have always done. They may introduce minor changes in the style of their products, they may serve new customers, or they may start contacts with new

160

suppliers, but individually these changes are rarely significant enough to warrant the name "innovation." For the latter, we would normally expect to find changes in the method of production, in the buyers perception of the product, or in the operating procedures of the firm.

However, even if, on average, innovation represents no more than a marginal use of resources, it can still have a major impact on growth and profitability. As Schumpeter had it: "What we, unscientifically, call economic progress means essentially putting productive resources to uses *hitherto untried in practice,* and withdrawing them from the uses they have served so far. This is what we call 'innovation'" (Schumpeter 1928, p. 378). New products and processes provide firms with new opportunities for growth, with some relaxation of market constraints, or at very least with a temporary assurance of competitive survival. The potential links between innovation and performance have been confirmed by a number of empirical studies in the United States, although it must be noted that these concentrated on technical innovation and generally related to the 1950s, when the opportunities for low-cost innovation may have been greater or less than at other times. In one study, Mansfield (1968) demonstrated that successful innovators could expect to grow more rapidly than comparable noninnovating firms during the five to ten years after an innovation. These differences were greater than those observed before the innovations and, not surprisingly, the impact of single innovations was greatest for smaller firms. Other studies indicate that, on average, sales and/or profits have been increased by additional expenditure on technical research and development (Minasian 1962, Branch 1974) or by an increase in the number of patents held by a firm (Baily 1972). The commercial benefits were found to follow patenting after a lag of three or four years (Scherer 1965) and are not confined to the science-based industries.

These data confirm that innovation can be beneficial. But the benefits are not guaranteed. U.S. data suggest that only twenty to thirty percent of new products can be rated as commercial successes (see below). Even when an innovation is eventually profitable, the time lag may be very much longer than the average of three or four years suggested by Scherer, especially for major innovations. For example, "R.C.A. had to wait nearly 15 years for a profit on television and again on colour television" (Freeman 1965, p. 62). Not all firms can afford to wait that long for the hoped for payoff, and the impetuous innovator may find his enhanced technical reputation small comfort to him in his bankruptcy. Further, a successful innovation may sometimes be unprofitable for the innovator if it simply defines a profitable market for attack by other firms. According to *Time* magazine (quoted by Berg and Shuchman 1963, p. 201), in the United States in the early 1960s this became known as the "Lestoil syndrome." Lestoil was a small company that pioneered the market for liquid household cleaners. Initially it was very successful, but its success attracted the attention of the giant detergent firms (Procter and Gamble, Lever Bros., and Colgate Palmolive) whose entry literally decimated Lestoil's market share.

For the rest of this chapter, we shall be concerned with the conditions which encourage innovation and accompany its success. Section 8.2 discusses the nature of the process in somewhat greater detail; 8.3 considers the strategic role of research and development, and some of the factors influencing the success and failure of innovations; 8.4 extends the discussion to allow for competitive pressures while 8.5 covers the reactions of potential customers. Finally 8.6 introduces one way of approaching the strategic and qualitative aspects of project selection. Following the pattern set by most empirical studies of innovation, the chapter concentrates on technical innovations, although most of its conclusions are perfectly general.

8.2 The process of innovation

The sequence of activities

Innovation is a continuous process rather than a discrete act. It starts with an idea or discovery, which may result from casual observation, direct experience, or formal research. Many firms prepare for innovation by investing in the generation of ideas, but it seems that most of the ideas on which firms base their innovations still originate outside the firm (see for example, Langrish et al 1972, or Mueller 1962). Sometimes these ideas appear to be going begging to anyone who has the foresight or imagination to grasp their potential, and firms may have a conscious or unconscious bias against ideas that they did not think up for themselves. The problem is sufficiently familiar for research personnel to refer to it as the "N.I.H." or "not invented here" attitude, but clearly awareness of the problem is no guarantee of a solution. Even the most progressive firms may sometimes turn away potential money spinners. For example, Chester Carlson's electrophotographic process, which has since become known internationally as "xerography," was rejected by more than twenty large firms in the early 1940s before it was taken up for development by the Batelle Memorial Institute and subsequently by Xerox, which was then the Haloid Company, a very small chemical manufacturer (Jewkes, Sawers, and Stillerman 1969).

However, a cautious approach to other people's ideas is not necessarily irrational. Many ideas originate in a primitive state, with no evidence to prove that they are either feasible or desirable, and there are undoubtedly many thousand questionable ideas for every one viable innovation. If an idea seems plausible, it must therefore be subject to further research and development (R & D) to test its technical and commercial viability. Many ideas die during this stage, partly because some were inherently unsatisfactory, but also because the opportunity cost of keeping a marginal product in the firm's portfolio will increase as the product matures: it may cost relatively little to investigate a number of possible starters, and even to keep some of the more promising ones ticking over to await the right moment for further development, but the costs escalate rapidly once it has been decided to test the idea under actual operating conditions or to develop the plant and equipment needed for full commercialization.

The total sequence of activities needed to test ideas is commonly subdivided into basic research, applied research, and development. Basic research is often described as the search for knowledge for its own sake, but in an industrial context it is usually restricted to those fundamental problems that are likely to be relevant to the firm's business areas. Sometimes such directed basic research is referred to as "background" research and contrasted with applied research, related to specific commercial objectives. Either or neither may be required for any one innovation, but every innovation will require some development work to define alternative specifications for the new product or process, to prepare ot test prototypes or pilot plants, and to identify a satisfactory specification for commercial use.

The projects which survive this investigation, seem technically feasible, and show sufficient promise to justify commercialization may then be introduced as new products offered to customers or new processes used by the manufacturing divisions. This will normally require capital investment. It will also require expenditure to cover the costs of starting up manufacturing and marketing operations, including the costs of training or retraining personnel and correcting early faults in the production process, together with the initial sales promotion needed to launch the product. Throughout, the innovation process will be relatively management intensive when compared with operating activities of similar cost, because it involves the redisposition of resources under considerable uncertainty, when previous experience may prove to be an invalid guide to current action.

Some of the projects will fail, but initially the successes and failures may be hard to identify, and in many cases the final outcome will not be obvious until use of the innovation has spread or diffused among a substantial proportion of the total population of potential users. Further, even the eventual successes will normally require further modifications to suit the needs of particular users, or to take advantage of improvements suggested by continued research and operating experience, and they may also be adapted or improved by imitators following the lead of the initial innovator. These modifications may well be as significant if not more significant than the original change (Rosenberg 1972) and a study of four processes in the U.S. petroleum refining industry (thermal cracking, polymerization, catalytic cracking, and reforming) suggested that the average annual cost saving due to the initial adoption of completely new processes was less than the saving that resulted from subsequent improvements (Enos 1958).

The industrial distribution of innovation

The significance of innovation varies considerably between industries. This is illustrated by the industrial distribution of technical and scientific research, which is heavily concentrated in the chemical, electrical engineering, and aerospace industries. In the United Kingdom, these three industries account for two-thirds of formal industrial R & D activity but only fifteen percent of industrial employment. This distribution is the net effect of several different influences. First, the level of expenditure is sometimes encouraged by the provision of Government finance, although this is not true of all industries: for example, the Government pays for over eighty percent of the R & D expenditure in aerospace, but less than one percent in chemicals. Secondly, the distribution may reflect the aims and objectives of the people employed in different industries: the industries which use a science-based production technology need to attract staff with a professional training, and often this encourages them to take a professional interest in the exploitation of new scientific developments. Thirdly, it may also reflect the competitive structure of the industries, although it is then difficult to say for certain whether the competitive structure causes the intense research activity or vice versa (see 8.4 below). Fourthly, it will reflect the conditions of supply and demand for innovations.

This is almost certainly the most important single factor. The supply conditions will be favorable in industries like chemicals and electrical engineering, where progress in basic science throws up a number of ideas for innovations. These ideas will sometimes spill over and affect less science-based industries, as when the advances in synthetic fibers encouraged the search for new techniques in user industries such as carpets. But, in general, it is the science-based industries that can be expected to provide a relatively elastic supply of innovations at relatively low marginal cost, in comparison with the craft-based industries, in which the existing techniques embody the currently perceived limits to knowledge or skill in the area. However, these supply conditions are not enough to provide a full explanation on their own. The profitability of innovations also depends upon the conditions of demand. Ceteris paribus, the demand for cost-reducing process innovations will be greater if product demand is fairly elastic, so that the improvement leads to significant increases in sales.

Further, the specific requirements of the user industries may generate a demand for innovations which can be met more easily with some technologies than with others. For example, the spread of mass-production techniques in manufacturing industry led to a demand for more standardized inputs, and thereby encouraged the development of synthetic products by the chemical industry to replace natural materials, whose quality could not be so readily controlled. Similarly, the electrical-engineering industry has probably benefited from an increased demand for compact labor-saving equipment in developed economies, which suffer from increasing shortages of time and space (Schmookler 1966). Further examples were included in our earlier discussion of the characteristics and national origins of multinational firms.

Innovation and the life cycle of industries

However, it would be wrong to suppose that the relative importance of innovation in different industries, and the relative contribution of different industries to the total innovation process, will remain unchanged for all time. A cursory glance at industrial history reveals the innovative role of textiles and heavy engineering in the early days of industrialization. The dominance of chemicals (especially organic chemicals) and electronics is a much more recent phenomenon. It seems that, like products, industries commonly follow a life cycle of growth and decay and the characteristics of innovation activity may differ between different phases of the cycle (Mueller and Tilton 1969).

Initially, there may be a fairly long lag between the germination of a promising idea and its subsequent flowering for commercial use. The impact of penicillin on the pharmaceutical industry was delayed for fifteen years after it was first discovered in 1928 until its therapeutic properties had been established and a commercially viable process had been developed. Similarly, the basic principle which ultimately led to radar was recognized in a German patent in 1904, although at that time it was not possible to produce a working prototype. The system was also foreseen in the United Kingdom by Marconi at least as early as 1922, and is foreshadowed in a U.S. patent in 1923. But no practical developments followed before special programs were sponsored by the British and German governments in the 1930s (Freeman 1965).

Once a significant breakthrough has been introduced by one innovator it will often be followed by subsequent imitators. Sometimes this will reflect a simultaneous approach to innovation by different firms. If several people work on the same problem, using the same basis of scientific knowledge, it is almost inevitable that some of them will approach similar conclusions, and the one who gets there first may be just a little more lucky, or a little less reticent, than the others. This may be why most countries claim their own national originator of the world's major innovations. Alternatively, the imitators may try deliberately to copy and improve upon the original innovation. By his success, the innovator reduces uncertainty and encourages imitation. Even if he appears to enjoy patent protection, the cover is unlikely to be comprehensive, simply because he cannot foresee all the relevant corollaries of the first discovery. At this stage, knowledge of the basic science underlying the innovation is often rudimentary. Much of the research will be done "by the seat of the pants" and the industry will be open to anyone with technological flair and good imagination.

Innovation is likely to become more formal as the industry matures. The accumulated results of background research will reduce the element of pure guesswork and allow firms both to develop specialized facilities and to exploit the specialist skills of their research staff more fully. These changes favor the larger established firms, who may also benefit from earlier experience in the development and commercialization of new products. Smaller firms may be able to make significant contributions by way of gradual improvements and may continue to dominate specific niches or segments, which are ignored by the market leaders (at least in the short run) as being too small or too unpromising to warrant more than a watching brief. Occasionally these contributions will have a major impact, but generally the increasing technological maturity will raise the costs of radical innovations until they are beyond the reach of small firms. Ultimately, as the industry continues to age, the prospects for radical innovation may become so remote that it no longer enters into the strategic planning of even the largest of the firms, unless it persuades them to diversify in search of more promising growth prospects.

The role of patents and licenses

Throughout this cycle, the incentive for innovation clearly depends upon the anticipated reactions of imitators. These competitive effects are discussed more fully in section 8.5, but we may note immediately that if the innovator is to recover the private costs of development, he must be able to retain some property rights in the outcome for long enough to allow him to appropriate a part of the total gain from his innovation. On the other hand, once it has been developed, an innovation has many of the properties of a public good: Imitators may have to meet the costs of their own learning before they can comprehend the innovation, but there will be no other opportunity costs because the innovation itself is not depleted by use. The result is a perennial dilemma for authorities wishing to encourage the development and use of new technology. The problem has been summarized succinctly by Johnson (1976, pp. 420–1) as follows:

The dual role of knowledge as a private good in production and a public good in consumption poses an insoluble problem for a private enterprise system. If the use of new knowledge is artificially restricted by the imposition and enforcement of a payment by the user to the producer, the producer is given an incentive to produce, though the incentive will be smaller, perhaps substantially smaller, than the knowledge-production is worth to society; and the level of use of the knowledge would be less than would be socially optimal. If, instead, a charge for the knowledge is either inherently impossible to assess or impose, or forbidden by law or social convention, what knowledge is created will be freely and fully used, to maximum social advantage; but the amount of knowledge available will be less than optimal, since no-one will have an incentive to produce it except as a by-product of his private satisfaction-maximising activities.

Johnson emphasized that the patent system represents an uneasy compromise between these conflicting objectives. The patent confers monopoly right on the patentor, but the rights are specific to a particular discovery and therefore do not rule out the possibility that it will be dominated by subsequent discoveries. Further, the rights are for a fixed maximum term, and although in principle the term is long enough to ensure that later changes will have little effect on the current value of the anticipated profits, nevertheless the discovery does eventually become available for use as a free good.

In practice, a firm owning property rights in a discovery may choose to sell those rights or to license others so that they may use the discovery without infringing the patent. Sometimes this may be done to reduce the risk of intervention by the antitrust authorities, or as a result of direct pressure from similar agencies, as happened when Roche licensed Berk Pharmaceuticals to produce diazepam (Valium) after it was ordered to do so by the Comptroller of Patents under section 41 of the 1949 Patents Act (Monopolies Commission 1973). Alternatively, a firm may choose to grant licences, especially to firms operating overseas, if it lacks the resources to exploit the patent right fully on its own. In such cases, licensing is unlikely to be highly profitable unless the licensor has done sufficient development work, and perhaps gained operating experience, so as to prove the operability and commercial viability of the process and reduce the technical risks of the licensee. As a third possibility, a firm may choose to negotiate cross-licensing agreements with other firms, simply because its own patents do not cover all the items that are needed. This is common, for example, for computers or other electronic capital goods (Freeman 1965). Such products are in fact complex systems of interdependent parts, and some of the parts may be impossible to make satisfactorily without access to other people's patents. As a result few firms can operate solely on the strength of their own R & D.

However, although licensing agreements may be fairly common, a firm would normally be unwise to rely wholly on licensing for access to the most recent technology, especially in the science-based industries. There are two main reasons for this. First, a firm which does no research may find it difficult to obtain the licences it requires on favorable terms. It has nothing to offer except cash, whereas a firm that can offer significant patents of its own in return is in a much stronger bargaining position. Second, and perhaps more important, a firm will normally have to undertake significant engineering and development work of its own if it is to assess, assimilate, use and (possibly) improve upon the licensed inventions, and it may lack the technical know-how which is needed for this unless it has undertaken some prior research in the area and is familiar with the state of the art.

The possible pitfalls may be illustrated from the experience of G. and E. Bradley (a subsidiary of Joseph Lucas) which first tried to enter the market for oscilloscopes in the early 1960s. Its estimate of market size and development cost indicated that the commercial success of the project was uncertain. To avoid the development costs, it chose to accept a licence from a French firm, Ribet Desjardins. But Bradley lacked the competence to assess the technical standard of the instrument, which had only been operated by the licensor in a development version, not in full production. Technical problems were revealed as soon as Bradley attempted full-scale production, but initially they lacked the expertise needed to "de-bug" the instrument without outside assistance (Layton 1972).

8.3 R & D within the firm

R & D as a fixed outlay

For some purposes, R & D expenditure may be considered as a form of investment, adding to the stock of usable technology and to the set of marketable products available to a firm. It therefore has something in common with capital investment, which increases the firm's productive capacity, and with expenditure on sales promotion, which increases the market space accessible to the firm.

In the longer term, these expenditures may be complementary. For example, process innovations may have to be embodied in new capital equipment, whereas product innovations may require both new capacity and additional marketing effort. The complementarity is readily seen in the pharmaceutical industry. New drugs have often had a very short market life before they have been superseded by imitations or improvements, and as a result the innovators have had to aim for very rapid market penetration to ensure a quick return. Successful innovation has therefore required intensive sales promotion (see Shaw and Sutton 1976). Further, although pharmaceuticals may be an extreme case, it is by no means unique: all studies of the characteristics of successful innovators have stressed the importance of effective marketing.

In the short term, however, R & D, sales promotion, and new capacity may appear to be alternative investments competing for scarce resources. This suggests that optimizing management would allocate expenditure among the alternatives until the marginal return per unit of expenditure was the same for each alternative and simultaneously equal to the marginal cost of additional investment funds. We might therefore suppose that the R & D budget would depend upon the list of projects which had been identified and upon the financial resources available to the firm, so that changes in these items would lead to changes in the allocation of funds for R & D. However, this does not seem to be generally true in practice. Most studies have suggested that total R & D budgets are fixed *before* specific ideas or projects are identified and assessed (Kay 1978), and that while the budgets may change slowly in response to anticipated changes in the overall profitability of past innovations, they do not normally respond markedly to short-term changes in the availability of finance (for example, Elliott 1971, Branch 1974).

The overall stability may conceal changes in the nature of the work. For example, priorities may be changed to favor projects with a short payoff period in times of financial stringency, whereas at the other extreme – especially in low-technology industries where R & D may seem to be more expendable – resources may be diverted to troubleshooting in periods of high demand in an attempt to overcome bottlenecks in capacity or in the supply of materials. It is clear, however, that the aggregate R & D budgets are likely to change fairly slowly. There are several arguments which may be used to explain such behavior.

First, R & D may be simply a special case of the general arguments for strategic decision taking which were discussed in Chapter 2. Uncertainty is generally very much greater for specific research projects than it is for simple extensions to existing capacity, or marketing programs linked to existing products, and so it is very difficult to make meaningful comparisons of the marginal benefits of alternative types of investment expenditure. On the other hand, although the benefits of a single project may be very uncertain, a firm may have a pretty good idea of the total strategic benefit to be gained from a portfolio of projects that, by the law of averages, can be expected to include some successes. The estimates may be based upon past experience or on a comparison with the activities of other firms, and may well be fairly crude. For example, a firm may believe that it can maintain its competitive position by allocating three percent of its sales revenue to R & D, but could not hope to survive if the allocation fell below two percent. Nevertheless, the estimates do provide a basis for quasirational decisions on the funding of total R & D. The basis is likely to be strongest for large organizations in science-based industries. For these firms, innovation has become an integral feature of corporate planning. On the other hand, smaller firms are more likely to be forced to adopt "bottom-up" planning, based upon the prior identification of individual projects, because each project has a much greater impact on the success or failure of the firm as a whole (Kay, 1976).

A second reason why firms will normally seek to change R & D funding fairly slowly is the high cost of rapid change. A research group must work as a team, or as a series of independent teams, and this means that rapid staff changes inevitably disrupt efficiency. Some marginal adjustments may be made through contacts with universities or similar independent institutions, but these will normally be restricted to fairly basic research, or to specific subcomponents of a total project, and cannot normally cover all the R & D stages. Given that staff costs represent a major part of total R & D costs, the staffing constraints must limit the scope for changes in total R & D spending. Further, cuts in expenditure may be deterred by the fact that redundancies may lead to a costly loss of information to competitors.

Thirdly, especially in small and medium-sized firms, it may be difficult to make downward adjustments in R & D budgets, because indivisibilities set a threshold below which R & D expenditure becomes too small to be worthwhile. This may happen because many research costs, including the cost of special equipment, will depend upon the nature of the project rather than upon the size of the firm financing the project. Further, the risks of concentrating upon a single research project will sometimes be prohibitive, so that a viable research program will need to bear the costs of a portfolio of several projects. This raises the threshold even further. However, it is probably more significant for major advances than for incremental innovations that build on an earlier breakthrough. These increments may only need a small design department without a full commitment to scientific R & D (Freeman 1974, Rothwell 1976).

The main evidence for threshold requirements in the United Kingdom relates to pharmaceuticals and to electronic capital goods. In pharmaceuticals, it was estimated that expenditure of at least £.5 million per annum in 1970 would be required for a research-oriented firm, although a smaller sum would be worthwhile, provided that the firm was simply looking for new formulations of other people's drugs whose patents had expired. On the other hand, the £.5 million only covered a narrow range of projects, and a satisfactory portfolio with eight to ten projects might have required as much as £2 to £4 million per annum (N.E.D.O. 1972). Estimates for electronic capital goods in the early 1960s also indicated a threshold level of R & D for any firm that wished to retain its market position, although these thresholds varied between different sections of the industry. They were higher for complex products, such as computers and electronic telephone exchanges, than for relatively simple instruments, such as marine radar sets and spectrum analyzers (Freeman 1965). Clearly, it would be wrong to assume that the thresholds are equally significant in all industries, or for all firms in the same industry, but they may well constrain those firms which seek to maintain a significant role in technologically progressive industries.

We may therefore identify three reasons (uncertainty, adjustment costs, and indivisibilities) that explain why research budgets may change relatively slowly, even though managers might wish to divert resources to expand capacity in periods of high demand, or to increase sales promotion in periods of depressed demand, in a search for more immediate profits. From time to time, this stability may mean that the firm takes on projects of doubtful worth in order to keep its research team together as an ongoing unit. If no other projects can be found, and the total budget is fixed, such projects may be justified in the short term because they involve a low opportunity cost. In the longer term, however, the low opportunity cost suggests a failure of strategic planning – either the R & D department has been allowed to grow too big, or its scope has become too narrow. For this reason, it is sometimes suggested that it may be easier to discover profitable research projects in firms that are already diversified, or at least have a clear policy in favor of diversification, provided that this does not lead to the dissipation of research effort between too many competing projects (Nelson 1959). There is, however, no general statistical evidence to indicate that the productivity of R & D is enhanced by diversification, although firms whose main base is in low-technology industries may be able to increase their research productivity by diversifying into other industries which are technically more progressive (Scherer 1965, Johannisson and Lindstrom 1971).

The allocation of R & D expenditure

In very small firms, the allocation of R & D resources to projects raises few management problems and will normally reflect the perception and personal interests of a single person or of a small group. Project selection will owe more to technical flair and less to market appraisal than it does in large firms (Langrish et al 1972, p. 81), possibly because a detailed appraisal seems to be prohibitively expensive. As a result, the small firms may face greater commercial risks, but meantime the small size of the organization and the personal commitment of the executives should help the technical progress of the project.

By contrast, larger firms may identify a wider range of opportunities and must be prepared to devote more time and effort to the initial selection and subsequent control of projects. For one thing, the organization's skills are likely to be diffused among a number of different departments (such as engineering, R & D, marketing, and finance) each of which has its own subobjectives and priorities. This makes coordination more difficult and may force the top management to set up interdepartmental task forces, or project teams, for each project, so as to pull together the skills of all relevant departments, ensure that each is identified with the project, and that all work together to further its progress (see, for example, Horwitch and Prahalad 1976).

Larger organizations will also need more complex selection procedures and must find some method both to compare projects in different business areas and to ensure that the project portfolio has a reasonable balance of general exploratory research. They must evaluate major or minor projects in support of existing business and projects designed to develop new business areas for future development. Numerous attempts have been made to provide formal, quantitative models for project selection, but these are never fully comprehensive. They are inherently unsatisfactory when dealing with intangible characteristics, such as the manager's experience in controlling different types of project, or the strategic balance of the total program. Taken together with the pervasive problems of uncertainty, these necessarily restrict the scope for quantitative analysis. As a result, the models are never used to provide anything more than a starting point for further qualitative discussions, and there have been several cases where quantitative models have been rejected after an early period of experimentation (for example, Allen 1970). In some cases, this may reflect the managers' reluctance to use formal techniques that are only imperfectly understood, and the acceptance or rejection of the models may depend upon the attitudes and training of one or two key personnel. However Baker and Freeland (1975, p. 1173) have identified two more common reasons for a cautious approach.

First, the existing models are incomplete in the sense that they do not include all the important, relevant aspects of the R. and D. environment. As a result, the manager is forced to adjust the recommended allocations in order to account for the often numerous environmental conditions not included in the model. The second reason is that the decision problem is characterised by multiple criteria, many of which are not easily quantified. The typical approach is to quantify preferences or subjective estimates of benefit with methodologies which are far from satisfactory. As a result, managers are highly skeptical of the validity of the estimates and of the subsequent allocation recommendations.

It therefore seems that managers typically reject mechanistic selection procedures. But they must still make a selection, and that will generally be based upon some estimate of the worth of different projects. In a study of the portfolio selected by one of the largest U.S. firms, Mansfield found that the expected profitability of alternative projects explained about half of the allocation of funds. As other major influences, he cited a preference for safe rather than risky projects, a predilection for projects satisfying scientific or technical as well as commercial interests, and a readiness to respond to persuasion or pressure from operating divisions or project advocates within the R & D department (Mansfield 1968, Chap. 3).

Some of these influences may seem at first to be irrational, and to have no place in a businesslike assessment. However, it would be wrong to dismiss them in this way. Pressure from operating divisions may be a good guide to the perceived needs of those divisions and so indicate their active support for a project: Mansfield and Wagner (1975) confirmed that a project was more likely to progress beyond the test market or pilot-plant stage to full commercialization if it was started to meet specific needs which were first identified outside the R & D department. Further, as was argued in Chapter 2, the nature of the total portfolio of projects may be a key factor in attracting or retaining research staff or line managers. In the extreme, a research manager who refused to admit the relevance of scientific curiosity for project selection might find that he had no research staff to manage. One possible way of trying to deal with the problem of intangibles is considered briefly in 8.6 below.

The cost of R & D projects

One United States study of a sample of firms in the chemical, electronic, and machinery industries has provided a breakdown of the total costs for completely new product innovations, allocated to six stages of the innovation process (Mansfield et al 1971, Table 6.2). In round figures the average share of total costs taken by each stage was (i) applied research, ten percent; (ii) preparation of product specifications, seven and one-half percent; (iii) prototype or pilot-plant development work, thirty percent; (iv) tooling and provision of manufacturing facilities, thirty-five percent; (v) manufacturing start-up, ten percent; (vi) marketing start-up, seven and one-half percent. These averages conceal wide variations even within the same industry. Further, they understate the true significance of R & D costs, because they do not include the costs of uncompleted projects that do not survive beyond the second or third stage. There are also significant differences between industries. In the chemical industry, work on applied research and on the preparation of product specifications is relatively important, and these two stages account for thirty percent of total innovation costs, on average. By contrast, in machinery and electronics, stages (i) and (ii) typically account for less than ten percent of costs, whereas over forty percent can be absorbed on prototypes and pilot plants. Additional data for a small sample of chemical firms suggest that the share taken by R & D (stages (i), (ii) and (iii)) will be greater for more significant innovations, but may be reduced as a result of learning-by-doing if the research staff have had prior experience of handling similar problems (Mansfield and Rapoport 1975).

In total, R & D costs are likely to be higher for more complex projects that involve a number of interrelated steps, and for projects which seek a significant advance beyond the existing state of the art. Further, when large and small firms attempt similar projects, the costs are often higher in larger firms (Cooper 1964), partly because they can afford to look at a wider range of alternative solutions, whereas smaller firms are forced to gamble on the occasional shortcut; and partly because of the more complicated control procedures that they require. However, the level of costs for a given project may also reflect the development strategy chosen by the firm, in the same way that manufacturing costs will be affected by the choice of technique. For R & D projects, there are two major choices to be made. These involve (i) the time period and (ii) the use of parallel projects.

The time period.   Innovation projects generally take a significant time, which may extend for several years. Any attempt to accelerate the process and shorten the total time period is likely to increase the total costs of the project. The reasons for this have been summarized by Scherer (1970, pp. 366–7) as follows:

"Accelerating the pace of development is costly because errors are made when one overlaps development stages instead of waiting for the information early experiments supply, because it may be necessary to support parallel experimental approaches to hedge against uncertainty, and because of conventional diminishing returns in the application of additional scientific and engineering manpower to a given technical assignment."

Estimates collected by Mansfield et al (1971) suggested that it may be more costly to speed up projects which attempt relatively large advances in the state of the art.

However, it is also possible for a project to be undertaken too slowly. Projects which are given a very low priority may be starved of resources needed for effective work, and may also suffer because of a lack of commitment by the staff concerned. Such projects may ultimately prove to be unnecessarily expensive.

Parallel projects. At the start of a project, it may be very difficult to make reliable predictions of its outcome. In some cases, it may be best to delay the start and collect more information, so as to improve the forecasts. But in other cases, it will be necessary to start immediately, either because competitive pressure makes delay intolerable, or because there is no other way to obtain the necessary information. In these uncertain conditions, it may be very difficult to choose between alternative product specifications or alternative production methods, and it may be appropriate to follow several alternatives in parallel until the research has made enough progress to allow a more confident choice of a single alternative (see, for example, Nelson 1961).

Parallel development, therefore, allows a firm to avoid premature commitment to a single route that could eventually prove to be a dead end. It may save time, because it reduces the risk that the work will have to be started again from scratch. It may also save money if some of the setup costs have to be repeated whenever the alternatives are followed sequentially. The savings are most likely to be realized when the alternatives are sufficiently distinct to allow a clear choice to be made as soon as specific uncertainties have been reduced or eliminated, and when the first stages of the development work can be undertaken at relatively low cost.

However, the case for parallel projects presupposes that the targets are already well defined, so that the decision problem becomes a simple choice between comparable alternatives. The case is very much weaker if the firm is operating in an unfamiliar area, because it may then have to undertake further analysis or research before it can identify the criteria which it should use for choosing between alternative projects. When this happens, it seems that a high priority should be given to developing one plausible alternative for an early test in a relevant environment, so that the project targets can be refined as soon as possible (Abernathy and Goodman 1972).

Uncertainty and the probability of success

Although firms can influence project costs by their choice of development strategy, they generally underestimate both the cost of the projects and the time needed to complete them (Mansfield et al 1971, Norris 1971). The cost estimates are often as low as forty to sixty percent of the actual costs, especially for the more ambitious projects that lie outside the estimator's previous experience. At the same time, however, it seems that most firms concentrate their R & D on projects which depend upon very small advances in the state of the art and have a high probability of technical success. Further, when a project does fail to reach its technical objectives, this is rarely due to technical problems alone. In most cases, the failure can be attributed to other causes: Either the project is stopped before completion because its commercial prospects are found to be unattractive (Mansfield et al 1971) or changes in priorities require a reallocation that leaves some projects starved of resources (Mansfield 1968, Wilkes and Norris 1972).

It seems, therefore, that the technical uncertainties involved in most industrial R & D are fairly small, and that firms are usually capable of finding technical solutions for most of the problems they choose to tackle. The projects are much more likely to fail for commercial reasons. One United States study suggested that while the majority of projects may achieve their technical objectives, only just over half of these "successful" projects are used commercially, and of those that are used, as many as sixty percent fail to give a return large enough to cover the opportunity cost of the resources used for their development (Mansfield et al 1971). However, the study also suggested that many of the projects fail to give an economic return simply because they offer no significant advances over existing alternatives. It seems that there may be a trade-off between the probabilities of technical and commercial success, and the market may reward the greater risk taken or the greater skill required to achieve more significant advances, provided that these are related to the needs of potential users.

A number of attempts have been made to identify the sources of success for the more profitable innovations, and for the more successful innovators. (A convenient summary of the main results of nine studies is given by Rothwell 1977. See also Rubenstein et al 1976). It is clear that there is no panacea. Success depends on a blend of many factors, which sometimes includes more than a reasonable share of good luck. Nevertheless it is possible to identify a number of points which seem to be more important than the rest.

First, all studies emphasize that the chances of success can usually be increased by taking care to relate the project to the needs of the final user, rather than to the technical interests of the innovator. The results have been summarized as follows.

The majority of *successful* innovations (on average, about 75 percent of successful innovations) arise in response to the recognition of a need of one sort or another (need-pull) as opposed to the recognition of a new technical potential (technology- push). In those cases where a new technical potential does become available first (which is more often the case with the technically more radical innovations) then successful innovators determine that a need exists before they proceed with the project and take great pains to determine precise user needs and to interpret them in the design of the new product or equipment. Failure is associated with the "we know best" attitude, which is fairly common among technical inventors, who often fail to see the need to consult potential users concerning their invention. A frequent consequence of this is the production of an innovation which, while being "technically nice," and while satisfying the ego of its inventor, has little to offer the user and so becomes a commercial failure. (Rothwell 1977, p. 201)

An example of success may be taken from Dow Chemical's early marketing program for their brand of polystyrene (Styron). The program included setting up a product-evaluation committee to check that Styron was appropriate for each application proposed by users, and to advise on the right chemical formulation for each use. Dow also undertook to develop different formulations to meet special uses. As a result of this integration of marketing and technical service, Dow established a commanding position in the market (Boyd 1968).

Second, the innovation studies have identified a number of organizational features which help to achieve success. Frequently, it seems that misdirected effort could have been saved if individual projects had been subjected to an independent appraisal at a fairly early stage. This should be done before too much has been spent on the project, and before it gathers the organizational momentum which makes ongoing projects increasingly difficult to stop, mainly because people begin to stake their reputations, and perhaps their careers, on a successful outcome. Even if the appraisal confirms that the project should continue, it may have helped to ensure that the problems and objectives have been specified correctly, and thus offset any risk of ivory-towered detachment in the research department. This risk can be further reduced if the management establishes a clear strategy and concentrates on projects which contribute to its objectives. The concentration cannot be total, partly because some projects are needed to investigate the technical and commercial characteristics of new product areas before the firm can define its strategic objectives, and partly because an R & D department can, and should, help to provide ideas to stimulate a periodic reappraisal of strategy. Nevertheless it is clear that a research project that is completely divorced from the established strategy is unlikely to be carried through to commercialization.

The innovation studies also stress the importance of internal cooperation between the R & D staff and the operating staff of the firm. In particular, cooperation with production and marketing personnel is needed to ensure that product innovations can be manufactured to the quality standards required by customers, or that process innovations are compatible with other facilities and can be operated on the shop floor by existing employees without excessive retraining. Even if the R & D staff have already got it right, so that the cooperation does not change the technical specifications, it may make the results more acceptable to the operating departments and reduce the not-invented-here bias against new ideas.

Frequently it is found that the benefits of an innovation are self-evident to people who have been working on the project from the outset, but are invisible to anyone who is presented with it as a fait accompli. The possible consequences were identified by Mansfield and Wagner (1975). Interviews with R & D *and* operating executives in eighteen U.S. firms suggested that the overall probability of commercial success might have been fifty percent greater than it was (that is, 0.5 rather than 0.32 for these firms) if the projects had been appreciated fully, and exploited correctly, by the production and marketing departments.

Clearly the chances of successful innovation can be influenced by the policies and characteristics of the innovating firm. But no firm is an island, and success must also reflect the reactions of competitors and the actions of customers. These responses will be considered in the following sections.

8.4 Innovation and competition

Rivalry and the technological imperative

It is commonly accepted that rivalry in oligopolistic markets will inhibit price competition, because firms believe that any immediate advantage gained by price cutting will be quickly reversed as competitors retaliate. At the same time, firms may divert their attention to product differentiation, advertising, or innovation partly because these activities create assets which are less vulnerable to immediate attack, and partly because the many alternative forms of nonprice competition make it more difficult to find a basis for the tacit collusion that helps to restrain price competition.

The pressures on firms are sometimes characterized by reference to what is known as the "prisoner's dilemma" (see, for example, Sherman 1972). The name arises by analogy with the drama of police interrogation, in which a prisoner or suspect may know that there is no case to be made against him, provided that he says nothing and his accomplices do the same; and yet at the same time, he may have little faith in his accomplices, and may believe that if anyone is going to "crack" and confess, it might as well be he, because he may possibly be treated more leniently as a result. A similar dilemma may face a firm that is trying to decide how much effort to devote to innovation. It could adopt a fairly leisurely pace if it could get a guarantee against rival innovations. Innovation might still be profitable; but if it did nothing, it would still be no worse off than it was before. By contrast, if the firm believes that its rivals are about to innovate, it may feel some pressure to step up its own efforts, so as to defend its existing market or to attempt a preemptive strike in a new business area. The incentive to do so will clearly be greater if delay is likely to lead to a permanent loss of market potential, but this depends upon the strength and success of its competitor's actions, and neither of these can be known with any real precision.

Some of the consequences may be illustrated by using a model developed by Scherer (1967, 1970). An immediate increase in the pace of innovation could be achieved either by increasing the number of projects that are started, or by accelerating the progress of existing projects. Scherer's model concentrates on the second alternative and assumes that the firm wishes to adjust the development time, so as to maximize the present value of expected profits. We have seen that accelerated development will usually increase the total costs of a project. Further, the limited statistical evidence in this area suggests that the elasticity of total cost with respect to development time increases as the time is reduced, so that the marginal cost of accelerating the project also increases (Mansfield et al 1971). The project cost function is therefore convex to the origin, as in Figure 7.

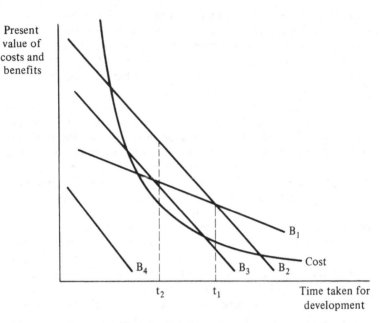

Figure 7. Project costs and benefits

The present value of the expected benefits will also vary with the expected development time. Clearly a project may be completed too soon if its profitability depends upon the prices or qualities of substitutes or complements which are slowly changing in the project's favor. In general, however, the project is likely to give a higher present value if the benefits can be realized more quickly, provided that this can be done without impairing its quality. The typical benefit/time trade-off may therefore be represented by a curve such as B_1 in Figure 7. A firm that wishes to maximize profitability will select the development time that offers the greatest margin between benefits and costs. Given the shape of the curves, this will occur when the marginal cost of reducing the development time equals the marginal benefit obtained by earlier commercialization. In Figure 7, this occurs when the total cost and benefit curves have the same slope, at development time t_1 for benefit curve B_1. Clearly the optimum time may vary if the shape or position of the benefit function changes. It will fall if there is an increase in the marginal benefit to be gained by accelerating development. This is represented in Figure 7 as a shift from B_1 to B_2 and a reduction in the development time from t_1 to t_2. Parallel shifts of B_2 toward the origin imply a lower total benefit but leave the development time unchanged, provided that the project remains profitable. Thus, curves B_2 and B_3 produce the same development time (t_2) because the marginal benefit at t_2 is the same in each case, but if the curve is shifted even further (say, to B_4), there is no development time for which benefits exceed costs, and the project would be dropped altogether.

It is therefore important to know how rivalry affects a firm's view of the benefits of innovation. There are no inevitable results, but the following suggestions seem to be the most probable. First, increased rivalry may mean that any delay will increase the risk of losing out to rival innovators. The firm may be able to rely on rapid imitation (see below), but otherwise the risk will encourage it to accelerate its own innovations. In terms of Figure 7, one effect of rivalry is to increase the elasticity of the benefits curve (say, from B_1 to B_2) and shorten the optimum development time. At the same time, however, the increased rivalry may mean that the firm must expect a smaller market and/or a shorter market life for its innovations, and so must anticipate a smaller total benefit. The result then depends upon the extent of this reduction. It will not alter the strategy provided that the project remains profitable, but a project will be abandoned if the benefits drop so far that they no longer cover the development costs. The net effect of increased rivalry would therefore depend upon a balance between two opposing changes: marginal projects may be abandoned, but the remaining projects will be developed more quickly.

The analysis therefore suggests that a firm should be prepared to adjust its development strategy in response to the rivalry encountered in each market. But it does not say how the rivalry is to be identified. Industrial economists generally stress the size distribution of firms in each market and the significance of any barriers to entry, but for innovative rivalry it may be necessary to look for alternative structural features (Kamien and Schwartz 1976) and especially (i) the technological base of the industry and (ii) the degree of product differentiation which can be achieved.

The technological base. Innovative rivalry is likely to be greater in industries which offer a rich base for innovation. In such industries the threat of innovation by rivals is more immediately credible, especially if earlier experience has shown that apparently monopolistic positions can be undermined rapidly by successful innovation.

This possibility has some support from empirical studies. Grabowski and Baxter (1973, p. 233) indicated that "as the decision-making environment shifts to one in which R. and D. becomes more important as a competitive weapon, the pressures and incentives for firms to react strongly to competitors' actions correspondingly increase." Similarly Scherer (1965) found that firms in high-technology industries tended to have very similar innovative intensities (measured as patents per billion dollars of sales revenue), whereas the intensity varied much more widely between firms in low-technology industries.

A further example is provided by the early post–World War II history of the pharmaceutical industry, especially in the United States. The introduction of penicillin and streptomycin in the early- and mid-1940s had a marked destabilizing effect on the structure of the industry. Licences were available for the manufacture of the two products, and the rapid entry which followed helped to encourage price reductions and undermined the position of the established market leaders. A rapid increase in research activity followed as firms sought new drugs that would be protected by patents and thus give some degree of monopolistic control (Comanor 1964). But it seems that some firms initially saw this as a temporary expedient: as soon as they discovered a patentable product with some market potential, they tried to cut back on their research (Costello 1968). They only recognized the need for continued innovation when it became clear that a single patent could not give a lasting monopoly, so long as competitors were actively searching for similar protection in a fruitful scientific area.

Product differentiation.   The type and, possibly, the amount of innovation will also be affected by the scope for product differentiation. Research is strongly motivated by the search for new or improved products. In a much-quoted survey by McGraw-Hill, which was undertaken in the United States in the early 1960s, eighty-seven percent of the responding firms said that the main purpose of their R & D was to improve existing products or to develop new products, whereas only thirteen percent emphasized the development of new processes for internal use in the manufacture of existing products (see, for example, Mansfield et al 1971, p.5). Frequently, as in the early development of the aluminum industry, the pace of process improvements may be set by the plant and equipment suppliers, for whom the new processes appear as new products (Peck 1961). The bias appears to reflect a search for the quasimonopolistic advantages of product differentiation. Exceptions can be found in the manufacture of established basic materials, which are sold in large volumes for a variety of end uses. The specifications of these products change slowly, if at all, and small savings in unit costs can have a large and lasting effect on profitability. But, in many cases, the benefits will be less secure and will disappear altogether if the market for the output is eliminated by someone else's product innovation.

This choice of particular types of innovation will also influence a firm's total innovative activity, because product differentiation can be established more easily by technical change in some industries than in others. Comanor (1967) has provided some empirical support for this view. He found that R & D expenditure was relatively high for more complex products like industrial machinery or consumer durables, where product differentiation is based primarily upon physical characteristics. By contrast it was relatively low both for standardized producer goods like pulp and paper, and consumer goods like foodstuffs, whose heterogeneity may be caused by advertising or image differentiation rather than by physical differences in product specification.

The residual effect of market concentration. The previous paragraphs suggest that if an industry offers the right conditions, innovative rivalry can develop regardless of the initial level of concentration. In such circumstances, it is clearly unwise for any firm to try to determine its own innovation strategy without also considering the incentives which may appeal to actual or potential competitors. On the other hand, a different situation may exist in the low-technology industries. Here the results are more likely to support the Schumpeterian view that concentration encourages innovation (Schumpeter 1942). Profitable innovations may be more difficult to find, but the profitability of individual projects may be higher if the market leaders can provide resources at relatively low opportunity cost and can expect further monopoly profits in return. In terms of Figure 7, concentration may shift the benefits curve from B_4 to B_1. That is, though it will allow innovation to proceed at a fairly leisurely pace, it may help to ensure that at least some profitable projects can be found in spite of the unproductive technology.

Innovation versus imitation

So far, we have assumed that firms would respond to rivalry by adopting an offensive strategy, and seeking to launch their innovations before their rivals, so as to preempt a part of the potential market. This strategy is often appropriate, but even in high-technology industries, the firms may sometimes be free to choose an imitative strategy, or what Baldwin and Childs (1969), following an unnamed businessman in an unnamed industry, have called the "fast second" strategy. This strategy allows other firms to innovate first in the belief that any worthwhile innovations can be copied and, perhaps, improved upon before there has been any costly loss of sales and before customers have developed a strong loyalty for the new product.

An imitative strategy will be impossible if the innovation is protected by strong patents, although as we have seen, competition-proof patents are rare. It may also be difficult if innovations occur in a continual stream and participation in one innovation is necessary to acquire the knowledge or skills needed for the next. Advocates of the imitation strategy therefore assume that the essential features of the design and manufacturing process can be discovered by analysis or reverse engineering of the competitor's product, and that the imitator can readily make the necessary adjustments to his production processes.

Given that an imitative strategy is feasible, it may be less costly than offensive innovation for several reasons. First, the imitator faces less uncertainty. He will still need to undertake some development, so as to refine his own version of the product and to define a workable manufacturing process, but he will be able to concentrate on a smaller portfolio of projects without an unacceptable increase in risk. Second, he may be able to learn from the innovator's mistakes. By basing his development upon the analysis of a proven product, he should be able to avoid blind alleys and so reduce development costs. Third, if the innovator has already "sold" the benefits of the innovation to potential users, the imitator may face less customer resistance with his follow-up product. These advantages all help to reduce the imitator's costs, and he may then choose to take a higher profit margin, to undercut the innovator's price, or to devote some additional effort to developing a superior product.

Taken to its "illogical" conclusion, this argument might suggest that no firm should innovate, but that all should wait for the others to act first, like a tennis match in which no one is willing to serve. In practice, however, this result is highly improbable, because the different strategies have different requirements, which may be met more easily by some firms than by others (see Baldwin and Childs 1969, Freeman 1974). As with any other strategic decision, each firm should first try to assess its own strengths and weaknesses relative to those requirements, before it decides on its strategy. It must also ensure that the chosen strategy is appropriate for its industrial environment. We have seen that cross-licensing agreements between firms are often important, especially in high-technology industries, and in such cases a firm which relied solely on an imitative strategy might eventually find itself excluded from the cooperative group of patent swappers.

An offensive strategy must be based on an ability to identify market needs and to discover new ways of meeting them. Some of the ideas may be generated internally, but others must be imported either by recruiting new staff or by contact with other technical and commercial organizations. Studies of successful innovations inevitably stress the importance of good external contacts, and of deliberate attempts to survey externally generated ideas. But the offensive firm must also be able to convert these ideas into marketable products and usable processes. It must have the facilities and skills to design, build, and test prototypes or pilot plants; it must be able to cope with the problems of scale-up or transition from pilot plant to full-scale operation; and it must have the ability to market a new product, simultaneously educating customers in the new features and reassuring them against the risks of newness. An offensive strategy must therefore be based on good contacts, a good marketing organization, and experience or flair in handling the unforeseen problems of development.

By contrast, an imitative strategy will be built on skills in production engineering and design rather than original R & D. Lead times can be reduced if the imitator can maintain a flexible production system, which can be adapted for new products without any loss of quality. Further, the risk of being left behind by the innovator will be less if the imitator has more extensive distribution facilities and has built a reputation for reliable service that will encourage customers to return from the innovator as soon as the imitator offers a comparable product.

These last points suggest that an imitative strategy may seem safer for established market leaders, who can rely on their contacts and reputation both to delay the innovator's advance and to speed their subsequent retaliation. These firms may also have a stronger incentive to play the waiting game, especially if the innovative products are expected to displace the existing products. Firms with no more than a moderate share of the existing market may gain significantly from an offensive strategy that enables them to gain sales from the market leaders, whereas the same innovation by the market leaders would simply enable them to take sales away from themselves. The leaders are therefore less likely to gain from an offensive strategy unless they can hope for an increase in the total market demand and/or an increase in profit margins. On the other hand, if others innovate, the leaders have a strong incentive to imitate in an attempt to protect their existing sales.

An example is provided by the dry-cleaning industry in the United Kingdom in the 1960s (Shaw 1973, Shaw and Sutton 1976). The nature of the industry was transformed when innovations allowed the earlier centralized dry-cleaning "factories" to be replaced by self-contained shops, where dry cleaning could be done on the premises. The market leaders had their capital tied up in factories and could see no immediate gain for themselves from the innovation. However, the innovations were adopted rapidly by new entrants, and eventually the leaders were forced to follow in order to protect themselves. Similar examples seem to have arisen in the motor industry. In this case, the larger firms compete in product design and have emphasized the development of mass-production assembly. But many of the developments which have involved substantial changes in the technical specifications of cars have been pioneered by smaller firms, who stood to gain more from increased market penetration. These innovations include front-wheel drive, automatic transmission, and power steering.

In many cases, however, especially in large firms, an appropriate strategy may involve a mix of offensive innovation in some areas and imitation in others: plausibly, a firm might adopt an offensive strategy in the areas which have been given priority in its strategic plan, while keeping a watching brief in other areas. Even when a firm plans an offensive strategy, the unpredictability of competitors' actions may mean that it should be prepared to adopt an imitative strategy at short notice. Similarly, in practice, a number of firms seeking offensive strategies may all produce similar innovations at about the same time and may then gradually seek to adjust their own innovations to incorporate the best features of the alternatives. Conversely, a firm which plans an imitative strategy in some area may still need to do some preparatory R & D if it is to keep up to date in the relevant area. For example, Layton (1972) reported that although General Motors could then see no commercial alternative to the present petrol- or diesel-fueled internal-combustion engine for use in cars and trucks (with the possible exception of the gas turbine engine for heavy trucks) it was continuing protective research into a wide range of alternatives, including the Stirling and Wankel engines, electric and steam engines.

8.5 Innovation and customers

We have stressed repeatedly that successful innovation requires close attention to user needs and marketing. Both market research and marketing are technical subjects which lie beyond the scope of this book. However, an understanding of innovation strategy is incomplete without some knowledge of the process by which innovations are adopted by potential users. The major characteristics of this process have been identified in a number of diffusion studies, which will be summarized in this section.

Diffusion may be measured by the cumulative number of adopters or the cumulative proportion of all potential adopters who have actually adopted the innovation by a specified date. Alternatively, for process innovations, it may be measured by the share of total production capacity taken by the new process. It is commonly represented by a diffusion curve which records the way in which the level of diffusion changes over time. Empirical studies generally identify S-shaped diffusion curves, of which a stylized example is given in Figure 8a. The curve is superficially similar to the product life cycle (see Figure 2), but the differences are important, especially for durable goods. The life cycle records annual sales, not cumulative values. A user who buys an innovative durable good in one time period is still recorded as an adopter in later time periods (unless he abandons the innovation after an early experiment) but will make no further contribution to the sales recorded in the product life cycle until he replaces or adds to his original purchase. As a result, annual sales of durable goods may reach a peak during the

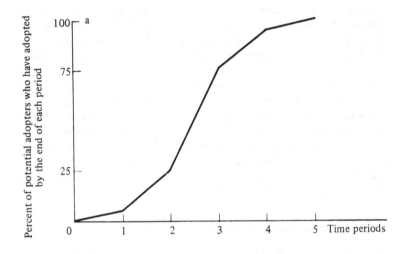

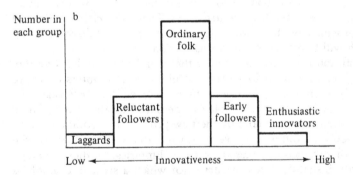

Figure 8. Stylized diffusion curve and stylized distribution of innovativeness

intermediate phase of very rapid diffusion, and thereafter the life cycle will decline and become increasingly dependent on replacement sales, while diffusion continues towards its maximum level.

Significant differences have been observed between the diffusion rates of different innovations. One U.S. study of the diffusion of twelve innovations in four industries (coal, iron and steel, brewing, and railroads) showed that although on average it took 7.8 years before half the relevant firms had introduced each innovation, the time for different innovations varied from 0.9 years to 15 years (Mansfield 1968). A similar range may be found for a single innovation between different countries (Nabseth and Ray 1974) or between different user industries, as with the use of numerically controlled machine tools by different sections of the engineering industry (Romeo 1975). Further, although it is convenient to talk of an S-shaped diffusion curve for all innovations, it seems that with more rapid diffusion the sharp "nose" of the diffusion curve may almost disappear (although the upper tail may be elongated). This is most likely to happen when the innovations are technologically simple and represent minor modifications of earlier breakthroughs (Robertson 1971, Davies 1976), possibly because they are then easier for the user to understand and are more compatible with his established operating procedures or life style.

The general S-shape may well reflect psychological or social, rather than economic factors. For example, assume that we can measure an individual's "innovativeness" or readiness to accept new ideas, and that (as with several other psychological characteristics) innovativeness is distributed normally throughout the population of potential users of an innovation (see Rogers 1962, Rogers and Shoemaker 1971). Even if we had no further information, this normal distribution would lead us to expect an S-shaped diffusion curve. This is easily seen if we take the distribution of innovativeness shown in Figure 8b as a very rough approximation to a normal distribution. The diffusion curve in Figure 8a is derived from Figure 8b on the assumption that the innovation is adopted by the five percent of enthusiastic innovators in period 1; by the twenty percent of early followers in period 2; by the fifty percent of ordinary folk in period 3; by the twenty percent of reluctant followers in period 4; and by the five percent of laggards in period 5.

Alternatively, diffusion curves may be explained by epidemic models similar to those used to explain the spread of disease (for mathematical treatment, see Mansfield 1968 or Davies 1976). The simplest approach is to assume that knowledge of the innovation is spread by word of mouth, and that one person can contact two others during any one time period. At the end of the first period, the innovator will have contacted two people. Each of these, plus the innovator, can contact two more during the second time period, giving six new contacts and a cumulative total of nine knowledgeable people. By the end of the third time period, the cumulative total may have increased to twenty-seven, and it will continue to increase at an approximately geometric rate for some time. But this cannot be sustained. The rate at which nonadopters are contacted must eventually decline, because an increasing proportion of the contacts will be with people who have already heard of the innovation.

Either of these alternatives (the distribution of innovativeness or the epidemic model) can therefore be used to give a simple explanation of the S-shape of diffusion curves. But on their own, these explanations are not very fruitful. They do little to explain the differences observed between different innovations. If we are to go further, we need to know how to distinguish between the early innovators and the laggards; to explain why the ordinary folk will follow the innovators more quickly in some cases than in others; or to say how much information is needed before those who already know of the existence of an innovation become convinced that it is worthwhile. Some progress can be made by looking in more detail at (*a*) the characteristics of potential adopters; (*b*) the attributes of the innovations themselves; and (*c*) the characteristics of the supplying firm.

The characteristics of potential adopters

All diffusion studies stress the importance of the relative advantage of the new in relation to the old: The greater is the advantage, the more rapid is the diffusion. The advantage will generally be easier to measure for producer goods, because the profitability or input saving of new processes can be measured more easily than (say) differences in the perceived qualities of consumer goods. However, in all cases it is the potential user's estimate of benefit which is important, not a quasiobjective estimate made by the supplier, or even by an impartial observer. The relevant estimates will therefore vary with the characteristics of different users. In part they will depend upon the quality of the available information, which is usually sparse and sometimes contradictory.

But even if there were no uncertainty, different adopters would still produce different estimates, because they would not all have the same strategic priorities; they would not all face the same costs when changing from a variety of existing methods to make use of the innovation; and they would not all have the same ability to exploit the innovation. The reasons for these differences may be discussed conveniently under four subheadings: (i) pressures of demand and competition; (ii) input supply conditions; (iii) complementarity with other products or processes; and (iv) attitudes of individual decision takers. The first two of these are fairly specific to the adoption of process innovations by industrial users, whereas the third and fourth relate to both industrial and private users.

Pressure of demand and competition. Among the major factors affecting a firm's assessment of a process innovation will be the present and expected future demand for its output, and its existing investment plans. New processes will be assessed more favorably if the firm was already planning to expand capacity or to replace existing facilities. In these cases, the new and the old technique can be compared as alternative investments on equal terms. But if the existing capacity is believed to be adequate and operable, the full cost of installing the new process must be covered by any subsequent saving in operating costs – in the jargon of elementary textbooks, the total cost of the new process must be less than the variable cost of the old. Taken on its own, this might imply that innovations would be adopted more readily in times of high demand, but in practice this conclusion may be too simplistic. It is true that the pressure of demand may favor innovation if it encourages an increase in capacity, but otherwise the firms would be reluctant to adopt innovations which might disrupt production (say) by diverting management's attention from current operations or by forcing a reorganization of an existing plant, because any loss of output would then have a high opportunity cost. If these considerations are significant, the firm might well appraise the innovations more favorably when it has some slack capacity, provided that this is not so great as to deter all investment.

Generally, it seems that larger firms will be among the earlier adopters of an innovation, at least on an experimental basis. This is because they can more easily afford a trial adoption, and may have a wider range of markets and capital vintages, so that at any one time they are likely to have some products for which the process is appropriate and some existing capacity that is due for replacement. On the other hand it may be that some innovations are only appropriate for some scales of operation, and this would influence the assessments made by firms of different size. For example, the basic oxygen steel process was originally developed in Austria for use in small plants. Inevitably, there were delays before the technique could be scaled-up for use in larger plants, and initially diffusion took place most rapidly in countries which, like Austria, were characterized by relatively small-scale operations (Meyer and Herregat 1974).

Though larger firms may be among the earlier adopters, however, the overall rate of diffusion is generally higher in more competitive industries (Mansfield 1968). This result reflects the net balance of two opposite effects. First, early adoption may be deterred by the fear of rapid imitation. Indeed, if firms are concerned by the prospects of future competition, early adoption will appear more profitable if subsequent diffusion is seen to be checked by licensing or franchise agreements that guarantee the early adopters a more lasting competitive advantage. On the other hand, once diffusion has started, the later adopters will have to adjust their assessment of the innovation to reflect the resulting changes in input costs or product prices, and may find that they have to adopt the innovation if they are to stay solvent. This pressure is likely to be strongest for major innovations that offer significant improvements over established techniques, whereas the late followers or laggards may more easily postpone their adoption of minor innovations.

Input supply conditions. Innovations normally involve some changes in the relative importance of different inputs. Sometimes, a change in supply is necessary to make the innovation profitable. For example, in the U.S. iron and steel industry, processes for pelletizing low-grade iron ore were adopted very slowly, but their use was eventually encouraged by increasing shortages of the high-grade ore that had required less preprocessing (Gold et al 1970).

Frequently, the different potential users of an innovation face different supply conditions, which may encourage or discourage adoption. For example, the adoption of numerical control for machine tools, which uses coded instructions on cards or tapes to lead the machines through a sequence of movements or operations, was generally encouraged by increasing labor costs and shortages of specific types of skilled labor, but "the influence of the labor market on diffusion may be specific to each company, depending largely on local conditions of labor supply" (Gebhardt and Hatzold 1974). Similarly, the diffusion of the tunnel kiln for brick making has been influenced by local input supply conditions in the United Kingdom.

In the tunnel kiln, the bricks are loaded onto special wagons which travel through the firing area in the central part of the kiln. But the kiln is not suitable for bricks with a high carbon content, because this makes it more difficult to control the fire. Further, the carbon can be exploited as a fuel in some alternative processes but not in the tunnel kiln; and as a result, the saving in fuel cost that would otherwise justify the higher capital cost of the tunnel kiln may be reduced or eliminated when the kiln is used for bricks with a high carbon content, such as those made with "lower Oxford" clay, which is used extensively in the Midland regions of the United Kingdom (Lacci, Davies and Smith 1974).

Complementarity. Supplies of complementary products or processes may also affect diffusion, and the innovation must also be compatible with the users' existing standards and equipment. For consumer products, there are obvious linkages between (say) the adoption of stereophonic record players and the availability and quality of stereophonic records. Perhaps a little less obvious is the acceptance of plastic for domestic buckets and bowls. Given that plastic buckets cannot be placed on the stove to boil the weekly wash, their adoption in place of metal buckets was aided by the diffusion of domestic washing machines (McCarthy, quoted in Bradbury 1969).

For industrial-process innovations, the linkages between successive processes are often important. For example, in the iron and steel industry, the efficiency of continuous casting machines, which permit continuous rather than batch production of steel slabs and blooms, depends upon the utilization rate. The rate can be higher if liquid steel is provided regularly at fairly precise intervals, and these conditions can be met more easily in plants which use the basic oxygen process rather than the open-hearth furnaces, in which the refining time cannot be so precisely controlled (Schenk 1974).

Attitudes of individual adopters. We have already suggested that diffusion will depend upon the innovativeness of the potential adopters. Sometimes, the suppliers of the innovation can exploit this by concentrating their early marketing on the more innovative potential users, who can help to demonstrate the worth of the innovation and so help to reduce the initial uncertainty felt by the ordinary folk. Further, the enthusiastic innovators may help to refine the initial innovation, and although this could prove to be a blind alley if their needs differ from those of other users, the refinements will often help to make the innovation suitable for more widespread use.

Most published studies attempt to identify the characteristics of the early adopters expost, when the diffusion process is well under way. They are more difficult to identify ex ante, but the studies do offer a few pointers. Sometimes, the early adopters may be identified by their size or competitive status: We have seen that large firms may be among the early adopters of process innovations, but that innovations which displace existing products or facilities may appeal more strongly to potential entrants than to established market leaders. In other cases, the studies may emphasize less tangible characteristics. In agriculture, it seems that early adopters are generally younger and more cosmopolitan, in the sense that they have a wider range of external contacts, whereas the tradition-oriented laggards are typically older and lower in social status (Rogers and Shoemaker 1971). Similarly, in manufacturing industry, innovativeness may be associated with a younger, more highly educated management and with ongoing expenditure on R & D (Romeo 1975). In general, technical innovations are probably adopted more readily by the scientific than by the lay community, provided that the scientists have not tied their professional reputations to the existing methods. In the early days of computers, for example, the advantages and operating requirements could be appreciated more easily by potential adopters in scientific institutions than by the general commercial customers, who needed more training, advice, and assistance from the manufacturers (Freeman 1965).

Observable attributes of the innovation

If an innovation is to be adopted, potential users must be able to see the possible advantages. In practice, however, the estimates of benefit will often be subject to considerable doubt and uncertainty. Given that the majority of potential adopters are likely to be risk averse, this uncertainty will reduce their subjective estimates of the value of the innovation. They may then react in one of two ways. Some may postpone a decision on adoption and wait until they can get additional information to reduce their uncertainty. Frequently, this can be done simply by waiting for feedback of the results of the more adventurous early adopters, and Romeo (1975) confirms that in the United States the later adopters of numerical control of machine tools were usually able to make more accurate estimates of the potential benefits. Alternatively, if the innovation can be tried out on a relatively small scale, potential adopters may undertake relatively low-cost experiments by limiting initial adoption to only a small part of their potential use.

Very often the significance of uncertainty will vary with the character of the innovation, and will be greater for the more radical innovations, which are less well understood by adopters and less closely related to their existing operating experience. Such innovations will therefore be accepted less readily, and their diffusion will be delayed. In the United Kingdom, this has been true, for example, of more radical changes in textile machinery (Rothwell 1976) and flour milling (Hayward et al 1976). The deterrent effect will also be greater for innovations that involve heavy capital expenditure on specialized, indivisible facilities (Mansfield 1968) or, as with the larger computer systems, require significant and possibly irreversible changes in operating procedures (Sutton 1975).

Further, even if potential adopters accept current estimates of the worth of the innovation, they may be reluctant to commit themselves prematurely to a process that, though satisfactory, may be capable of considerable refinement. "The decision to undertake innovation X today may be decisively affected by the expectation that significant improvements will be introduced into X tomorrow (or by the firmly held expectation that a new substitute technology, Y, will be introduced the day after" (Rosenberg 1976, p 525). This also has implications for competitive suppliers. We have seen that rivalry among suppliers will encourage technical progress. However, we must now add that it will simultaneously discourage early adoption if potential users decide to wait for the improvements that may be made by imitators.

The same argument may apply to substitute products, whose suppliers may react to the innovation by cutting prices or increasing services and so changing its relative advantage. Their reaction will be particularly important if the innovator is diversifying into a new business area, in which customers are reluctant to break their long-standing contacts with existing suppliers. Alternatively, instead of cutting prices, the suppliers of substitute products may be provoked to accelerate their search for product improvements to protect their existing markets. This appears to have been the reaction of natural fiber producers to the inroads made by man-made fibers, for example, in the production of shirts. Initially, nylon shirts offered better easy-care properties and by about 1960 they provided generally acceptable standards of comfort. These advantages encouraged rapid penetration, but also provoked improvements in the easy-care properties of cotton or of blends of cotton and polyester, which enabled the natural fiber to recover some of the ground lost to nylon during the 1960s (Catling 1972).

The characteristics of the supplying firm

We have already seen that potential innovators pay more attention to user needs, marketing, and after-sales service. Diffusion may therefore take place more rapidly if the innovation originated from a firm that has already established good contacts with potential users and has earned a reputation for reliability. In turn, this suggests that the more successful innovations are likely to be those that are related to the firm's existing skills and experience, and so, hopefully, are most closely tied to its strategy.

This link between strategy and innovation is probably the most important single factor explaining the IBM Corporation's domination of the computer industry: IBM has supplied over sixty percent of the value of general-purpose data-processing equipment installed in the noncommunist world. It was not the first firm to enter the industry, nor was it the most technically creative, but is was able to exploit its earlier experience in the market for electromechanical tabulators and calculators. As a result, IBM had a prior understanding of the new area's marketing requirements, and of the need to develop software and service support for the commerical users. Further, for many users, a small IBM computer seemed a natural progression after their existing IBM equipment. This appreciation of the needs of the nonscientific community enabled IBM to build such a reputation that potential users were sometimes reluctant to adopt innovations introduced by other firms until they had been given the "seal of approval" that was implied when they were taken up by IBM. On the other hand, if IBM announced a new product, other firms had to be prepared to divert resources to match it if they were to stay in the hunt (Stoneman 1976). To this extent IBM may have been able to act as a technological leader, controlling, or at least influencing, the pace of technical progress in the industry, even though its technical standards are not necessarily higher than those of its competitors, in spite of its higher aggregate research expenditure.

8.6 Strategy and project assessment

Previous sections of this chapter have stressed that although innovations can be profitable, the proces by which they emerge from the welter of operating experience and research is often protracted and rarely follows a predetermined route. It therefore involves considerable risk. Sometimes, a successful outcome appears to depend on good luck rather than on skilled management, but in general it seems that the incidence of good luck is greatest in firms that focus their resources in an appropriate way and that have the know-how to exploit their luck when it arrives. Success can never be guaranteed, but the chances can generally be improved if the innovator follows a balanced program that pays attention to all relevant factors, exploiting those that are favorable and (if possible) alleviating those that are unfavorable.

Our objective in this chapter has, therefore, been to identify those factors that are most likely to be significant. We have seen that the pressures and opportunities for innovation will vary between product areas, and will depend on the needs of the environment, the stage in the product's technical life cycle, and the pressures of competition or technological rivalry in each area. Firms that operate in several areas cannot hope to impose a common pattern on them all but must identify and respond to the needs of each area. Further, although there are good reasons for arguing that a firm cannot change its total R & D budget at short notice, it must be prepared to respond to changes in the needs of different areas, and to the lessons learned from the experience of individual projects. It is clear that such projects are more likely to be completed successfully if they are well matched to the firm's existing skills and to its recognized needs and objectives, and so have the committed support of both the R & D personnel and of the relevant operating departments. Successful projects must also be matched to the needs of customers, either as a specific response to requests from users or as part of a deliberate process to ensure that a new technical idea can be made suitable for a particular end use. Further, the timing and, perhaps, the selection of projects must allow for the expected behavior of actual or potential competitors.

The variety of these influences on innovation and the uncertainty of their effect make it very difficult to establish rigorous procedures for the initial appraisal and subsequent monitoring of research projects. In particular, it is often difficult to make precise quantitative estimates of a project's worth. Some estimate must be made for those projects that are directed at specific commercial applications, if only to ensure that if everything does go right, the project can cover the opportunity cost of the resources it uses. But, in the early stages, the forecasts of costs and benefits are usually so crude that it would be unwise to base decisions solely on numerical estimates of the likely outcome.

On the other hand, the evidence suggests that an R & D portfolio is more likely to be profitable if the projects are subjected to some formal assessment at an early stage. This assessment should seek to weed out those projects that represent an obvious mismatch with the firm's chosen strategy, and those that have been supported by technical faith but must hope for commercial charity if they are to succeed. Further, for the projects that are retained, the assessment should identify the areas of existing weakness that must be researched and corrected before the innovations can fulfill their promise. The assessment should therefore attempt to make explicit the intangible factors that are not included in a quantitative appraisal, and it is commonly guided by some form of checklist, which identifies the range of problems or characteristics that should be considered.

Some writers have argued that the checklists can be used as part of a scoring system for project appraisal. In such systems, a score has to be assigned to each characteristic. For example, the characteristic "compatibility with existing distribution channels" may be given a score of 1, 2, or 3 depending on whether it is thought to be bad, indifferent, or good. Each score is then weighted to reflect the importance of the characteristic and the aggregate weighted score, expressed as a percentage of the total possible score, is taken as an index of the worth of the project (see, for example, O'Meara 1961).

The discipline needed to assign realistic scores for the many characteristics can help to identify the major strengths and weaknesses of the project, but unfortunately it is rarely possible to devise an appropriate set of weights. This is partly because the relative importance of the characteristics cannot be expressed precisely in quantitative form without a fully specified model of the process of innovation, and partly because some characteristics, such as legal requirements, may be no more than permissive, carrying an effective veto if they are "bad" but making no positive contribution to success if they are "good." For these reasons checklists are best used as guides to management appraisal rather than as formal tools.

For illustration, we shall simply note one possible system of checklists, proposed by Bradbury, Gallagher and Suckling (1973). The authors stress that their proposals are intended to complement quantitative evaluations, not replace them. Their system is based upon three checklists, which fall into two groups. The first, the viability checklist, is intended to identify problems that are likely to arise at a fairly early stage in the development and commercialization of the project. The second and third checklists, on the other hand, are intended to cover the contribution that the project makes to the firm's overall objectives and to identify the potential synergy between the project and the firm's existing activities. These checklists are therefore more obviously concerned with the long-term consequences of the project.

The viability checklist is intended to identify current problem areas that could have an adverse effect on the eventual payoff. The possible areas should be listed before the assessment is started, but the list would vary between different industries, and between firms in the same industry, and should include those factors that experience or analysis had identified as being critical for success. The list proposed by Bradbury, Gallagher, and Suckling is divided into three sections. The first relates to the manufacturing process and covers items such as raw-material procurement, effluent treatment, and process reliability. The second relates to the product and covers such items as quality, compatibility with the users' existing behavior or facilities, and ease of imitation by competitors. Finally, the third relates to the market and includes reference to sales promotion and distribution channels, among other items. In each case, it is suggested that the items should be classified as "no problem"; or as "problems" which may be, but have not yet been, solved by research; or as "threats" for which no ready solutions are apparent. No weighting system is proposed for the different items, but clearly the major "problems" help to identify the priority areas for further research, whereas a number of major "threats" could indicate that the project is simply too risky to be worthwhile.

Longer-term effects are covered by the objectives and synergy checklists. The objectives checklist is designed to record the specific contribution that the project is expected to make to the overall objectives or goals of the firm. Clearly, the list will depend upon the goals which the firm has already set as part of the process of strategy formulation, and may include (say) growth of sales, stability of cash flow, or flexibility in the face of competitive threats.

The check can still be made informally even if the firm does not have a formal statement of objectives, but there is then the danger that the objectives considered will be those that happen to be met by the project, rather than those that would be preferred by the firm.

Finally the synergy checklist is designed to identify possible instances where the firm's existing skills in general management, research, production, and marketing appear to be particularly well matched with the attributes required for successful completion and commercialization of the project. The approach is therefore very similar to the strengths-and-weaknesses analysis already discussed in Chapter 5, and as with that analysis, it is essential that the checklist should compare the firm's attributes and advantages against those of identifiable competitors. It is always possible that what appears in isolation to be a very significant advantage may be no more than the minimum necessary for survival in a competitive environment and, conversely, some relatively minor experience of a unique problem may provide the basis for a commanding lead in a new area.

A system of checklists of this type can help to ensure that the project appraisal does not overlook essential features of the project or its context. However, the checklists cannot guarantee that all the relevant factors will be covered in an uncertain world, simply because the world is uncertain. They may aid decision taking, but they cannot take the decisions. As we have argued throughout this book, the essential feature of decision taking under uncertainty is that there can be no "right" decision. The best that analysis can do is to reduce the range of ignorance and to identify the key features of each decision problem so that an informed judgment can be made. It cannot provide a substitute for judgment.

Appendix A: Myopic monopoly and joint maximization

Consider an intermediate product which is supplied only by firm B and purchased only by firm A, which uses the intermediate to produce a consumer good of which it is the only supplier. Define

q_a, q_b = number of units produced by A, B
p_a, p_b = price per unit of sales by A, B
c_a, c_b = cost per unit produced by A, B
c_a' = additional cost per unit by A to convert intermediate into final product.
P_a, P_b = profit earned by A, B

Assume

$$c_a = c_a' + p_b \tag{1}$$

c_a', c_b are constant

$$p_a = m - nq_a \quad \text{where } m, n \text{ are constant} \tag{2}$$

$$q_a = q_b$$

We shall consider only the first-order conditions for an optimum.

Case 1: Myopic monopoly

$$P_a = q_a p_a - q_a c_a \tag{3}$$

substituting (1) and (2) in (3)

$$P_a = mq_a - nq_a^2 - q_a(c_a' + p_b)$$

If the price set by firm B is taken as a parameter by firm A, then firm A will assume $dp_b/dq_a = 0$, and given that c_a' is constant by assumption, then the first-order condition for firm A to maximize profits is

$$\frac{dP_a}{dq_a} = m - 2nq_a - (c_a' + p_b) = 0 \tag{4}$$

Solving (4) for p_b gives

$$p_b = m - 2nq_a - c_a' \tag{5}$$

Given that $q_a = q_b$ by assumption, then (5) is the derived demand function facing firm B. Firm B's profit function will be

$$P_b = q_b p_b - q_b c_b \tag{6}$$

and replacing q_a by q_b in (5) and substituting the amended (5) into (6) we have

$$P_b = mq_b - 2nq_b^2 - q_b(c_a' + c_b)$$

The first-order condition for maximizing P_b is

$$\frac{dP_b}{dq_b} = m - 4nq_b - (c_a' + c_b) = 0 \tag{7}$$

Solving (7) for q_b gives

$$q_b = \frac{m - (c_a' + c_b)}{4n} \tag{8}$$

Case 2: Joint maximization

For joint profit maximization, given $q_a = q_b$, the objective is to maximize

$$P_t = P_a + P_b$$

where P_t is the joint profits of the two producers A and B. In this case, revenue comes from the sales of firm A. The total costs of the two producers is the sum of their separate production costs. Hence P_t can be written

$$P_t = R_t - C_t = q_a p_a - q_a(c_a' + c_b) \tag{9}$$

where R_t and C_t are the total revenues and costs of the two producers. The first-order condition for maximizing P_t is

$$\frac{dP_t}{dq_a} = m - 2nq_a - (c_a' + c_b) = 0 \tag{10}$$

Given that $q_a = q_b$ by assumption, solving (10) for q_a gives

$$q_a = q_b = \frac{m - (c_a' + c_b)}{2n} \tag{11}$$

Comparing the two solutions given by (8) and (11) then it is clear that q_b must be greater in Case 2 than in Case 1: that is, myopic monopoly leads to a restriction of output and a failure to maximize joint profits.

Bibliography

Aaronovitch, S., and M. C. Sawyer. 1975a. Mergers growth and concentration. *Oxford Economic Papers* 27:136–55.

1975b. *Big business.* London: Macmillan.

Abernathy, W. J., and R. A. Goodman. 1972. Strategies for development projects: an empirical study. *R & D Management* 2:125–9.

Abernathy, W. J. and K. Wayne. 1974. Limits of the learning curve. *Harvard Business Review* 52:109–19.

Adelman, M. A. 1955. Concept and statistical measurement of vertical integration. National Bureau of Economic Research, *Business concentration and price policy.* Princeton, N.J.: Princeton University Press.

1972. *The world petroleum market.* Baltimore, Md.: Johns Hopkins.

Adler, L. 1968. *Plotting marketing strategy.* London: Business Books.

Allen, J. M. 1970. A survey into the R & D evaluation and control procedures currently used in industry. *Journal of Industrial Economics,* 18:161–81.

Andrews, K. R. 1971. *The concept of corporate strategy.* Homewood, Ill.: Dow Jones–Irwin.

Ansoff, H. I. 1965. *Corporate strategy.* New York: McGraw-Hill.

1969. *Business strategy.* Harmondsworth: Penguin.

1972. Strategy as a tool for coping with change, in Taylor and Hawkins (1972), pp 3–8.

Ansoff, H. I., R. G. Brandenberg; F. E. Portner; and R. Radosevich. 1972. *Twenty years of acquisitive behaviour in America.* London: Cassell–Associated Business Programmes.

Bailey, M. N. 1972. Research and development costs and returns: the US pharmaceutical industry. *Journal of Political Economy* 80:70–85.

Baker, N., and J. Freeland. 1975. Recent advances in R & D benefit measurement and project selection methods. *Management Science (Applications)* 21:1164–75.

Baldwin, W. L., and G. L. Childs. 1969. The fast second and rivalry in research and development. *Southern Economic Journal* 36:18–24.

Baumol, W. J. 1959. *Business behaviour, value and growth.* New York: Macmillian.

Berg, T. L., and A. Shuchman. 1963. *Product strategy and management.* New York: Holt, Rinehart and Winston.

Bernhardt, I., 1977. Vertical integration and demand variability. *Journal of Industrial Economics* 25:213–29.

Berry, C. H. 1975. *Corporate growth and diversification.* Princeton, N.J.: Princeton University Press.

Birley, S. 1976. Acquisition strategy or acquisition anarchy? *Journal of General Management* 3:67–73.

Blair, J. M. 1972. *Economic concentration.* New York: Harcourt Brace Jovanovich.

Boyd, H. W. 1968. Concentration, in Adler (1968).

Boyle, S. E. 1974. US v IT&T – incompetence, irrelevance and confusion. *Antitrust Bulletin* 19:327–62.

Bradbury, F. R. (ed.). 1969. *Words and numbers.* Edinburgh: Edinburgh University Press.

Bradbury, F. R.; W. M. Gallagher; and C. W. Suckling. 1973. Qualitative aspects of the evaluation and control of research and development projects. *R & D Management* 3:49–57.

Branch, B. 1974. Research and development activity and profitability: a distributed lag analysis. *Journal of Political Economy* 82:999–1011.

Brooke, M. Z., and H. L. Remmers. 1977. *The international firm.* London: Pitman.

Brooks, D. B. 1965. *Supply and competition in minor metals.* Baltimore, Md.: Johns Hopkins.

Buckley, A. 1972. A profile of industrial acquisitions in 1971. *Accounting and Business Research,* Autumn, pp. 243–52.

Cantley, M. F. 1972. The choice of corporate objectives, in Taylor and Hawkins (1972), pp. 9–22.

Carruth, E. 1976. The nervous capital boom in chemicals. *Fortune,* February, pp. 96–101 and 156–9.

Catling, H. 1972. Conditions for innovation – with particular reference to textiles. *R & D Management* 2:75–82.

Caulkin, S. 1974. Wilkinson makes a safety match. *Management Today,* November, pp. 74–81.

    1975. The merger aftermath. *Management Today,* February, pp. 58–65.

C.B.I. 1973. *The responsibilities of the British public company.* London: Confederation of British Industry.

Chandler, A. D. 1961. *Strategy and structure* Cambridge, Mass.: M.I.T. Press.

Channon, D. F. 1973. *The strategy and structure of British enterprise.* London: Macmillan.

Christensen, C. R.; K. R. Andrews; and J. L. Bower. 1973. *Business policy.* Homewood, Ill.: Irwin.

City Code. 1976. *The city code on takeovers and mergers* (Revised edition, April 1976). London: Issuing Houses Association for The City Working Party.

Coase, R. H. 1937. The nature of the firm. *Economica,* 4:386–405.

Cohen, K. J., and R. M. Cyert. 1973. Strategy: formulation, implementation and monitoring. *Journal of Business,* 46:349–367.

Comanor, W. S. 1964. Research and competitive product differentiation in the pharmaceutical industry of the United States. *Economica* 31:372–84.

1967. Market structure, product differentiation and industrial research. *Quarterly Journal of Economics* 81:639–57.

Conn, R. L. 1973. Performance of conglomerate firms: comment, *Journal of Finance* 28:754–8.

1976. Acquired firm performance after conglomerate merger. *Southern Economic Journal* 43:1170–73.

Cooper, A. C. 1964. R & D is more efficient in small companies. *Harvard Business Review* 42(3):75–83.

Cosh, A. 1975. The remuneration of chief executives in the United Kingdom. *Economic Journal* 85:75–94.

Costello, P. M. 1968. The tetracycline conspiracy: structure, conduct and performance in the drug industry. *Antitrust Law and Economic Review* 1(4):13–44.

Crew, M. A. 1975. *Theory of the firm.* London: Longman.

Cyert, R. M., and J. G. March. 1963. *A behavioral theory of the firm.* New York: Prentice-Hall.

David, R. 1976. Picking the winners, *The Times,* January 6.

Davies, B. J. 1976. *The regulation of takeovers and mergers.* London: Longman.

Davies, S. 1976. The diffusion growth curve for process innovations. Discussion Paper No. 76.2. Univeristy of Sheffield, Division of Economic Studies.

Davis, W. 1970. *Merger mania.* London: Constable.

Day, R. H. 1967. Profits, learning and the convergence of satisficing to marginalism. *Quarterly Journal of Economics* 81:302–11.

Devine, P. J.; R. M. Jones; N. Lee; and W. J. Tyson. 1974. *An introduction to industrial economics.* London: Allen and Unwin.

Drucker, P. F. 1974. *Management; tasks, responsibilities, practices.* London: Heinemann.

Dunning, J. H. (ed.). 1974. *Economic analysis and the multinational enterprise.* London: Allen and Unwin.

Edwards, R. S., and H. Townsend. 1962. *Business enterprise.* London: Macmillan.

Elliott, J. W. 1971. Funds flow vs. expectational theories of research and development spending in the firm. *Southern Economic Journal* 37:409–22.

Enos, J. L. 1958. A measure of the rate of technological progress in the petroleum refining industry. *Journal of Industrial Economics* 6:218–41.

Foster, G. 1976. Eastwood's golden eggs. *Management Today,* October, pp. 51–8 and 128.

Franko, L. G. 1976. *The European multinationals.* London: Harper and Row.

Franks, J. R.; J. E. Broyles; and H. J. Hecht. 1977. An industry study of the profitability of mergers in the United Kingdom. *Journal of Finance* 32:1513–25.

Freeman, C. 1965. Research and development in electronic capital goods. *National Institute Economic Review* 34:40–91.

1974. *The economics of industrial innovation*. Harmondsworth: Penguin.

Gay, P. W., and R. L. Smyth. 1974. *The British pottery industry*. London: Butterworth.

Gebhardt, A., and O. Hatzold. 1974. Numerically controlled machine tools, in Nabseth and Ray (1974).

George, K. D. 1972. The changing structure of competitive industry, *Economic Journal* 82 (March, supplement): 353–68.

George, K. D., and A. Silberston. 1975. The causes and effects of mergers, *Scottish Journal of Political Economy* 22:179–93.

George, K. D., and T. S. Ward. 1975. *The structure of industry in the E.E.C.* Cambridge: Cambridge University Press.

Gold, B.; W. S. Pierce; and G. Rosegger. 1970. Diffusion of major technological innovations in US iron and steel manufacturing. *Journal of Industrial Economics* 18:218–41.

Gorecki, P. K. 1975. An inter-industry analysis of diversification in the UK manufacturing sector. *Journal of Industrial Economics*, 23:131–46.

Gort, M. 1962. *Diversification and integration in american industry*. Princeton, N.J.: Princeton University Press; N.B.E.R. General Series No. 77.

1969. An economic disturbance theory of mergers. *Quarterly Journal of Economics* 83:624–42.

Gort, M., and T. F. Hogarty. 1970. New evidence on mergers. *Journal of Law and Economics* 13:167–84.

Grabowski, H. G., and N. D. Baxter. 1973. Rivalry in industrial research and development: an empirical study. *Journal of Industrial Economics* 21:209–35.

Grant, R. M. 1977. The determinants of the inter-industry pattern of diversification by UK manufacturing enterprises. *Bulletin of Economic Research* 29:84–95.

Green, J. 1971. That bureau business. *Data Systems*, February, pp. 19–35.

Gribbin, J. D. 1974. The operation of the mergers panel. *Trade and Industry* 17, January, pp. 70–73.

1976. The conglomerate merger. *Applied Economics* 8:19–35.

Guth, W. D. 1976. Towards a social system theory of corporate strategy. *Journal of Business* 49:374–88.

Hannah, L. 1974. Mergers in British manufacturing industry 1880–1918. *Oxford Economic Papers* 26:1–20.

Hannah, L. 1976. *The rise of the corporate economy*. London: Methuen.

Hannah, L., and J. A. Kay. 1977. *Concentration in modern industry*. London: Macmillan.

Harman, A. J. 1971. *The international computer industry.* Cambridge, Mass.: Harvard University Press.

Hart, P. E.; M. A. Utton; and G. Walshe. 1973. *Mergers and concentration in British industry.* Cambridge: Cambridge University Press.

Haugen, R. A., and T. C. Langetieg. 1975. An empirical test for synergism in mergers. *Journal of Finance* 30:1003–14.

Hayward, G.; D. H. Allen; and J. Masterson. 1976. Characteristics and diffusion of technological innovations. *R & D Management* 7:15–24.

Helleiner, G. K. 1973. Manufactured exports from less developed countries and multinational firms. *Economic Journal* 83:21–47.

Hogarty, T. F. 1970. Profitability of corporate mergers. *Journal of Business* 43:317–27.

Holl, P. 1975. Effect of control type on the performance of the firm in the UK. *Journal of Industrial Economics* 22:257–71.

Honeycutt, T. C. 1975. Comment (on Lev and Mandelker 1972). *Journal of Business* 48:267–71.

Horwitch, M., and C. K. Prahalad. 1976. Managing technological innovation – three ideal modes. *Sloan Management Review* 17:77–89.

Jewkes, J.; D. Sawers; and R. Stillerman. 1969. *The sources of invention.* London: Macmillan.

Johannisson, B., and C. Lindstrom. 1971. Firm size and inventive activity. *Swedish Journal of Economics* 73:427–42.

Johnson, H. G. 1976. Aspects of patents and licenses as stimuli to innovation. *Weltwirtschaftliches Archiv* 112:417–28.

Kamien, M. I., and N. L. Schwartz. 1976. The degree of rivalry for maximum innovative activity. *Quarterly Journal of Economics* 90:245–60.

Kay, N. 1976. R & D budgeting in Swedish firms. *R & D Management* 7:45–6.

   1978. *The innovating firm: a behavioural theory of corporate R & D.* London: Macmillan.

Keeling, B. S., and A. E. G. Wright. 1964. *The development of the modern British steel industry.* London: Longmans.

Kelly, E. M. 1967. *The profitability of growth through mergers.* University Park, Pa.: Pennsylvania State University Press.

Kitching, J. 1967. Why do mergers miscarry? *Harvard Business Review,* 45:84–101.

   1974. Why acquisitions are abortive. *Management Today,* November, pp. 82–7 and 148.

Knickerbocker, F. T. 1973. *Oligopoly reaction and multinational enterprise.* Boston: Harvard business school.

Knight, A. 1974. *Private enterprise and public intervention: the Courtauld's experience.* London: Allen and Unwin.

Kuehn, D. 1975. *Takeovers and the theory of the firm.* London: Macmillan.

Lacci, L. A.; S. W. Davies; and R. Smith. 1974. Tunnel kilns in brick making, in Nabseth and Ray (1974).

Laffer, A. B. 1969. Vertical integration by corporations, 1929–65. *Review of Economics and Statistics*, 51:91–93.

Langrish, J.; M. Gibbons; W. G. Evans; and R. F. Jevons. 1972. *Wealth from knowledge*. London: Macmillan.

Layton, C. 1972. *Ten innovations*. London: Allen and Unwin.

Lev, B., and G. Mandelker. 1972. The microeconomic consequences of corporate mergers. *Journal of Business* 45:85–104.

Levitt, T. 1962. *Innovation in marketing*. New York: McGraw-Hill.

Loasby, B. J. 1976. *Choice, complexity and ignorance*. Cambridge: Cambridge University Press.

Lowes, B. 1977. The changing role of business in society, in Taylor and Sparkes (1977).

Lynch, H. H. 1971. *Financial performance of conglomerates*. Boston: Division of Research, Harvard Business School.

McGowan, J. J. 1971. International comparisons of merger activity. *Journal of Law and Economics* 14:233–50.

Mandelker, G. 1974. Risk and return: the case of merging firms. *Journal of Financial Economics* 1:303–35.

Mansfield, E. 1968. *Industrial research and technological innovation*. New York: Norton.

Mansfield, E., and J. Rapoport. 1975. The costs of industrial product innovations. *Management Science* 21:1380–6.

Mansfield, E.; J. Rapoport; J. Schnee; S. Wagner; and M. Hamburger. 1971. *Research and innovation in the modern corporation*. New York: Norton.

Mansfield, E., and S. Wagner. 1975. Organisational and strategic factors associated with the probability of success of industrial R & D. *Journal of Business* 48:179–98.

Markham, J. W. 1955. Survey of the evidence and findings on mergers, in N.B.E.R. conference report *Business concentration and price policy*. Princeton, N.J.: Princeton University Press.

Marris, R. 1964. *The economics of managerial capitalism*. London: Methuen.
    1971. An introduction to theories of corporate growth, in Marris and Wood (1971).

Marris, R., and A. Wood. 1971. *The corporate economy*. London: Macmillan.

Martin, L. G. 1975. What happened at N.C.R. after the boss declared martial law. *Fortune*, September, pp. 100–4 and 178–81.

Mason, R. H., and M. B. Goudzwaard. 1976. Performance of conglomerate firms: a portfolio approach. *Journal of Finance* 31:39–48.

Mead, W. J. 1969. Instantaneous merger profit as a conglomerate merger motive. *Western Economic Journal* 7:295–306.

Meeks, G. 1977. *Disappointing marriage: a study of the gains from merger*. Cambridge: Cambridge University Press.

Meeks, G., and G. Whittington. 1975. Giant companies in the United Kingdom 1948–69. *Economic Journal* 85:824–32.

Melicher, R. W., and G. H. Hempel. 1971. Differences in financial characteristics between conglomerate mergers and horizontal or vertical mergers. *Nebraska Journal of Economics and Business* 10:61–74.

Melicher, R. W., and D. F. Rush. 1973. The performance of conglomerate firms: recent risk and return experience. *Journal of Finance* 28:381–8.

   1974. Evidence on the acquisition-related performance of conglomerate firms. *Journal of Finance* 29:141–9.

Meyer, J. R., and G. Herregat. 1974. The basic oxygen steel process, in Nabseth and Ray (1974).

Minasian, J. R. 1962. The economics of research and development, *in The rate and direction of inventive activity*. Princeton, N.J.: N.B.E.R. – Princeton University Press.

Minchington, W. 1957. *The British tinplate industry*. Oxford: Oxford University Press.

Monopolies Commission. 1972. *Beecham Group Ltd and Glaxo Group Ltd, the Boots Company Ltd and Glaxo Group Ltd; a report on the proposed mergers* (HC 341). London: H.M.S.O.

   1973. *Report on the supply of chlordiazepoxide and diazepam* (HC 197). London: H.M.S.O.

Mueller, D. C. 1969. A theory of conglomerate mergers. *Quarterly Journal of Economics* 83:643–59.

Mueller, D. C., and J. E. Tilton. 1969. Research and development costs as a barrier to entry. *Canadian Journal of Economics* 2:570–9.

Mueller, W. F. 1962. The origins of the basic inventions underlying Du Pont's major product and process innovations 1920 to 1950, in *The rate and direction of inventive activity*. Princeton, N.J.: N.B.E.R. – Princeton University Press.

Nabseth, L., and G. F. Ray. 1974. *The diffusion of new industrial processes*. Cambridge: Cambridge University Press.

N. E. D. O. 1972. *Focus on pharmaceuticals*. National Economic Development Office, Chemicals Economic Development Committee. London: H.M.S.O.

Nelson, R. R. 1959. The simple economics of basic scientific research. *Journal of Political Economy* 67:297–306.

   1959. *Merger movements in American industry 1895–1956*. Princeton, N.J.: Princeton University Press.

   1961. Uncertainty, learning and the economics of parallel research and development efforts. *Review of Economics and Statistics* 43:351–64.

Newbould, G. D. 1970. *Management and merger activity*. Liverpool: Guthstead.

Norris, K. P., 1971. The accuracy of project cost and duration estimates in industrial R & D. *R & D Management* 2:25–33.

Oi, W. Y., and A. P. Hurter. 1965. *Economics of private truck transportation*. (Chapter 2, pp. 31–67, reprinted as "A theory of vertical integration in road transport services" in *Economics of industrial structure,* ed. B. S. Yamey. Harmondsworth: Penguin, 1973.)

O'Meara, J. T. 1961. Selecting profitable products. *Harvard Business Review* 39:83–9.

Peck, M. J. 1961. *Competition in the aluminum industry.* Cambridge, Mass.: Harvard University Press.

Penrose, E. T. 1959. *The theory of growth of the firm.* Oxford: Blackwell.

Pickering, J. F. 1974. *Industrial structure and market conduct.* London: Martin Robertson.

Pratten, C. F. 1970. A case study of a conglomerate merger. *Moorgate and Wall Street Journal,* Spring, pp. 27–54.

  1971. *Economies of scale in manufacturing industry.* Cambridge: Cambridge University Press.

Radice, H. K. 1971. Control type, profitability and growth in large firms. *Economic Journal* 81:547–62.

Reekie, W. D. 1975. *Managerial economics.* Oxford: Philip Allan.

Reid, S. R. 1968. *Mergers, managers and the economy.* New York: McGraw-Hill.

  1976. *The new industrial order.* New York: McGraw-Hill.

Rhys, D. G. 1972. *The motor industry.* London: Butterworth.

Richardson, G. B. 1960. *Information and investment.* Oxford: Oxford University Press.

  1972. The organisation of industry. *Economic Journal* 82:883–96.

Robertson, T. S. 1971. *Innovation behavior and communication.* New York: Holt, Rinehart and Winston.

Rogers, E. M. 1962. *Diffusion of innovations.* New York: Free Press.

Rogers, E. M., and F. F. Shoemaker. 1971. *Communication of innovations.* New York: Free Press.

Romeo, A. A. 1975. Interindustry and interfirm differences in the rate of diffusion of an innovation. *Review of Economics and Statistics* 57:311–19.

Rosenberg, N. 1972. Factors affecting the diffusion of technology. *Explorations in Economic History* 10:3–33.

  1976. On technological expectations. *Economic Journal* 86:523–35.

Rothwell, R. 1976. Innovations in the UK textile machinery industry: the results of a postal questionnaire survey. *R & D Management* 6:131–8.

  1977. The characteristics of successful innovators and technically progressive firms (with some comments on innovation research). *R & D Management* 7:191–206.

Roy, A. D. 1952. Safety first and the holding of assets. *Econometrica* 20:431–9.

Rowley, A. 1976. Flurry of mergers. *The Times,* November 12 (Special Report on Insurance Broking, p. II).

Rowthorn, R. 1971. *International big business 1957–1967.* Cambridge: Cambridge University Press.

Rubenstein, A. H.; A. K. Chakrabarti; R. D. O'Keefe; W. E. Souder; and

H. C. Young. 1976. Factors influencing innovative success at the project level. *Research Management* 19(3):15–20.

Rumelt, R. P. 1974. *Strategy, structure and economic performance.* Cambridge, Mass.: Harvard University Press.

Samuels, J. M., and J. Tzoannos. 1969. Takeovers and share price evaluation. *Business Ratios* 2:5–16.

Schenk, W. 1974. Continuous casting of steel, in L. Nabseth and G. F. Ray (1974).

Scherer, F. M. 1965. Firm size, market structure, opportunity and the output of patented inventions. *American Economic Review* 57:1097–125.

1967. Research and development resource allocation under rivalry. *Quarterly Journal of Economics* 81:359–72.

1970. *Industrial market structure and economic performance.* Chicago: Rand McNally.

Schlaifer, R. 1969. *Analysis of decisions under uncertainty.* New York: McGraw-Hill.

Schmookler, J. 1966. *Invention and economic growth.* Cambridge, Mass.: Harvard University Press.

Schumpeter J. 1928. The instability of capitalism. *Economic Journal* 38:361–86.

1942. *Capitalism, socialism and democracy.* New York: Harper.

Scott, B. R. 1973. The industrial state: old myths and new realities. *Harvard Business Review* (March/April), pp. 133–48.

Servan-Schreiber, J. J. 1967. *Le defi American.* Paris: Editions de Noel.

Shaw, R. W. 1973. Investment and competition from boom to recession: a case study in the process of competition – the dry cleaning industry. *Journal of Industrial Economics* 21:308–24.

Shaw, R. W. and C. J. Sutton. 1976. *Industry and competition.* London: Macmillan.

Sherman, R. 1972. *Oligopoly, an empirical approach.* Lexington, Mass.: Heath.

Simon, H. A. 1952. A behavioral model of rational choice. *Quarterly Journal of Economics* 69:99–118.

Singh, A. 1971. *Takeovers.* Cambridge: Cambridge University Press.

1975. Take-overs, 'natural selection' and the theory of the firm. *Economic Journal* 85:497–515.

Solow, R. M. 1971. Some implications of alternative criteria for the firm, in Marris and Wood (1971).

Steiner, G. A., and J. B. Miner. 1977. *Management policy and strategy.* New York: Macmillan.

Steiner, G. A., and H. Schollhammer. 1975. Pitfalls in multi-national long range planning. *Long Range Planning* 8(2):2–12.

Steiner, P. O. 1975. *Mergers; motives, effects, policies.* Ann Arbor: Michigan University Press.

Stigler, G. J. 1950. Monopoly and oligopoly by merger. *American Economic Review* 42:23–34.

1951. The division of labour is limited by the extent of the market. *Journal of Political Economy* 59:185–93.

Stoneman, P. 1976. *Technological diffusion and the computer revolution.* Cambridge: Cambridge University Press.

Stopford, J. R. 1972. Organising the multinational firm: can the Americans learn from the Europeans? in *The multinational company in Europe,* ed. M. Z. Brooke and H. L. Remmers. London: Longman.

Stopford, J. M., and L. T. Wells. 1972. *Managing the multinational enterprise.* London: Longmans.

Sutton, C. J. 1972. Management behaviour and a theory of diversification. *Scottish Journal of Political Economy* 20:27–42.

1975. The effect of uncertainty on the diffusion of third generation computers. *Journal of Industrial Economics* 23:273–80.

Taylor, B. 1977. The concept and use of corporate planning, in Taylor and Sparkes (1977).

Taylor, B., and K. Hawkins (eds.) 1972. *A handbook of strategic planning.* London: Longman.

Taylor, B., and P. Irving. 1971. Organised planning in major UK companies. *Long Range Planning* 3(4):10–26.

Taylor, B., and J. R. Sparkes (eds.). 1977. *Corporate strategy and planning.* London: Heinemann.

Thune, S. S., and R. J. House. 1972. When long range planning pays off, in Taylor and Hawkins (1972).

Tilles, S. 1963. How to evaluate corporate strategy. *Harvard Business Review* 41:111–121.

1966. *Making strategy explicit* (Boston Consulting Group); excerpt reprinted in Ansoff (1969), pp. 180–209.

Tisdall, P. 1977. Branching out at W. H. Smith and Son. *The Times,* February 21.

Tugendhat, C. 1971. *The multinationals.* London: Eyre and Spottiswoode; Harmondsworth: Penguin, 1973.

Tzoannos, J., and J. M. Samuels. 1972. Mergers and takeovers: the financial characteristics of companies involved. *Journal of Business Finance* 4(3):5–16.

Utton, M. A. 1969. Diversification mergers profit. *Business Ratios* 1:24–8

1971. The effects of mergers on concentration: UK manufacturing industry 1954–65. *Journal of Industrial Economics* 20:42–58.

1974. On measuring the effects of industrial mergers. *Scottish Journal of Political Economy* 21:13–28.

1977. Large firm diversification in British manufacturing industry. *Economic Journal* 87:96–113.

Vaizey, J. 1974. *The history of British steel.* London: Weidenfeld and Nicolson.

Vance, S. C. 1971. *Managers in the conglomerate era.* New York: Wiley-Interscience.

Vancil, R. F. 1976. Strategy formulation in complex organisations. *Sloan Management Review* 17(2):1–18.

Vaupel, J., and J. Curhan. 1973. *The world's multinational enterprises: a sourcebook of tables.* Boston: Harvard Business School.

Vernon, R. 1971. *Sovereignty at bay: the multinational spread of US enterprise.* New York: Basic Books.

1974. The location of economic activity, in Dunning (1974).

Wall, J. L. 1974. What the competition is doing: your need to know. *Harvard Business Review,* November/December, pp. 22–38 and 162–6.

Weinberg, M. A. 1971. *Takeovers and mergers.* London: Sweet and Maxwell (3rd Edition, with M. V. Blank and A. L. Greystoke).

Weston, J. F., and S. K. Mansinghka. 1971. Tests of the efficiency performance of conglomerate firms. *Journal of Finance* 26:919–937.

Whittington, G. 1971. *The Prediction of Profitability* Cambridge: Cambridge University Press.

1972. Changes in the top 100 quoted manufacturing companies in the United Kingdom 1948 to 1968. *Journal of Industrial Economics* 20:17–35.

Wilkes, A., and K. P. Norris. 1972. The accuracy of project cost and duration estimates in industrial R & D. *R & D Management* 3:35–6.

Williamson, J. 1966. Profit, growth and sales maximisation. *Economica* 33:1–16.

Williamson, O. E. 1964. *The economics of discretionary behavior: managerial objectives in a theory of the firm.* Englewood Cliffs, N.J.: Prentice-Hall.

1971. Managerial discretion, organisation form and the multi-division hypothesis, in Marris and Wood (1971).

1975. *Markets and hierarchies.* New York: The Free Press.

Index

217